Zsolt

Living, Loving,
and Other Heresies

ZSOLT

LIVING, LOVING,
AND OTHER HERESIES

WITH A FOREWORD BY
DAVID J. ROTHMAN

CONUNDRUM

PRESS

Conundrum Press, Crested Butte, Colorado 81224
© 2003 by Zsolt

Cover photograph by F. Scott Swearingen © 2003

Library of Congress Control Number 2003106879

ISBN 0-9713678-0-9 (pbk)   ISBN 0-9713678-1-7 (cloth)

For
The Z Team

CONTENTS

FOREWORD

Every manuscript has a story, but our interest in that story varies in direct proportion to the strength of the manuscript. As this book is the strongest piece of work of any kind to cross my desk in twenty-five years as an editor, the story is worth telling.

On January 12, 2002, I received an e-mail from Anna Kaltenbach, whom I had met a few years before when she was working at the Colorado Center for the Book and I was serving on the Board of Directors. Anna asked me if I would be willing to read a manuscript for Conundrum Press by someone she knew. His name was Zsolt, and when she was growing up in northern New Mexico she had taken piano and ballet lessons from him. As she described it:

> He turned out to be much more than a teacher—a best friend and a great influence on my life, outlook, and capability to giggle. Also, incidentally, he's the reason I drink vodka martinis. When I was a teenager, I'd arrive at my piano lessons some days and he'd say, "Let's skip the lesson today and just go somewhere and have vodka and chocolate!" Of course, we never did, but when I grew old enough to drink vodka I did so—and still do—in the spirit of Zsolt.

All very charming, of course, but not exactly a guarantee of good writing. Nevertheless, Anna was adamant about the quality of Zsolt's work, so, in the rather exasperated and distracted manner of editors everywhere, I encouraged her to send some of it along.

Obviously, the story did not end there. As Anna told me more about Zsolt's life, I grew more curious. She explained that although Zsolt is only in his forties, he suffers from a progressive, debilitating, and almost surely fatal neuropathy whose diagnosis is still unclear. By the time I started reading his work his disease had already deprived him of most of his physical ability, while leaving his mind untouched. As letter writing and even individual e-mails became too much of a burden, he had begun writing group e-mails which evolved into essays not only about his disease, but also about life in general. While not maintained on a website, his entries functioned as a kind of blog—with the exception that as Zsolt was writing the entries, he was simultaneously losing the ability to play music, ride a bike, walk, speak, and even take care of himself in the most basic ways. Indeed, many of the essays in this book were written using word-recognition technology on a keyboard, one very slow letter and return keystroke at a time. It is surely one of the first, if not the very first book ever written largely in this way.

Still, to be blunt, none of the foregoing would have mattered in the slightest to me as an editor if the writing were mediocre. As it is, I vividly remember the first essay by Zsolt which I read, #62, which came to me like this, sans capitals (difficult for Zsolt to type). Here is how it begins:

> the walls of a room.
> a clothed bed.
> one's body.
> each of these, for the terminally or chronically ill, or for the severely disabled person, constitutes more than a noun, more than an objective space.   each, in its subtle and enigmatic shadows, is a sanctuary within which each sound, each touch calls us to witness, here amid the ever changing light infusing the windows, the walls, the linens, and the flesh.

The rest of the essay fulfills the promise of this astonishing beginning, which both focuses the mind by the evocation of pain and suffering, yet soothes it by invoking the power of a spirit to respond to that suffering simply through the force of its own meditative consciousness. The fact that the entire thing is written from within the situation it describes—not from a place where the disease has receded or been cured—only makes it that much more compelling. Indeed, more: it is written in the knowledge that an already advanced disease is only likely to continue to advance to its end. As far as I know, few if any have ever written from such a place (let alone done it so eloquently), because the available technology simply did not exist to allow anyone in that situation to convey such nuanced thoughts and feelings.

One quality of Zsolt's writing evident above is that, like every strong essayist, he is astonishingly attentive to his subject. Some essayists attend primarily to politics, others to ideas, still others to history, or religion, or ethics, and so on. As his accurate title indicates, Zsolt attends passionately to living and to loving, and to the moments in which they occur, meaning he ranges across all these subjects and more, from the personal to the political and back again. In his prose and his poetry, he strives always to be in relationship: with others, with nature, with art, with the passage of time, all in the context of living and loving, further tempered by his stark acknowledgement that our precious time in the world must eventually end. In his choice in life and as a writer to open himself to encounters with the world and his ability to savor those encounters—even the painful realizations of his own illness and mortality—he avoids simple reductions. Like Whitman, he is filled with multitudes and contradictions.

Even Zsolt's life (let alone his work) bears some surprising parallels with Whitman's. Zsolt, like Whitman, is deeply engaged with and knowledgeable about music, including Whitman's beloved opera; like Whitman, he is very much a free intellectual and creative spirit, sporting no institutional affiliations; like Whitman, he worked as a nurse; like Whitman, he is carefully discrete about his personal life at the same time as he mines it for larger truths. Most significantly, Zsolt is a writer of sublime American exuberance, who finds joy and solace in the world—even in a sickbed—despite understanding its failings and his own. He is a poet of reality and its contradictions in the tradition of praise. Unlike Whitman, however, he is emphatically a poet of specifics, of details, of contours, in addition to the larger truths which grow out of them.

Living, Loving, and Other Heresies is a testament to a carefully examined and purposeful life. It is a book of witnessing and testifying, intensely personal and yet expansive, characterized by careful art throughout. Like any such work, it seems to touch upon things which the author does not even discuss. Far more than merely a significant contribution to writing about disease, it articulates the experience of living a full, creative, joyous and caring life in our time.

The examined life has been a dangerous enterprise since Socrates defined it. The word "heresies" is therefore appropriate in Zsolt's title. "Heresy" ultimately derives from the Greek, meaning "a taking," in the sense of being "able to choose," and it therefore indicates a factious nature, the idea being that a heretic is to be condemned because he is free to choose and has knowingly and willfully taken a position that is generally viewed as wrong. And indeed, the world usually reacts with discomfort when confronted by spirits as stubborn, keen and ardent as Zsolt, in whom the imperfect burns so hotly, whose choices are so passionate and insistent. For it is in the nature of societies to create and require order, and prophets of vitality and compassion tend to exude more energy and questions than orderly social institutions can readily absorb. But that of course is exactly why the world needs its heretics, its Whitmans and Beethovens, its Picassos and Martha Grahams, its Gandhis, Martin Luther Kings…and Zsolts. For Zsolt, like these others, heretically reminds us of something that it is otherwise strangely easy to forget: that even though each of us will inevitably die, we must love one another if anything larger is to survive.

Near the end of "Democratic Vistas," Whitman prophesies the future of America's "works, poems, philosophies," tying them closely to democracy's best hope:

> Intense and loving comradeship, the personal and passionate attachment of man to man—which, hard to define, underlies the lessons and ideals of the profound saviours of every land and age, and which seems to promise, when thoroughly develop'd, cultivated, and recognized in manners and literature, the most substantial hope and safety of the future of these States, will then be fully express'd.

In its passion for life and its love of other people and the world, this book is a fulfillment of that prediction and a vindication of its terms.

David J. Rothman
Publisher/Editor, Conundrum Press
Crested Butte, Colorado
June 8, 2004

PREFACE

You are holding in your hands a selection of forty-six essays, poems and fragments culled from one hundred e-mail letters, eponymously called Zsoltgossips, written over a four year period beginning on my fortieth birthday and ending on September 24, 2003.

By way of preface to this selected collection of Zsoltgossip letters, let me elucidate the title of the book you are now reading.

Zsolt is my name.

It is a Hungarian name.

I am not, however, Hungarian.

Nonetheless, Zsolt is my name.

Unlike the precocious Mr. Mozart with his six names, I have only one— short, simple, monosyllabically strong.

My father, blessed be his name, in a moment of tender camaraderie, once remarked, "Zsolt is a beautiful name."

And so it is.

Nowhere in my reminiscences, oral or written, have I fully related the remarkable story of my cherished name, a richly interwoven narrative which shall ultimately go to the grave with me, blessed be our memories.

Until that fine moment, its mutely comforting presence accompanies me, a gentle reminder from the muse that not everything a person experiences can be put into words.

Or needs be.

Living is my being.

It is not merely something I hope to achieve in some nebulous future; nor is it something I must now regret having never accomplished.

For aliveness is my very being, an electricity of music ever coursing through my veins.

As Gwendolyn Brooks writes at the end of a poem entitled "Speech to the Young,"

> *Live not for the battle's end.*
> *Live not for the-end-of-the-song.*
> *Live for the along.*

Such has it been for me, living the along-song all along.

Thus it is and shall continue to be, this living a mad old habit nestled in my pulsing blood.

Loving, for lack of a less tattered and abused word, is my way, my journey.

Truly, every bird, every blossom, each sudden breeze, the touch of a comrade's hands, the scent of his arrival, the very song of life are my beloved.

Perhaps it is because of this journey, this way of mine that the final words of this book express so much of my self, I who can no longer *speak* of love, but must instead *dwell* in love.

I urge you, however, not to peek ahead, for those words shall have more meaning when read at the end, rather than the beginning of your reading journey.

Heresies. It is quite impossible to defend myself on this issue. You see, for me to say that ordinary menfolk are finely capable of caring for one another, of compassionately nursing the ill, the diseased, the elderly;

to speak of compassion not as emasculating pity, but as a powerful force of community;

to speak of community not as family, religion, nationality or color, but as the interstices of an entire humanity, of life itself;

to insist that the complexities of disability and disease can yet allow for lives that are vibrant, meaningful, delightful, intellectually rich and sensually alive with fragrant sounds, delectable visions, and ever the touch of the beloved;

to deny nostalgia for the past and hope for the future in favor of the great irruption of life that is this moment, this event, this warmth, this song-of-now;

to insist that dying is intrinsically bound to living, thereby no less absurd, no less hauntingly beautiful;

to laugh in the midst of pain, and weep in the midst of joy;

to persistently act against injustice, even within the confines of a mute wheelchair;

to live vulnerably, humbly;

to tenderly touch, to kiss my beloved in each strange and unexpected gesture of the turning earth;

to espouse all of these and more, is to stand guilty of heresies against a pantheon of narrower notions of life and love.

Yet I cannot retreat from the intensity of my living, beastly iconoclast that I am.

Thus my heresies remain lovingly intact, word for word, to titillate you in your reading pleasures.

On an entirely different matter, I cannot depart this Preface without acknowledging the dedicated efforts of David J. Rothman, the publisher and editor of Conundrum Press, and Cath Sherrer, Princess of the Moon, who have never stopped believing in the words of an unknown rogue of a writer. In addition, I am indebted to Lyn Brown, who tirelessly read and critiqued every one of the one hundred Zsoltgossips.

I would also like to express deepest gratitude to my representative, Peter Fant. Through his selfless efforts, royalties from the sale of this book will go directly to furthering the educational needs and dreams of impoverished children throughout the world.

Lastly, though this book is dedicated to the men of the Z Team—that marvel of a crew of volunteers who routinely assist me with my personal care needs—I would here like to also honor their spouses and children, who have so generously supported the efforts of these devoted, loving men. My general well-being is also maintained by many assorted people, from strangers opening doors, to friends, family and agencies providing supplies, to the generosity of my dentist and others in the community, some of whom you will read about in the following pages.

And now, dear Reader, the journey is yours to live and to love; to cherish all the sublime heresies woven into the name of your soul and the soul of your name, blessed be its song.

I love you all,

Zsolt

Santa Fé, New Mexico
May 3, 2003

1. ZSOLTGOSSIP

It has occurred to me over the past several months that I am becoming less and less able to keep up with my correspondence with all of you in the detailed and in-depth manner I would like. After mulling over various options, I have decided to try sending letters en masse, something made infinitely easier through the technology of the Internet. While this does not allow for as personal a message as I would wish, it nonetheless offers some degree of ongoing communication. A year ago I could write several long and involved letters per week, often several in one day; now it is down to one per week or two per month. This is not due to any lack of desire, but simply the realities of my life. This last statement, of course, begs the question, "Are there any realities in Zsolt's life?" I, unfortunately, am in no position to answer this and must leave it for you.

While some of you have been acquainted with me for years, and in fact longer than you probably thought possible; others are more recent acquaintances. Regardless, I welcome you to ZSOLTGOSSIP. I realize that this is perhaps an incorrect use of the term gossip, for it ought not to be one's self who gossips, but someone else. However, having never been known to use the English language correctly, I shall abscond with the transitive nature of the verb and turn it reflexive. Who ever said a person cannot gossip about him- or herself? Indeed are not we the best ones to do so, for you cannot ever believe a word a person says about him- or herself, making all personal revelation nothing more than gossip. This is due to the fact that the source is never reliable.

Thus, on the first day of my fifth decade I begin this exercise in Selfgossip. How long it lasts depends on several factors, one of them being the calculation of which life I am currently living; in other words, of the nine lives I have been allotted, am I on the seventh or the eighth? Using a perverse form of trigonometry, some pundits have calculated it to be the eighth; others, using nothing more than the average density of the tea I drink, have returned with a figure of seven. Neither of these methods actually disallows for the fact that I may in truth be on my ninth life, the most sublime; though by nobody's calculation am I still on life number six, regardless of how childish I may act at times. On the other hand, there is some debate as to whether or not I am living those nine lives sequentially. It may yet be that after I have finished life number

1

nine I will need to go back and tidy up life number two. Nonetheless, and regardless of the days, months and years remaining to me, I shall for the foreseeable future try to send you messages from the World of Blather on a regular basis.

October 20, 1999

3. GIFTS OF OUR HANDS

I look down at my hands. For forty years they have been part of my life. In them are etched enough stories to fill volumes, stories that will for the most part remain untold at the time of my death, for in order to tell in detail even the most elegant, the most sublime, the most heroic of the stories would require yet another lifetime. While generally speaking the human hand is a remarkable instrument, one that brings to each of us a treasury of sensations and stories, I feel inordinately lucky in the sheer diversity of gifts my hands have brought me. If one were to search for a meaningful symbol of my life one would need go no farther than my hands; in them I find mirrored most everything of value to me.

And now I must admit to you, in the hope that only a few of you will flee in disgust, that I am at this very moment listening to selections from Tchaikovsky's ballet *Swan Lake*. I am well aware that such a confession may send some of you to the delete button, and others to sigh fretfully and murmur, "Dear Lord, what are we to do with that girl?" Admittedly it is some of the most worn-out, melodramatic music in the library—in some of its phrases there is enough crashing of cymbals to wake the dead of the past and the dead to come all at once. Yet, for my hands this music is nothing less than an exhortation to dance, to unfold, to unveil a story. In the past my whole body would have been prancing about the room, carried on the wings of this music; today it is only my hands and arms which move, while I remain seated.

Actually, this is not entirely correct, for it is not only with my hands that I dance, it is in my heart, my soul. From this vantage point in my life it is almost incomprehensible to me that I once had such precision and strength in the movements of my body; indeed I would now have to pass off such memories as merely culled from an old film, except for one thing...my hands. In them memories are alive in ways that my mind cannot bring fully to life by itself. And oddly enough the tears falling from my eyes are not tears of sorrow, nor of remorse, but of joy, and more so, of gratitude. Even when my hand, in an attempt to do something exquisitely beautiful, instead hits me in the head, I am undeterred. Rather I find myself feeling intense admiration for that boy who long ago overcame so many obstacles in order to become a Swan. Yes, I was always a better Swan than a Prince, though of late I find myself attaining the kind of dignity that might one day bring me the role of the Prince's mother, namely, the Queen.

This morning, however, all that remains of that boy's dream are these hands, as well as a wondrously naive belief that the music is not, and never was, about Swans and Princes, but about life itself.

Yes, somehow the naivete endures.

And so does the life.

Late October, 1999

8. THE PIPE ORGAN

At this moment the sun is beginning to set across the late autumn horizon. Earlier this afternoon I took two beets given me by a friend and carefully cut them into large pieces, admiring the color and the grain. I then put those pieces into the food processor along with an onion, the first steps in making a pot of borscht. After tossing this grated mess into the boiling broth, I added oil, dill, garlic, salt and pepper, along with a leftover cup of tea. This is the most extravagant cookery I have managed in months. Splash and burn cookery, one might call it. One never knows what the results will be and whether or not they will add to the problem of global warming.

It was while cutting the beets that I thought of my friend Juan. For years our routine followed the same pattern. After getting him out of bed and making certain he got onto the toilet safely, I would go into the kitchen and prepare his breakfast. On the stove was a double boiler, more or less the only cooking vessel in the whole house. To simplify things, the water in the basin of the double boiler was changed only when it began to go bad; several days in winter, perhaps only a day or two in summer. Why waste water when all one needs it for is steam? Into the top of the double boiler went a variety of root vegetables: carrots, yams, burdock and beets. Occasionally a bit of fish or chicken. Juan would generally specify which combination of vegetables he preferred that day and how much of each one to prepare. He was very particular about the whole process, nutrition being an important part of his health maintenance regimen. Much of what he did and believed in concerning his diet made complete sense; some of it, on the other hand, seemed concocted from nothing more than personal mythology. I always prepared the food as he requested, however, rarely asking him why it mattered to eat one thing or another in one way or another; after all, it was his body he was feeding, not mine. One day, after months of cutting the vegetables in a certain specified way, he requested I cut them differently, on the diagonal. Wondering if somehow, in his head at least, doing this would make the vegetables more nutritious, or more easily digested, or some such reasoning, I couldn't refrain from asking him why he wanted the vegetables cut in this new shape. He smiled his famous and infinitely charming smile and replied, "Because I'm tired of the old shapes." Even in the midst of trying to reason through and make sense of living with a debilitating disease, there are decisions and actions predicated on nothing more complex than the desire for a new shape, a new texture on the tongue.

My housemate in Switzerland was a very nice young physicist from India. He rarely dined in, and seldom used the kitchen at all, with one exception: every morning he would boil an egg in a small pot. The pot was never washed; he merely added new water when necessary. Over time, between the minerals in the water and the minerals in the eggshells, there developed a calcified coating on the inside of the pot, a coating which grew infinitesimally thicker with each boiling of a morning's egg. I often tidied up the kitchen for the two of us, though it never even entered my mind to wash up that small pot. In some perfectly acceptable way its layers were a testimony to the rituals of this man's life; to have washed them away would have been unnecessary, if not unduly brutal. It felt as though, by microscopically searching through those layers of sediment, one might recreate the morning thoughts of a person's life. In all likelihood there was no reason for this habit of his other than its utter simplicity; after all, he had much more on his mind than the bother of washing up a pot that anyway didn't need washing up. Even if his scientific work did not require his attention, there was always the remarkable scenery of Switzerland to enjoy before returning to India within a couple of years.

Several weeks ago Hart's parents were passing through town on their way to a new home in a new city. Along with their overloaded car they had with them a rental van, a truck really. Inside the van, on top of everything else, was his mother's electric keyboard, the one she had purchased some years ago when they had moved into a smaller house and needed to get rid of her big organ. Now relocating once again, they had loaded the keyboard last in order to leave it with Hart, a means to store it temporarily, due to limited space in their future home. Additionally they thought I might be able to make use of it, hoping that it would be easier for me to play than a regular piano. Personally, having never been overly fond of electric keyboards, I thought it would merely sit in a corner taking up space. Nonetheless, because leaving it here seemed convenient for them, the instrument was duly brought inside, bench and all. Several days after their visit I decided to try it out; after all, on some of these electric keyboards the harpsichord setting does not sound half bad. Pulling out some pages of Bach, I sat down to play this new harpsichord, and to my delight found it rather enjoyable.

After a week of harpsichord sounds, Hart suggested I try out some of the other buttons, most of which made us laugh uproariously: Bach played on the vibraphone, for instance. Quite another reaction ensued, however, when I pushed the pipe organ setting and proceeded to plunge into a prelude by the great Meister B himself. Well! If that wasn't a splendid shock. With a bit of technology who needs St. Paul Cathedral? On second thought, I wouldn't mind the dome, if anybody's out shopping.

With the pipe organ button securely in place I pulled out my beloved and battered volume of "The Well-Tempered Clavier," recalling that Herr B was himself an exceptional organist. Taking a few breaths to gather up my pluck, I returned to the keyboard in readiness for the thrilling sounds of a Pipe Organ. (For those of you who might be curious, I hereby admit that I did indeed move the volume lever to FULL.) With the first note I was unstoppable. Did it matter that my fingers digressively fumbled around and often hit notes that presumably belong to other pieces of music? Did it matter that my shoulders began burning? Did it matter that my mouth drooled uncontrollably even as I ploughed my way through those incredible preludes and fugues? Did it matter that because of my audacity today I will awaken tomorrow with fingers gnarled into contortions of stiffness? No, it did not. Why? Because life is precious, but only if it is lived. Admittedly, that small bit of me which still maintains a sniff of rectitude kept telling the rest of me to stop playing, to take a break; nonetheless, the river of the music continued to well over me, page after page, until I was having a hard time even breathing. Why did I continue? Because, awash in music, I was alive. More than alive, I was bursting into new realms, new configurations, new ideas. Yes, there will come a day, as there must for every musician, when I will no longer be able to sit and play music. Even then, however, a wonderful melody of Schubert will still drift through my blood, its idiosyncratic modulations bringing me a sense of vitality. I know that for me the day the music stops flowing through my veins, I will be dead, whether my heart still beats or not.

Beyond the immediate enjoyment of playing music, sitting at this electric "pipe organ" brought back wonderful memories of playing a variety of real pipe organs across Europe. For some reason I have always had a penchant for going into churches and asking the caretaker or priest if I could play the organ. Making such a request could often be a complicated procedure, due either to language barriers or merely the queerness of my request, or both. Undaunted I would persevere until I got permission to climb step after step into the organ lofts of churches large and small, and with a bemused priest or cleaning woman looking on, I would begin with a bit of Bach before moving into full throttle improvisations on any theme I happened to be humming that day. The most remarkable thing is that not once was my request ever denied, though it often took a bit of cajoling. Perhaps it was a pride in their instrument, perhaps it was curiosity, and perhaps it was nothing more than a love of music brought to the forefront by an opportunity to hear Bach in the middle of a mundane hour which had originally been set aside for more prosaic encounters. Once, after a particularly rousing round of improvisation, I lifted my hands triumphantly from the keyboard only to find, in the wake of the echoing chords, that one pipe still rang out its note. Looking down at the keyboard I noticed one of the keys sticking, and no matter what I did I could not unstick it. Petrified, and concerned that I had damaged it, I turned an apologetic face to the priest in attendance, who merely leaned over the organ and by wiggling something caused the key to return to its place. In the now quiet loftiness of the large church he said matter-of-factly, "It happens all the time."

Some years ago, here in Santa Fé, I was asked to play for an AIDS memorial event at the cathedral. Obviously I needed to go in several days beforehand in order to practice on the organ. Having met with Father Pat to get the key, I ascended the steps to the choir loft, and diligently set to work deciding which pieces would sound best, and how best to present them. Upon finishing my thoughtful rehearsal, I pulled out every damn stop on that old pipe organ and lunged into five minutes of hell-raising improvisation on a theme I can no longer recall today, though it may have been a fragment of Dvorák or Berlioz. Finishing my little impromptu earthquake, I turned to find Father Pat standing behind me, solemnly berobed and appropriately thoughtful. I wondered to myself whether I had disturbed someone's prayers, or committed some other transgression against the sanctity of the day. Father Pat's face then opened into a great smile and, with all the certainty that comes of any intimate relationship with the divine, said to me, "God loves it when the windows shake."

One of the most remarkable things about lighting a single candle is the sudden sense it enlivens of beginning anew, a pleasant reminder that with each day we can yet again illuminate the darkness. While there is an awesome grandeur to a mass of candles burning at once, such a sight does not compare to the simplicity of watching darkness dissolve in the halo of a flame blossoming from a wick embedded in a piece of cold wax. Moments like this, rather than gripping the heart with furious ecstasy, have the propensity for returning us to a shimmering genesis, the meeting place of dark and light.

Travelling along the back roads of Ecuador, in that deepest moment of twilight before it is consumed by night, we passed a simple house. Through one of the windows could be seen a single flame, probably of a lantern rather than a candle. What was most extraordinary about that one flame, however, was not that it was alone, but that its light counterbalanced all the darkness enveloping the earth. The only other light for miles was the spray of light coming from the headlights of our bus. To this day, I do not know anything about the inhabitants of that cottage—nor even what fuel burned to create that single, miraculous flame—yet I have ever after felt connected to them, whoever they were. The same desire and need to light a candle, a lantern, a fire, and in doing so feel again the ability of a small flame to illuminate an entire night of darkness, belongs to us all. For this reason the stars exert a power on us which is in excess of their tiny dots; for seeing them piercing the indigo sky, who can be afraid of the night?

Once, after not seeing Juan for some time, I went to visit him in his humble room at a nursing home. At that point in his illness he could not speak very well and generally responded with short, simple answers to my questions. After a few minutes of introductory comments I looked at him lying almost immobile in his bed and asked him how he was doing, to which he replied, "Okay." Assuming that this was merely a polite response to put me at ease, I told him he did not need to gloss over things with me; after everything we had been through together, I felt I could hear whatever he had to say, no matter how distressing or depressing. Yet, and with his ever gracious smile, he looked at me and reiterated, "I'm okay." With this I was convinced, though it was not the words which caused me to believe him, it was his smile. You cannot induce or fake a smile like that, a smile which illuminates the darkness.

Few of us would willingly opt to live the kind of life that became Juan's life. Why? Perhaps because we so often forget that it is we who light the first candle; it is we who can dare to shake the windows with music, and in doing so allow love to be expressed through us. I cannot imagine that Juan sat down on a day in his early twenties and said, "I think I'll spend the last sixteen years or so of my life slowly deteriorating from the effects of multiple sclerosis." Nonetheless, when it came, and when it became more than a mere inconvenience, a mere stumble here and there, he did opt to remain ever alive, ever smiling and continually shaking the windows. Perhaps because, after all was said and done and diagnosed, he had grown tired of the old shapes.

December 12, 1999

10. JOY

On 13 April 1742, George Frederick Handel's great oratorio, *Messiah*, was premiered in Dublin, Ireland. After an orchestral overture, the first words of the work issue from the mouth of the Prophet Isaiah. "Comfort ye," he sings. At least, that is how he would have put it had he been speaking with Handel over a pint of ale in a Publick House in London. The words are sung *mezzo voce*, neither loudly, nor softly; the dramatic gesture expressed not through the thundering skies nor the eternal body of God, but through the mouth of a human being, a comrade, as it were. Following these first words the oratorio continues through various arias and choruses which, over the next couple of hours, relate the pivotal events in the life of a man known as Jesus Christ. Nonetheless, and taking into account the lovely music that follows, I am not sure there is a more sublime gesture in the entire oratorio than the moment when the Prophet Isaiah sings, "Comfort ye." For these words speak to us all, regardless our birth, our life, or the death that awaits us.

In the same year, far away to the east, the Baal Shem Tov, born Israel ben Eliezer—and also son of Sarah, by the way—then approximately forty-two, was bringing a similar message to Eastern European Jewry, mired as it was in hopeless poverty, its spiritual leaders in a state of conservative paralysis following the debacles of the preceding century. The Baal Shem's iconoclastic words of comfort and hope, however, along with his legendary actions, were not meant as prophesy; his interest lay not in what would be, but in what is, in man's direct relationship to God here and now. The way the Baal Shem interpreted that relationship had little to do with scholarship or privilege, but rather with something more personal and readily accessible to anyone, joy. Not only was his message one of joy, it was meant to be heard across barriers of class and caste. For him knowledge of God was not limited to the province of the Talmudic scholars nor to the ruling Rabbis. According to the Baal Shem one needed neither special language, nor esoteric prayers, nor arcane knowledge. Every soul who so desired could involve him- or herself in a relationship to and with the divine. A person needed only his or her heart. One needed only to respond. The simplicity of this message, brought to a downtrodden populace, was a fervent spark which lit a brilliant flame of hope, of renewal.

Several decades later, in the swirls of the Sturm und Drang movement that was then sweeping through the German Principalities and beyond, Johann Christoph Friedrich von Schiller wrote a poem called "Ode to Joy," a lengthy poem most of us would probably not even notice today if it had not captured the interest of the young Ludwig van Beethoven, who, as early as 1796, was trying to set parts of it to music; later it would be the text around which both the "Choral Fantasy" of 1808 and the final movement of his Ninth Symphony (1822-1824) would revolve. Schiller's poetic concept that all mankind could become brothers and sisters through joy, that "brilliant spark of the gods, daughter of Elysium," was seductive to a man influenced by the ideals of the French Revolution which were prevalent in Europe during Beethoven's early years. What I find interesting, however, is not that he was influenced by these ideals, but that he did not abandon them as did many others. Incensed by what he believed was an act of betrayal on the part of Napoleon Bonaparte—namely the act of having himself crowned Emperor— Beethoven nonetheless doggedly persevered in expressing his own fervent ideals, not only in 1808, but again in his last years. Furthermore, these ideals of Fraternity and Liberty were variously expressed not merely in the aforementioned works, but in page after page of his *oeuvre*.

Toward the end of his Heiligenstadt Testament of 1802—a letter written to his brothers, though never sent—in which he bemoans the sorry state of his life and the horrible reality of his encroaching deafness, we find him begging Providence for one day of pure joy, just one. As most of you know, he did not have an especially lovely childhood, and adulthood was made difficult not only by his increasing deafness but by other health problems, as well as the lack of a soul mate and the self-incurred legal struggle to gain custody of his nephew. It is highly doubtful he ever got his one day of pure joy. In an odd way, however, he may have, though it was a day shattered into many shards and strewn over a lifetime, minutes of joy etched into the structures of his music; moments which radiate nothing if not joy; moments we find impossible to listen to without responding with joy. While these waves of joy are most obvious in such works as the finale of the Ninth Symphony when the chorus shouts out, "Freude! Freude!" backed by a full orchestra, nevertheless the "brilliant spark of the gods" is palpable throughout his entire *oeuvre*.

Herein lies his genius, that in all the muck and mess of his life he persevered in his search for that one day of pure joy, and while he may not have found it in the living reality of his life, he left behind a pilgrimage littered with clefs and notes and rests which when listened to bring us not the sounds of a demigod, but of a human being struggling with the same issues each of us today struggles with. Whereas in Handel's oratorio the words of Isaiah are sung with a gesture of comfort, in Beethoven we are confronted not with what might be little more than hollow prophecy, but with the same immediacy as that of the Baal Shem, a call for passionate involvement not only with life but with the divine. And how is that involvement to be expressed? Through joy, among other things.

Looking at our contemporary world, it appears we are only able to relate to joy either through flaccid superficiality, or with cynical resignation, a shrug of the shoulders, a denial that it even exists. After all, advocates of the latter will tell us, of what concrete use were the Baal Shem's ideals as millions of Jews were being murdered during the Shoah? And, the music of Beethoven prevented neither the hideousness of Hiroshima nor the quagmire of Vietnam, events which, even as they were perpetrated, were couched by their espousers in terms of goodness, of the future peace and happiness of humankind. Unable to discover in ourselves a river of dark, ominous, exultant joy, we destroy it in others. Perhaps this is because we've forgotten that joy is an encompassing gesture: within its waters are not only delight and rapture, but also anguish and despair. The brilliant spark of joy cannot exist without the fuel of our anguish, and every time we push away the anguish through denial or resignation, joy is pushed farther from our lives. Joy wraps itself around anguish not in order to eradicate it, but to comfort it, as it were. Remove the sorrow from within joy and you are left with a shell; remove the radiance from our sorrows and we are left with nothing but cold cinders.

Years ago I read a book by Thich Nhat Hanh in which he wrote of how a simple smile can be the first step toward peace. At the time I thought sarcastically, *Oh great, a bit of chipperness and all the world's problems are solved.* This, of course, is not at all what he was advocating. Thich Nhat Hanh, we must remember, is a man who knew firsthand the horrors of the Vietnam War, a Buddhist monk who, when he smiles radiates what can only be described as joy, not in spite of the anguish in his heart—sorrows which, after all, will remain with him for the rest of his life—but alongside, above and around the darkness, encompassing it, illuminating it. In this way a smile born of anguish, a joy arising from within the despair of what life brings to all of us in one form or another, is a foundation upon which peace can exist. Without that foundation, which is nothing more than a life fully lived, we are forced to choose between superficiality and cynicism. Each time Beethoven set Schiller's "Ode to Joy" to music, the results were ever more bizarrely radiant, jaggedly joyous; not because he became a more perfect composer, but because the hues of his life had deepened, ever shaded by the events of that same life. The power of this lies not in its idealism, but in a persistent engagement with life which surfaces generation after generation, though it is often little more than a tiny spark.

One of my friends is severely disabled. A combination of cerebral palsy and brain damage at birth left him incapable of speaking, walking, chewing, or feeding himself. As an infant he even had difficulties swallowing. To this day he wears a diaper at all times, except when he is being bathed. Though the doctors recommended he be placed in an institution as an infant, where he would then live out his life in a more or less vegetative state, the boy's family refused to part with the child. At the age of fifteen or so he underwent an operation which allowed his legs to straighten enough for him to walk, though not without

12

constant assistance and supervision. In fact, the whole reason I know him is because I used to go to his house several times a week in order to bathe him, feed him, and walk with him up and down the streets of his neighborhood.

During the years when I helped him with his hygiene and his therapies, he was prone to intense outbursts of anger, frustration, and confusion, as well as of joy, exultation, and delight. His emotions were as straightforward as they were enigmatic. One could never exactly locate their origins. For instance, on Monday the water pouring out of the shower would delight him. On Tuesday it would only enrage him. When angered he would bite down hard on his hand and violently shake his body or stamp his feet. His face would contort into a visage of unfettered emotion. Interestingly enough, joy was expressed in the same manner, without restraint, without subtlety. As an example, he is quite fond of ice cream, and often when out walking we would take the opportunity of a respite to buy an ice cream. Usually, as soon as he had figured out what the plan was, he would lift his head back with a great smile and scream at full voice, his torso swinging back and forth in a sort of dancing/boxing motion.

Whenever my friend expresses extreme emotions such as rage or joy, his initial body language is precisely the same; in other words, when an emotional outburst comes it is quite difficult to tell from the contortions of his face whether he is experiencing rage or joy. For several moments they are indistinguishable one from the other, and, believe me, the joy is as formidable as the anger. I am always relieved for his sake if it turns out to be the former. When it is anger, the people around him can attempt to find a solution and perhaps fix the problem. Just as likely, however, they remain in a state of unknowing, even though something real or imagined is obviously causing my friend intense anguish. While most people seem perfectly capable of expressing unbounded rage, my friend is one of the few human beings I have ever met who can embody unbridled joy, a joy as frightening as it is ebullient. In fact, his expression of joy is what once precipitated our being thrown out of a local cafe for "frightening the tourists."

The Prophet Isaiah saying, "Comfort ye."

Beethoven practically screaming at us through the choruses and orchestras of his deafness, "Freude! Freude!"

The Baal Shem joyfully singing and dancing with God in the very arms of misery.

All of these are encompassed in joy, though none of them is made any more comprehensible by being touched with its radiance. It remains, however, within the incomprehensible where we may most powerfully discover our own joy.

December 18, 1999

13. BUMPER STICKERS AND BACH

The other day I noticed a bumper sticker—complete with an icon of Albert Einstein's portrait—which read, "Imagination is more important than knowledge." If truth be told, I can hardly imagine a more preposterous notion. It isn't that I do not believe Mr. Einstein said such a thing—indeed, I would be more skeptical had it been stated the other way around—rather, I wonder whether, having these words taken out of their original context and now expected to stand for his beliefs, Einstein himself would invest them with any more purport than his daily laundry list. For, distilled from the lifework of a great mind, the above snippet does not seem an especially intelligent thing to say. Agreeably, within the context of, say, the genesis of a scientific theory, Imagination does take on immense importance as the driver of the vehicle of Knowledge. But does it have MORE importance than Knowledge? Of course not. After all, where, pray tell, does one go without the vehicle itself? Without a sound foundation of Knowledge, would the architect's building stay up, would the painter know which colors she needs to combine in order to make purple? Certainly Einstein himself understood this: upon comprehending the imaginative insights which lead him to his General Theory of Relativity he knew damn well he hadn't the mathematical foundation to fully express his theory, therefore he went to his friend Marcel Grossman, who did have that knowledge, and with his help Einstein worked to strengthen his own Knowledge in order that the flight of his Imagination could alight securely in his 1915 paper, a paper in which he manages to pull together gravitational physics with the geometry of curved space. The fullness of life consists of a marvelous interplay between Imagination and Knowledge; one WITH the other, however, rather than one OVER the other. The above words of Einstein, taken out of the context of his life, lead us to the latter preposition: over. His life and work place him firmly within the former preposition: with.

With this in mind, what I find most troublesome about the aforementioned bumper sticker is its inherent divisiveness, whether intentional or not. Bumper stickers, after all, are meant to catch our attention, to provoke us toward one side or the other of any given issue, even if it be nothing more than trout fishing. While this is often done with humor it can also be accomplished through wit, shock, disorientation, or even intimidation, though in almost every instance we will place ourselves either pro or con on the issue; at fifty or sixty kilometers per hour in separate vehicles there can be little if any room for discussion, for context, for expression. (How aptly this reflects much of our current cultural climate is a worthy enough subject for its own extended exposition.) In this particular case, after reading Einstein's words we are confronted with having to make a needless choice between Imagination and Knowledge, pitting the Imaginationists against the Know-It-Alls—although some might question whether those Know-It-Alls who do not actually know anything ought instead be placed with the Imaginationists. Therefore those who side with Imagination will relievedly applaud the words of a great scientist brought to bear witness for their cause, while those who side with Knowledge will feel abandoned by a genius who had hitherto embodied the very notion of pure Knowledge. This is ridiculous, of course, because Imagination and Knowledge, while not the same phenomenon, are yet two sides of a Moebius strip. This is worth considering for a moment. Are there two sides to a Moebius strip? Yes? No? At once Yes and No? At some point Yes, and another No? Does the actualization of the Moebius strip destroy the very hypothesis placed within its mystery? Perhaps, having used this metaphor, it is now possible to comprehend the symbiotic relationship between Imagination and Knowledge.

Fortunately, it takes little effort on our part to become aware of the fortified divisions artificially set up between all manner of otherwise innocuous concepts: Intuition and Logic, Spontaneity and Method, Rationality and Irrationality, Masculinity and Femininity. . .

How often have I heard one polarity say, in effect, "I hate math." "I don't understand physics." "Why do people insist I think that way?" While the other is grumbling, "I'm not creative." "I can't write poetry." "The wife takes care of those things." (You may think I have added this comment about the wife for dramatic color, but truth be told, I actually heard a man once say it.)

All of this divisiveness is reinforced each time a person pigeonholes him- or herself into categories such as Right Brain, Left Brain, Linear, Abstract, Rational, or Emotional. I can hardly think of a more insidious way to insult one's self, for immediately upon pasting such labels on our own foreheads we impose upon ourselves the most feudal of restrictions: Here is your tiny plot of land, and if you dare to step beyond its limits you will be boiled in oil.

Now, in these finely enlightened times it is often advertised that such categorization provides tools for self-awareness out of which self-knowledge can arise, followed either by a lifetime of prosperity, happiness or well-being. Would that this were true, I would have little complaint about it. Unfortunately, I observe such labels doing little more than serving to keep most people in ruts, albeit it ruts with chic and clever names. Having once figured out or been told into which category a person's thought process, emotional state or physical abilities fall, the remainder of a person's life often becomes preoccupied with little more than hunkering down and defending the fortress, wherein the innocent word becomes an ever more self-imposed dungeon. One can imagine the person who slapped the above bumper sticker on his car stepping back and saying, "There!" as though it were himself and not a scrap of paper he had just pasted onto the proclaiming bumper.

Yet while defending our dungeons—yours and mine—it is easy to succumb to antagonism and atrophy, rather than striving toward symbiosis and synthesis. Slapping that bumper sticker onto one's car may make a person feel good for a moment. I fail to see, however, how it can possibly bring about any true understanding of the symbiosis of Knowledge and Imagination.

As I have mentioned in a previous writing, someone has loaned me an electronic keyboard with the hopes that I will find it easier to play than an acoustic piano. Making use of it as a Faux Harpsichord, I have for several weeks been pleasantly playing music by Johann Sebastian Bach. Set out on the music stand is a volume of music purchased some years ago, which includes his French Suites, English Suites, The Partitas, Inventions and Sinfonias, along with a work generally referred to as the *Goldberg Variations*, a set of thirty variations on an original aria. Written for one of his finest keyboard pupils, Johann Gottlieb Goldberg, they were composed at the request of a count who needed music to solace his sleeplessness, and are punctuated by canons, a fughetta, an overture and a quodlibet before finally returning to a reprise of the original aria. The entire reason I bought the above collection of music was for these *Goldberg Variations*, my desire to learn them a life-long dream. Nonetheless, and in spite of having made a brave incursion into a page or two of this challenging music, I have never actually learned the entire set of variations. Not only are there thirty of them, they also vary in remarkably inventive and often intricate ways. For instance, having been written for a double manual harpsichord—one with two claviers—it is not always an easy task to figure out how to play some of the variations on the single keyboard of a piano, or, in my case, an electronic keyboard vainly imitating the sounds of the early eighteenth century. Because of this fact—that they were composed for an instrument different than what I am playing them on—the hands often find themselves colliding as Bach sends them in flights up and down the keyboards, a simple enough situation when each hand has its own manual or keyboard. Not only does such inventive writing create difficulties in reading the music, but in manual cooperation as well as musical decision making.

During the past weeks, following the arrival of the Faux Harpsichord, I have spent hours playing through The Partitas and French Suites, English Suites and Sinfonias, all of them learned throughout a lifetime of studying music. Not only does this activity satisfy a longing to play music I know and enjoy, these pieces are also what are now easiest for my hands. Somehow music that already resides in my fingers is still relatively accessible to me, though the more complex or difficult a work is, the less of it I can play at a single sitting. There is, of course, a lot to be said for having such a treasury in one's fingertips, and also a lot to be said for being at peace with what one has. Truly, would there be anything wrong with spending the remainder of my days playing through the well-stocked library of music I have spent a lifetime learning? No, and in fact, with each newly arriving day those old pieces can become ever new again if I allow them to well up from an interior which is being continuously transformed by life. In the last decades of his long life the great Spanish cellist Pablo Casals would begin each day by sitting at the piano and playing the First Prelude and Fugue of "The Well-Tempered Clavier," Book One, by J. S. Bach. He referred to this habit of his as a benediction on the house. Because he was such a fine human being, I simply cannot imagine that it was ever the same piece of music twice; yes, the same notes, but not the same music.

No, my dilemma did not have anything to do with playing the music which still exists in my fingertips, nor was it a problem of accepting the truth that to learn pieces of complexity or difficulty is now almost beyond me. Rather, one day I realized that in trying to come to terms with my disability I had gradually allowed it to define the limits of playing music. While the *Goldberg Variations* is a massive, complicated piece of music, it is also broken up into many smaller units of varying levels of difficulty. Recognizing this, I opened the book of music and proceeded to begin learning the aria which commences the work, and by playing a single note in the right hand and a single note in the left hand began fulfilling a dream. I have now successfully made my way through the entire work, thirty-six pages of tightly spaced notation, seventy-two pages of material when performed with all repeats. Needless to say there will continue to be problems to solve, explorations and learning, but in the midst of everything that is now my life I have allowed myself to redefine the boundaries, altering even my definition of music making. There remain reams of musical material which are simply out of bounds for me, works that only a few years ago would have been playable on first sight or with the mildest of effort. Nevertheless, in looking deeply within myself, in clarifying my situation, I have uncovered a dream which was and is still fulfillable, and in doing so have become intimate with one of the great keyboard works of all time. Does it matter that in two months' time I may no longer be able to play it? No.

Years after Bach's death, in the second decade of the nineteenth century, Ludwig van Beethoven referred to several of his later piano sonatas as *Hammerklavier Sonaten*, a term used by him to distinguish between the piano of his time and its older and distant relative, the harpsichord. The term has since become linked to one sonata in particular, the Opus 106 (1817-1818), longest and arguably most difficult of Beethoven's thirty-two piano sonatas. It demands not only technical virtuosity from the performer but resources of stamina and strength. More than anything, however, it requires an astute and agile musical mind to solve its compositional vagaries. During the past year I have played very little of Beethoven's music on the piano. This has been mostly an issue of stamina, because my favorite works of his are strung out page after page, requiring both clarity in the hands and strength in the body. Whereas Bach can be played at a variety of tempi, including slow and slower, and still bring aural harmony, doing the same to Beethoven's surging movements not for the purpose of practice but simply because I no longer have the physical resources, does little more than remind me of how much my body has deteriorated. Yes, I have continued to listen to Beethoven on disc and to converse with friends about his music, thus maintaining some connection to his *oeuvre*, his life. Doing so, however, is not the same as playing the music itself.

Recently I have been craving the feel of this man's music in my fingers. No longer willing to put aside this yearning, what options are available to me?

1. I could play only a page or two of a given piece of his music, leaving the remaining ten or fifteen for another day.

2. I could simplify the music somehow.

3. I could play shorter, easier pieces, even though they are not among my favorites.

4. I could try some of the slow movements of the sonatas which, while they may be long, do not present the same problems of sustained technical virtuosity.

The first three of these options, while valid enough in their own way under current circumstances, were anathema to me, particularly the first two because of the obvious evisceration of the music. What remained, however, was a perfectly valid alternative, namely to play some of the slower movements of his sonatas. Accordingly, I dragged out my ragged, broken-spined Volume II of "Beethoven Sonatas" in order to look at the lovely slow movement from his Opus 90, and in the process stumbled upon and was reminded of the great, unwieldy adagio of the Hammerklavier Sonata, Opus 106. While in the past I have spent a fair amount of time with this sonata, in particular the adagio, it has been some years since I have played any of it. The adagio itself begins humbly enough with a single note played in unison in four octaves, A-A-A-A, as though sung by soprano, alto, tenor, and bass. These notes are held for three beats before each voice moves upward to C-sharp. At this point we have little notion of the immensity of architecture which Beethoven is going to erect out of these simple utterances. Or do we? In an incomprehensible way it is possible, even in those first notes, to sense what will follow—our task is to rise and meet it face to face, soul to soul, over an increasingly spellbound architecture which is often so transparent as to almost disintegrate. (In my edition, in which the notation is squeezed together as a space-saving device, this movement still occupies eleven pages, taking me about twenty minutes to play.) What keeps it from completely disintegrating is a melding of Imagination and Knowledge; stated another way, in order for us to not collapse beneath the immensity of this music, we must come to it with equal parts Imagination and Knowledge.

What I have found most interesting in coming anew to this music is how much more accessible it now is, both technically and musically, even though I have not looked at it for years. This facility is due in part to my intensive studies of Bach, allowing many passages of the adagio now to fit quite readily into my hands; furthermore, though it is something of a cliché, age has brought with it a maturity which gives me the courage to place myself within the music rather than outside of it or against it. The love which has always been present in my relationship to these notes still remains, deepened by the rarity of the experience, even by the discomfort within my body reminding me of the physical limits now existing for me, limits which while they may constrict the amount of time I can sit at the piano or the kind of music I am able to play cannot imprison the artistry of my soul. True, I can no longer even consider playing the other three movements of this notoriously challenging sonata. Nonetheless, by making the decision to leave them behind, letting them exist in a different part of my life, I may yet step onto the deck of the ship which remains and in pulling up the anchor may sail into waters charted and uncharted. Does it matter if by chance I have chosen to sail upon a ship which will never return? No. For in truth we can never return. To summon one's soul and play those first notes is to lift the weight, to break open the stone fortress, is to journey into and beyond the remarkable expanses of the human mind, the human soul as they strive to Know through Imagining, and to Imagine through Knowing.

Writing about my experiences of learning the *Goldberg Variations* and of returning to the adagio of the Hammerklavier Sonata does not alter the truth that the musical technique is slowly and undeniably ebbing from my fingers. Having left behind three of the movements of Beethoven's Opus 106, I shall inevitably one day sail away from the notation of the fourth. Where the music remains, however, and where it may remain, is in my Knowledge *and* in my Imagination, its unbounded song breaking through the stone walls of insularity. And regardless of the deterioration of a person's body, or the decay of his or her mind, it is in the heart where Imagination and Knowledge may ever and again playfully, fruitfully interact one WITH the other.

In our hearts, we are both and therefore more, as is the Moebius strip.

January 7, 2000

15. PEARLS

Recently there has been a spate of pearl tragedies in my life. To begin with, while I was travelling in December my most favorite set of pearls simply disappeared. I lifted my hand to my chest in order to make a decorative gesture underlining the sincerity of whatever the hell I was then expounding, only to feel something missing, as though my chest had, unbeknownst to me, been shaved. With a gasp I rather indecorously whispered, "My pearls!" Yes, just as in a tawdry novel. While the most likely solution to the mystery is that the clasp broke and the string of pearls merely slid unnoticed to the street, the thought of such a reality is simply too horrifying to contemplate. Much better to imagine them disappearing into the hands of a handsome man who just happened to be near enough to put his fingers to the nape of my neck to unfasten the pearls and, with his sweet smile distracting me, pocket them for his own use that very night. Yes, this is a much nicer thought than thinking of them being trod upon by an ugly pair of ordinary running shoes. Whatever did happen, they seem to have gone for good, and many memories with them.

Only a week later, on a day when substitutes filled in for both of my regular pool buddies, my nicest everyday pearls vanished. At first it was assumed the guy who took me to the pool had put them out of sight of the guy who later came to fetch me. Alternatively it was thought that the latter, not alert for such accessories as pearls, simply did not think to search for them, nor I to mention them to him. Once again, part way through the day I felt a sudden lack and realized the pearls were gone. On my next visit to the pool I asked the staff if any pearls had been found either by a swimmer or by one of the janitorial crew. None had, leaving me to hope and pray they had left the building on the chest of a kind man who would treat them well. This particular episode happens to have a happy ending, however, because the pearls were later found in my jacket pocket, placed there by a conscientious substitute pool buddy who did not know where else to put them, but failed to let me know of his wonderful solution to the problem. By the time the missing pearls were discovered, however, I had already substituted another set of everyday pearls. I was therefore now wearing two strands doubled into four, which seemed a nice change.

Yesterday, while leaning over to do some minor task, both sets of pearls caught on something without my being aware of it and upon straightening up the strings of pearls broke, both of them. This, fortunately, has not left me depleted of pearls, though what remain are either the crown jewels—not to be worn for just any old occasion—or are really rather cheap, having come to me through thoughtful people who evidently thought this girl would wear anything. Which, when it comes to pearls, is close enough to the truth.

Learning to get about with walkers and wheelchairs is one thing. Having to give up one's pearls is quite another, though I suppose it must be done at some point and better strand by strand than all in a lump. THAT would devastate. I am afraid it will not help for you to say, "But Zsolt, my dear, they were mere costume jewelry." This is rather like the Prince saying of a woman who has just died, "Oh, she was just the milliner." Milliner or not, she had her stories.

Regardless, all of these pearly tragedies are leaving me feeling as though I have become immerged in a poorly written mystery novel.

I suppose the above tragedies point up the fact that it is always easier to dispose of things oneself than to have them wrenched away by the hand of Destiny. Somehow, at times like this, when you thought you knew Destiny well, the feel of his hand is not quite what you remember.

With this in mind it is a queer thing that we continue obsessively living an illusion of Life as Accretion and Ownership: how we painstakingly accrue degrees, years, objects, wrinkles, honors; we have children, grandchildren, defenses, spouses, houses, sex. In fact we are so damn confident of the ownership of our accretion, rather like plaque on the teeth, that it is quite a joke when, somewhere in all the fuss of Having, we begin to find that the dominant feature of life is not Accumulation, but Loss. Quite likely in our earlier years we lost a kitten, or a toy, or a friend, or a grandparent, even a parent. As we age, however, and even with the persistent amassing of birthdays, we find ourselves losing everything from muscle tone to memory, pearls to hair. As the dust piles up and inflation grows, as undone chores multiply and wrinkles are added daily, many of us begin questioning whether our glittering personal empires are stable enough to maintain themselves to the end.

For a year and a half I have been going through, sorting out, and tossing away the most incredible rubbish from my life. How I ever thought it was anything worth saving, I do not know. Boxes and boxes have gone off to the thrift shops. Bags and more bags have been sent to the Dumpster, everything from water-damaged magazines to worn-out clothing—since most of my clothing comes to me from thrift shops, by the time I am done with it the earth wants it back. Nicer objects have gone to charities for fundraising purposes; other things, now ruined beyond recognition, were simply thrown into trash bags. My health beginning to fail, I was determined to do as much as I could while I was still able to sort through things, simplifying my own glittering empire. The thought of people I care about having to go through all that muck and decide what was what and whether it was important or not, shamed me into action, albeit at a Herculean turtle's pace. It did not happen all in a weekend, of course, but over a period of months, now becoming years. In an odd way I feel as though I am returning to a prior time in my life when everything I owned could be carried across the earth on my back and in my hands. There is still much to be rid of before reaching that state, however, and anyway by the time I get there I will not be able to lift anything, therefore I suppose it does not especially matter whether it is all gone by the time I am all gone. I do find the whole process, regardless of the progression of my condition, healing. There have been so many goodbyes, so many little lead weights dropped to rest where they lie, somewhere back there next to the pillar of salt. And truly, there is no looking back, is there, darling?

An inventory of what has gone might be of interest you:

A rack of wedding gowns. Some years ago, while with a group of friends on our way to a fundraising ball, our car was hit by a motorist from California. Climbing out to assess damage and injury, it happened that I was the last one out, replete in wedding gown, much to the amazement of the children in the offending vehicle. I don't suppose it would have made matters any clearer if I had confessed to owning a pair of Levi's which actually made me look rather butch, but only so long as I stood still and did not walk. Once in motion, the Swan cannot be camouflaged.

A horribly moth-eaten poncho purchased in Ecuador—one which I had owned for more than twenty years—was recently discovered and resolutely given back to the earth. I suppose it is not quite right to say it was discovered, because I knew all along where it was and even that it was gradually being reduced to dust by the vital forces of nature. Something, however, kept me from being rid of it, and at the same time it seemed useless to try and salvage it; so there it sat at the bottom of a pile of cloth, occasionally reminding me of how well it had kept me warm on three continents. Its memorable mantling has since been replaced by other articles of clothing, its stories incorporated into a greater scheme than was predicted at the time of its purchase, myself then only a teenager.

Stacks of magazines filled with important articles about how to battle squash bugs in the garden, or about the origins of the Steinway Piano Manufacturing Company; or containing interesting facts concerning the Masai people, complete with gorgeous photographs. Long ago all of these topics seemed worthy of future study, of being returned to in the hopes of actually quashing the squash bugs or merely in order to gaze at the face of a beautiful man from another realm. Needless to say, the stacks of magazines, seldom touched after being earnestly put aside for future use, became nothing more than a confusion, for there was no simple way of cataloging them, of facilitating access to their wisdom. Hence, many of these were given to a teacher in the public school system. Better they be used there, even if it be for making collages in art class, which is, in many respects, the best possible use for them. Interestingly, the memories held within their covers are different than those of other objects I have disposed of; for the memories of a magazine article are of a future that never came to pass. Rather than being a relic of a moment frozen in my history, those magazines were a hint of plans made and for one reason or another never executed.

Coins and paper money gathered up from around the world, now mostly meted out to young friends who are enchanted with the quaintness of having either an old coin, or a coin from a country which no longer exists. To them the words schilling, pengö, Soviet Union, Yugoslavia are remnants from an encyclopedia whose pages have been randomly torn out and speak less of geography and history than of magic.

Grainy photographs of vegetation that might have depicted part of a landscape or might merely have been a close-up of a tossed salad served at a long-forgotten dinner party.

Piles of notebooks, reams of poetic fragments, bundles of manuscripts, some so weathered that the ink had almost vanished. Thousands of words scrawled across pages which were themselves strewn across my life, now gone, their bits of dialogue, their long stretches of narrative, their poetic whispers buried in the flesh of a god who gave birth to their spidery existences without my knowing about it.

And so many motley things, you cannot imagine, you simply cannot imagine what a life this has been.

Even with all the cleanings and purges, some of them quite dramatic, one of the most hallowed parts of my collected life had until recently remained firmly intact: my library of printed music. Last week I dutifully began to work my way through an undergrowth of notes and clefs, of the ornate names of composers and compositions, printed and bound by publishing houses near and far. I had always assumed that when I died this entire library would be as it has been, complete, along with any music that would be further added between now and then. In these past weeks, however, I have felt a great desire to see some of it rescued from the dark morasses of filing cabinets and placed into the hands of people who, even if they themselves do not have the capacity to play the music, might marvel at the notation, might feel a kinship with the composer as have I. The music chosen to be given away now sits in a large pile awaiting decisions about distribution: some to this friend, some to that friend; some to a library, some to a chorus having a fundraiser...

Within that extensive library, however, there is one section which shall remain intact, to be given away whole at some future date. This is my collection of keyboard works by women composers. To date eighty-five women are represented, spanning four centuries and six continents, their music ranging from early Baroque through Rococo, Classical through Romantic, Impressionist, Serial, Ragtime, Blues, Jazz, and Folk. It has taken fifteen years to amass this collection, which even now continues to grow. Some of it, taken piece by piece, is rather dubious as concerns its musical integrity; a lot of it is enjoyable to play; and a few of the works are truly masterpieces. Broken apart it is an eclectic collection, much of which, when seen alone, presents a pale complexion. Together, however, it is a remarkable documentation of the struggles and triumphs of women who desired to create music, often against the most daunting and even vicious obstacles. Gustav Mahler was so intimidated by his fiancée Alma's exceptional compositional skills that he made her agree to forego composing once they were married. Even when looking at an obvious "parlor piece" of sentimental persuasion, I am astonished; for here is the audacity of a woman who, desiring to write music, found an arena in which she could, and did.

Yes, I am growing accustomed to living life without the exuberance of dancing, without the thrill of bicycling, without a rack of wedding dresses, without coins that are no longer even exchangeable, without dimly-imagined futures that never came to pass, and as I contemplate my own future I am gradually coming to peace with the thought of living without this object or that, without the full use of my legs, without the playing of music, without much of what has previously defined me, both in my eyes and in the eyes of others. Oddly enough, though, this persistent dissolution of things, whether real or conceptual, is leaving me feeling ever more alive, not less. What remains, however vulnerable, is yet tough and brilliant as a diamond. And on each facet of that diamond is reflected the face of someone I love.

It is here where I most resist having to dismantle my life: those I love. Thankfully there is no need to dismantle them at this point. And perhaps there never will be. While we are often told that we will have to take that last step alone, I wonder if this is true, for in some queer way the love we have been given, part of a magnificent universe, as well as the love we have lived and shared is not only who we are but also that into which we will step at the threshold of death. Even if it be dust to dust, some kind friend is bound to plant a seed in it and watch with awe as it sprouts into luxuriant growth whose berries vaguely resemble pearls.

So toss out the old toaster ovens, throw away the clothing that no longer fits, burn the moth-eaten years of your youth, your life, but the people you love, take them with you, for it is into their love that you will dissolve at the threshold.

Oh hell, take along a string of pearls, too.

January 16, 2000

17. THE BICYCLE MECHANIC

For years my main source of transportation around town was my beloved bicycle. My first good bicycle was purchased from a friend who was moving to Sweden. It was a Raleigh ten-speed he had used for racing of some kind, as well as for his own personal enjoyment. It was not a new bicycle, yet it was finely made and rode wonderfully. Additionally, it was lovely to look at, with ornamental details one would not find on most bicycles today. In due course I became very attached to it, the two of us having one adventure after another. Early on I learned to ride without use of my hands so that I could better view the passing scenery, feeling almost as though I were flying. I thrilled at going so fast that the pedals could no longer keep up with the wheels.

Though I was constantly having flat tires, often from the thorny goatheads sprinkled about the roads, I never quite grasped how to fix a flat or change a tire. My bicycle mechanic, the kindly Aunt Art, would patiently show me the procedure and I would diligently pay utmost attention—for it did interest me—and yet, the next time I had a flat, whether within weeks or months, I would find myself walking the bicycle to Aunt Art's shop, knowing that I would no more remember how to fix it than win a decathlon. In a heroic attempt to circumvent the problem without alluding to the fact that I was a total idiot when it came to tire culture, my mechanic over time suggested various options, such as thicker inner tubes or more knobby tires, which solutions, while they were probably of immense help, failed to curtail my occasional visits to Aunt Art.

A couple of years later, Jeremy came to work with Aunt Art and quickly became Uncle Jeremy. Thereafter, whenever my bicycle had problems I would take it to Aunt Art and Uncle Jeremy who between them never failed to not only fix the immediate problem but also to make the bicycle run ever so much better. Was it because they had done some extra bit of tuneup, or was it simply because they were such nice guys that the bicycle was invariably easier to ride after being in their capable hands?

One sad day, however, I was riding along having just had a new derailleur put on, when of a sudden things went awry. Getting off the bicycle I looked down to find that a small, albeit crucial, part of the frame had broken. Hauling it up onto my shoulders I carried it to Uncle Jeremy who gave the grimmest of diagnoses, one without even a prognosis. My beloved bicycle had succumbed to Death by Zsolt. Well, only the frame; the rest of the parts were just fine, including the new derailleur. Relating this story to a friend, he mentioned that he had an old frame from his former days of riding, and if the two bicycles were compatible, perhaps Uncle Jeremy and Aunt Art could combine them into one. This new frame was an Italian frame made in Greece, or some such combination—perhaps it was a Greek frame made in Italy. A week after dropping off this frame, I returned to pick up my new bicycle. There it was: blue, not red, and in perfect working order. Aunt Art showed me his workmanship, explaining his decisions about which parts he kept as well as those that had been added. Then he went over to the work bench, picking up an object which he then handed to me. Looking at it I recognized it as part of my old bicycle. He had cut the frame up for use as fireplace utensils, leaving for me the most beautiful part, the section I had always liked best. While I certainly enjoyed having this memento—and have it still, even following a year and a half of dismantling my material world—what impressed me most was that he had paid attention. Aunt Art KNEW how much that bicycle meant to me, and he understood why. Furthermore, he also knew precisely the focal point of my relationship to that bicycle, and it was this piece of metal he now gave to me.

Soon enough I came to enjoy my new bicycle as much as the old. Perhaps this was because of its stories. Before I even sat on my new bicycle it had a history which included me and my friends.

My routine in those years, since I did not live in town, was to be dropped off early in the morning, sometimes as early as 6:30 A.M., near the highway that runs along the edge of town. Then I would ride all over the place to work, to study, to do errands, before joining up with my ride in the evening, as late as seven or eight, sometimes nine o'clock. This procedure was a year-round routine, summer, autumn, winter, and spring, regardless of weather conditions. There were only a few days when I ended up on foot rather than bicycle. In many ways I was in the better position when it came to road hazards such as blizzards, because I could always pick up my vehicle and move it to the side of the road and from there continue on my way, walking the bike beside me. Being on a bicycle in a snowstorm often brought about some interesting encounters. I would often stop to help push cars out of snow drifts or give them a shove over some ice, then get back on my bicycle and pedal away.

One day, during a particularly nasty blizzard, I was as usual getting out of a warm vehicle to fetch my bicycle from the rack on the back when I realized I did not have any shoes on. I had left home wearing only my socks—though, not to worry you, I was wearing trousers, shirt, etc. There I was, ready to pedal off, and my shoes were thirty kilometers away. What else to do but get on the bicycle and ride into the 7:00 A.M. traffic. Several hours later, in the hopes of procuring shoes, any shoes, I found my way to a thrift shop. At that point I would have taken whatever shoes fit my feet and my meager budget, even if they had been bright red four-inch pumps. Alas, there was nothing, absolutely nothing in my size. Therefore, in place of shoes I bought several pairs of old socks and wore every damn one, pretending they were warm, felted arctic boots slathered in water-proofing goose grease, which fantasy worked well enough and got me through the day without frostbite.

In the spring were the winds.

In the summertime thunderstorms would come of a sudden, quickly leaving me drenched—an interesting aspect about such deluges is that you get exactly one second between being dry and being wet, and thereafter you are simply more wet and more wet.

Autumn was generally a pleasant time to ride.

Parking was rarely a problem; neither were traffic jams. If I got stuck in traffic I picked up the bicycle, set it on the sidewalk and rode off, an option which, though it may be illegal, at least got me to where I was going. If there were no sidewalk and the terrain were too rough for riding, I could still walk my bike alongside the stalled traffic and was comfortably able to get past the accident or whatever was holding up traffic.

Last spring I was attending a performance of Bach's great Mass in B Minor. Afterwards, while getting ready to depart on my motorbike—I was still riding my motorbike then—I happened to meet up with Uncle Jeremy and his wife. At that point, not having ridden my bicycle for a while, I hadn't had much contact with either Uncle Jeremy or Aunt Art, though I would occasionally see Uncle Jeremy in his truck and wave greetings toward him. There in the lobby of the church where the concert was held it was good to reconnect with him, particularly after hearing the music of J. S. Bach.

At that time I was trying to come up with ways to exercise my increasingly weakening body; more precisely, ways to get to the swimming pool where I hoped I would be able to develop a workable regimen of exercise. Riding home on my motorbike that April night I wondered if I ought to contact Uncle Jeremy to ask for his help. Not knowing his telephone number or even his last name, I had a friend contact him at his bicycle shop in order to ask if he would be willing to do what might now be called pool duty. As he was more than willing to help, a schedule was arranged and that was that. Well, it was not quite so simple. While my entire life at that time was filled with unexpected and novel situations, it must be admitted that having one's former bicycle mechanic help one out in the locker room requires a definite shift of perspective. I suppose it might be easier for you to grasp the situation if I underscore the fact that we were not there for a recreational swim together, nor was I an old man who finally at the end of a long life needed a bit of help;

indeed I had only six months earlier turned thirty-nine. From years of highly disciplined dance training and performance; from years of bicycle riding and jogging, I had the body of an athlete, though, due to neural degeneration, it was no longer coordinated like that of an athlete. Add to this that it is not an ordinary thing to be thirty-nine years old needing to ask your mechanic to help you out in the locker room. This among so many shifting relationships in which what had come before had simply laid a few stepping stones toward what is now by necessity a more intimate and inevitably more profound relationship.

While there were often confusing moments for me in those months, and moments of frustration or despondency, Uncle Jeremy, in his own inimitable style, would not let go. I mean this in the best possible sense. At times when I wanted to give up—or worse, in moments when I had not a clue what was up and what was down—he remained firmly beside me, in body and in soul. As I was trying to get some sense of what was happening to me and my body, Uncle Jeremy never expected me to do or be anything more than what I was in any given moment. Due to the proximity of his shop, there came a spate of times when he was called up by the pool staff to come rescue me when other helpers failed to show up. Never once did he complain about these sudden requests which inevitably pulled him away from work and customers.

Among other things, Uncle Jeremy is also a brew master. One fine day he showed up a few minutes late for his usual round of taking me to the pool. Getting into his truck I was greeted with a most delicious aroma—though not the aroma of his usual morning coffee. Commenting on the luscious fragrance, I was told that one of the tubes on the huge brewing vats had only moments earlier broken or come undone or some such mishap, causing beer to spew all over him. Well, I certainly did not mind, and made a comment about the possibility of selling the beer as a cologne. For the next twenty minutes, as we went through our routine at the pool, in among the odors of chlorine and soap, I had the wonderful opportunity to enjoy the fragrance of this man's life, of his work, of one of the things he really enjoys doing. I use this example to illustrate how my life now unfolds not only in unexpected ways but in ways beautifully constrained by living with a disability, a condition which itself is structured by the continuing decline of my body. You see, in the very narrowing of my world it is becoming expansive in the most subtle of ways, ways that have nothing to do with distance, momentum, or duration. Had not my needs become quite specific, confined to a place and a point and a need for help, I would forever have known Uncle Jeremy only as a kind, intelligent bicycle mechanic. Instead I have become closely acquainted with a remarkable human being.

I do not know why I tell you about this man, other than to invite you to turn off your television or radio with all of its artificial news and to step outside, to look into the night sky, to contemplate the enigma of one man helping another, of one human being helping another. In looking up at the deep expanses of stars above you, or at the luxuriant clouds reflecting the bright lights of your city, the marvel of one man giving selflessly to another finds an apt environment in which to dwell, namely within your heart.

That, my friends, is the news.

January 26, 2000

23. THE TRAIN

—For Jane Diggs

There are doors a person goes in and out of as easily as waving a hand. Such doors are routinely structured into our lives as marvelously convenient landmarks. One has only to think of one's front door. In the morning a person uses it to go out into the big world and in the evening one returns through it in order to enter the sanctuary of the home. There are many such doors in our lives, so many, in fact, that we seldom think of a door as anything at all, that it might perhaps be other than what it appears, or, in an odd twist, that a very undoorlike experience might in fact be a door. Because, you see, there are also doors one passes through never to return. It is not merely that one chooses not to go back over its threshold. It is that one is unable to, is forbidden to.

It is arguable that, due to the explicit arrow of time itself, every moment of our lives is a doorway of the latter not the former quality. Yet, on a macroscopic level we find ourselves quite capable of passing many times back and forth through the doors of our lives with minimal enough deviation in the structure of the universe that it is as though the door is the same door and we the same people. When I speak of a door through which a person goes only once, it is not of these subtle and barely recognizable changes I am referring, but of a profound meeting with the unknown, a relationship which we must then become, or perish.

In some inexplicable way I feel as though, over the past weeks, I have gone through such a door. In retrospect it was a vast, unbounded doorway that did not make its existence known until I had turned around to look at something else, at which point the carved, wooden door became small and fixed, even ordinarily knowable. Set into its hard wooden surface is an ornate window of leaded glass through which I am still able to see what remains on the other side, which—I ought not be surprised—is quite a lot, and, as you can well imagine, quite a lot of familiar faces and places. Looking around me here in this new expanse, however, I recognize very little.

I am not, however, alone, for it has gradually dawned on me that I have not crossed the threshold by myself. And while those who have accompanied me might themselves have made mention of the door, in truth the journey was accomplished with such apparent effortlessness that I am not sure any of us quite realized we were in a different experience until I myself looked back and saw the past settling into the very ordinary form of a door, a door through whose glass I can still see people frenetically going about their lives as though each of my gestures and those of the men and women surrounding me were invisible to them. Furthermore, as the days advance, it is becoming ever more clear that I and those with me have not come here on holiday, to loll about a while before going back through that door, a door which, if we could reopen it, would bring us once again into that before-world. No, the door has ineluctably been shut tight by some unseen hand.

And how to describe the expanse in which I find myself? It feels very like an infinite, unwalled train compartment, its seats having been gradually filled by the people who have accompanied me through the door, the door itself being now closed by the conductor in preparation for the blowing of the whistle.

I have always found something heartrendingly beautiful about the blowing of that whistle, signaling as it does the lurching forward of a monstrous, human-made engine coupled to a long chain of wagons which enclose people whose destinations vary, whose pasts intermingle or not, and yet who for the foreseeable future are bound by the journey of the train on its tracks. At various moments during the past weeks, in the subtle and barely perceptible boarding process, I have found myself gazing at the face of this man, or that woman, or a child standing beside me. Looking thoughtfully at the lines of these faces, the textures of their stories, the thought continually comes to me, whispering in my ear, *This is the face of Buddha.*

Then I turn to look through the beveled glass of the door to see what and who, for whatever reason, remained on the other side, their faces and bodies and fragrances fading with each moment, becoming lifeless while remaining incessantly active. Having begun to grasp what has happened, I am gradually realizing that as those faces behind the beveled glass fade from view, whether faces of people or faces of places or faces of ideas, I must allow myself to grieve for them. While for many months my life has been held in a prolonged suspension between past and future, somehow the equilibrium of that stasis has now been tipped, setting in motion not only the recent passage across a profound threshold, but the motion of the train itself.

I am perhaps fortunate in that I am very fond of trains, and while most travelers have a sense of departure whenever an airplane lifts off the earth or their car turns a corner, there is something unique about a train's departure; perhaps because, due to the nature of train travel, there will inevitably be so many departures along the route, most of which do not belong to us, but to someone else. Nonetheless, we find ourselves players in a remarkable ebb and flow of arrival and departure, of participating in something inclusive of humanity; never is a train ride purely one's own. So, as this rather indescribable train gathers enough momentum to carry itself on, I find myself waving goodbye to people behind a piece of leaded glass, people who are so preoccupied that they are not even aware a train has come into the depot and is now departing; I wave my hand at ethereal places and people who are now farther from me than the white clouds in the blue sky, farther than the great arms of the Crab Nebula.

Taking a deep breath and lowering my hand, I turn to survey the occupants of this particular carriage and am astonished at the faces of Buddha. I want to say to this one or that one, *What are you doing here?* Or, *Who would've thought you would be here!* Ah, the mysterious Divine has a wicked sense of humor, and a rather improper sense of propriety. Where, for instance, are all those faces that were supposed to be here, who either said they would be here or whom I expected would be here? Such a joke upon my presumptuous ego! And to add jest to jest, one of the faces is a loaf of banana bread. Yes, a loaf of banana bread, and I am not trying to be sacrilegious, my friends. At the very last second, between the blow of the whistle and the lurch forward of the great universal engine, a charming postman arrived with a parcel from a woman I have known since she was ten and who is now twenty-four. Upon opening the parcel—which might have been books, since she is a writer, or might have been a collection of tattered *pointe* shoes, since she was also a ballerina—I discovered yet another face of Buddha, namely a bubble-wrapped, foil-shrouded loaf of banana bread baked by my friend.

Then, nestled in among the faces, there is Sweet Will. In these two words are three distinctly unconnected faces of Buddha: a book, a man, and a concept. The book is a gift. The man a fellow human being. The concept a luminously lit lamp. If none of this makes sense to you, it isn't necessarily supposed to. How, indeed, is it possible to explicate in words the remarkable convergence that is a hand span of the Bayeux Tapestry? Nonetheless, in the same way that we may find truth in the sublime, I hope you shall discover beauty in the presence of Sweet Will, a book, a man, and a concept.

Additionally, though the seats in this wagon seem well enough occupied, I do not doubt that some impish rogue of my acquaintance will have jumped onto the end of the train just as it left the depot and before it had gathered enough energy to prevent communication with the past; yes, a roguish villain of my own ilk who will at some near moment drop down the side of the train and enter mischievously through the window, an act that will no doubt endear him or her to me for the remaining hours, days, months, and years of this journey.

Perhaps now you can see how at once there is a grieving and a celebrating, these two fundamental aspects of life intermingling so deeply that the expression of each is, for all intents and purposes, the same. The idea of celebrating a loss may seem queer to some folk, but I think there is no other option, because in celebrating a loss we refuse to deny it. In other words, our loss cannot be brushed under the rug or hidden in the closet when it has been made the guest of honor. Second, by celebrating our losses we pay homage to the hours spent together, the things shared, and whatever happenstance brought such living into contact. Ah, to be sure, there is much to grieve for, so much life lived, that I am likely to spend an eternity celebrating it. Yet, I cannot do so just now, because a man has come to sit beside me, to remind me that it is time to go to the swimming pool (evidently there is a swimming pool on this train), and to help me up from the upholstered seat. Yes, the celebration of my grieving must be inextricably woven into the small steps, one after another, which take me down the train, out of this man's hands and into the embrace of the water, all the while a fragment of melody sweeping in through the open windows.

Compassion.

At the root of this word is another word: Passion, which originally meant, and still means in certain situations, agony or suffering, as in J. S. Bach's "St. Matthew Passion," referring to St. Matthew's view of Christ's suffering. Adding the prefix *com-*, we find ourselves with a much misunderstood word which means to suffer with or alongside of. Note that it does not mean to suffer for or in place of, but with and alongside. The act of compassion is necessarily one of relationship. If ever you have walked beside other human beings, supporting them because they cannot walk by themselves, or have helped transfer a bedridden person into a wheelchair or onto a portable toilet, you will know the truth of this, though such a truth can only be illuminated if the relationship pierces the flesh and flows from heart to heart. Otherwise it remains merely a chore from which we desperately want to be relieved as soon as possible. Though the foundation of the word, and of such a relationship, resides in suffering and agony, in practice if two people walk together in compassionate love, then a mysterious thing ensues: the suffering dissipates. Oh, not that there is no longer pain or difficulty—nor has some miraculous healing occurred—only that sorrow is sublimated in joy, and ordinary suffering cannot exist in such a communion of love.

Yes, the whistle has blown.

The train lurches forward. I look about me at the myriad faces of Buddha, I marvel at Sweet Will, I patiently await the arrival of an unguessable rogue, I nibble at a slice of banana bread and know that all is.

Is what?

Is.

February 20, 2000

32. WHEELCHAIR ETIQUETTE

ased on experiences garnered from years of caring for people in wheelchairs and also from using one myself I have compiled the following guidelines. The ideas contained in it are not comprehensive nor are they universal; some apply to certain situations and not others. There are probably as many emendations as there are people in wheelchairs.

AUNT ZSOLT'S GUIDELINES FOR WHEELCHAIR ETIQUETTE

Let us start by giving a name to the person in the wheelchair. How about we call her Naomi. (While in my wheelchair I have been called everything from Rollergimp to Cutie, Sweetie to Heyyou. Once someone called me Pumpkin, but I think she was referring to my dog.) The following ideas are not ranked in any particular order.

1. When speaking with Naomi, it is an excellent idea to come down to her level. This can be done by squatting, kneeling, or pulling up a chair. Personally, I have been considering finding a way to attach a small, portable camp stool to my wheelchair so that when I am with people who cannot get onto the ground (or cannot get up) they will have somewhere to perch. If you cannot sit, leaning over can be useful, so long as you do not hover like a vulture over carrion.

2. Unless you are actually in the act of pushing Naomi's wheelchair, step in front of her to express yourself. It is nice for her to be able to see the person with whom she is communicating; in this way she can observe body language as well as delight in the visual aspect of the relationship. Also, this allows her to save energy by not having to project her voice to reach around behind her. Two additional points here: do not walk away while you are speaking, and do not turn your back. While Naomi may still be able to hear you, she is once again put into the position of having to project her voice farther while at the same time losing the opportunity to use non-verbal body language to communicate her ideas or needs.

3. When pushing the chair for Naomi, if you find yourself utterly intent on doing wheelies, or skipping along behind the wheelchair, or running REALLY fast simply because you need to release some pent up energy, ask her beforehand. It is not a good idea to assume that she shares your idea of a fun time; nor is it

wise to assume that she is not interested. A good wheelie may be just what Naomi is in the mood for. To complicate things even more, one day she may say yes and the next day she may say no. Or, she may say no to you and yes to your sister, simply because she likes the way your sister does wheelies. No need to take offense.

4. Communicate clearly. Listen attentively. When around others, let Naomi communicate for herself whenever possible. Even if she needs to use alternative forms of communication such as a word board.

5. Please do not blather on about other peoples' disabled situations, or about how well you have dealt with those situations in the past. Naomi is Naomi and not Percival. In other words, what worked with Percival will not necessarily work with Naomi; it is a good idea to observe and listen carefully to Naomi's needs, then adapt what you learned from helping Percival. While it is certainly important to utilize what you have learned from prior experiences, each person with a disability is a marvelous new frontier, as is each person without a disability, for that matter.

6. I would not automatically assume Naomi is miserable in her wheelchair, but if you speak and act as though she is, she probably will be, if for no other reason than that she cannot stand being around you. Conversely, she may be utterly miserable in her wheelchair and having someone prance about on healthy legs saying, "Oh, it really isn't so bad, is it?" is likely to make Naomi suicidal. That said, you need not tiptoe about on eggshells; just observe her own attitude and respond accordingly. If you are uncertain, it doesn't hurt to ask, "What are your feelings about your wheelchair, Naomi?" Do not ask, however, unless you are truly interested in listening to the answer, because she may tell you things you are unprepared for and which you would rather not hear.

7. Neither you nor Naomi are super-humans. If you get tired pushing her wheelchair around, or dealing with Naomi's demanding ways, tell her. Bottling it all up inside of yourself will only lead to burnout, at which point you will be totally useless to Naomi, and you may never want to help another person as long as you live. In other words, take care of yourself. While the relationship may be physically lopsided, there is no need for it to be emotionally or spiritually lopsided. This is a good place to remind you that you need not be afraid of making mistakes. Even when they annoy the hell out of Naomi, you have the right to make mistakes. Most of my caregivers can tell you about the day(s) they forgot to show up, or some other infraction of duty. My own philosophy in these situations is, "If I can't accept that you'll make mistakes, then I've no right to ask you to help me." Obviously there is a break-even point, and after too many mistakes Naomi may ask you to move on. If this happens, be as gracious as you can about it, even if she is not as composed and respectful as you might wish.

8. Offer to massage Naomi's feet, legs, arms, back, hands, scalp, even her butt and her tummy. There are medical reasons for this, as well as any psychological benefits to be obtained. It is important to remember that Naomi is

sitting a lot, maybe most of the time. Massaging her butt can help prevent pressure sores, which can be a very serious health problem, gently massaging her tummy can aid in digestion and elimination, rubbing her hands and feet can assist in circulation. Here we can keep in mind the words of the anthropologist Claude Lévi-Strauss, "An impropriety is no longer improper when it possesses its own logic—a logic that differs from that of the discourse in which it is first introduced." Once again, ASK FIRST before you rush in and start rubbing away. If Naomi has a tendency to form blood clots in her legs, massaging them may loosen the clots, sending them toward her brain where they may cause a stroke. Massage may also cause her pain. If you are uncertain, and if Naomi is herself not sure, ask her physician or her physical/massage therapist. Also, everyone's reaction to being touched is quite different; so be attentive to how you ask and how you touch. On the other hand, a caring touch may totally transform Naomi's day, particularly if she has lost the ability to initiate it herself. As in other situations she may say no to you and yes to your spouse or to a complete stranger. No need to be offended. Naomi knows what feels right for her, even if her choices do not make sense to you.

9. If she can stand at all, ask her if she wants to do so with your assistance. While you are up there, she may appreciate a great big hug. Or she may not, and might just like the opportunity to hold on to you simply in order to be out of her wheelchair. Being able to stand, if only for a few moments, can help with blood circulation, bone mass conservation, and the prevention of edema.

10. Offer to clean Naomi's wheelchair once in a while. She may already have someone doing it on a regular basis, but if not, it will be a nice treat for her. Also, if you see some modification you think might make Naomi's life in her wheelchair easier, offer to make it. Again, DO NOT automatically do it without asking her or someone close to her. While it may be the most brilliant idea ever, she may not necessarily be prepared for it psychologically, financially or physically.

11. Offer to take her out somewhere, particularly somewhere you think others will not. For instance, if you are strong and wheelchair savvy, suggest taking Naomi along a mountain trail or to the beach. If you think of an expedition which you feel she would enjoy but which is not wheelchair accessible, round up some people willing to help you lift the wheelchair past the inaccessible zone. If it looks impossible, look again.

12. Take your time. Unless Naomi says, "We gotta get the hell out of here," there is no need to rush. (I am blessed with a great group of caregivers who rarely hurry. Even when things get complicated, causing them to be late for work or late for a date with girlfriends or spouses, they generally stay completely focused within the timelessness of the task. This is not to say that my caregivers are slothful, or that you need to be. It is a matter of attitude, not of tempo.)

13. Learn early on where the brakes on the wheelchair are, and make sure to use them, particularly if Naomi is not capable of doing so herself. Even if she is,

however, it does not hurt to double check to make sure they are secured, because she may be assuming you have taken care of it. Also, this is not an especially good time to be cavalier, thinking that you need not bother with the brakes because, after all, you are standing right there and what could possibly go wrong? Believe me, lots can and will go wrong. If you are going to be around Naomi more than once or twice, take some time to familiarize yourself with her particular wheelchair. If possible let her tell and show you, instead of swaggering in pretending you know everything about wheelchairs. Even if you do know a lot about wheelchairs, it is a nice opportunity to let her know she has something to offer to the world. Here I might mention that it is wise to use your knees and not your back when transferring Naomi. Even if she is a slight person, you can cause a lot of injury to yourself if something goes awry. If you are going to be doing a lot of transferring, learn the proper techniques, for your own safety as well as Naomi's.

14. If you are Naomi's motor, meaning that you are the one pushing the wheelchair, back her into elevators so that when the doors open at your destination both she and you are looking toward where you will be going. Whatever you do, do not park her facing a wall—unless she requests you do so. This may seem the most obvious thing in the world, and yet I am surprised at how often it happens to me, or something similar. When necessary, turn her toward the people she is conversing with. Also, it is a good idea to be constantly aware of how far the footrests stick out in front of the wheelchair, else you will hit a lot of unsuspecting people in the backs of the legs. This is not bumper cars, you know.

15. While there is a lot of information here, the most crucial thing to remember is to be yourself. Be open. Be open to your own feelings. Be open to humor, to joy, to distress, to despair. Be open to the opportunity for a remarkable relationship. Be open to the touch of the divine, because, if you are, one day in your indescribable journey with Naomi, you will encounter it.

When that day comes you will turn around in order to see who is touching you and you will meet yourself.

July 5, 2000

33. BREATHING, THE SONG OF LIFE

It is amazing how a lowly visit to the pulmonologist can utterly transform a person's life. One day I am loping about haphazardly, either in my wheelchair or with the assistance of my walker, and the next I learn that my maximal respiratory pressures are, on average, thirty percent of normal, leading the kind doctor to speak quaintly of Tracheostomies and Ventilators as though we were discussing what flavor of cake to order for his daughter's wedding. This last comment is not meant to illustrate any cold-heartedness on the part of the doctor, rather the opposite, to show both his ease and his genial accessibility. Indeed, I find that I quite like the man. Before going further, I will clarify that my lungs themselves are healthy. It is the underlying musculature that has weakened, thereby making it difficult to breathe smoothly and deeply.

(I am sitting on a train. Across from me a woman cradles a baby in her arms. Perhaps she is the mother or the aunt of the child. Maybe she is a fellow passenger who has offered to hold the baby while the mother goes in search of the loo. Regardless, and as she gently rocks it back and forth, the woman begins to sing softly. As the fields and trees outside fly past us, an uncomplicated melody flows across the woman's tongue, her lips, words interwoven with sounds rippling out from a single breath. Sitting nearby I not only hear and feel the lyrics and the tune of the lullaby, I am also touched by and made to understand in some small way the life of the woman who transforms those words and harmonies within her breast before setting them ever and again afloat on the breath of her life.)

Breathing—is there any more fundamental act of living?

One of the first things done to each and every one of us out of the womb is the infamous slap on the back to encourage our first breath, our first transaction with the atmosphere of earth. One of the last things we do—after the last scenic drive, the last cigarette, the last morsel of food, the last mumble, the last gaze—is to breathe one final breath. Little, if anything, follows this ultimate breath. Perhaps one final aural reception, or a sensation of touch. I think most of us agree that whatever ensues from this point, and whatever form a person's life takes, it is no longer a life of and on this planet.

Exhalation ever succeeding inhalation.

Inspiration transpiring into expiration, two hands between which we are balanced in a miracle called life, an ebb and flow between the inner self and the divine other, forever expressed as inhalation flowing into exhalation, the continuum of this cycle the most intimate of our relationships.

Breathing—the song of life.

The opposite of death (expiration) is not life, but creation (inspiration), for life itself encompasses both creation and death, and therefore cannot be the opposite of either one. The fundamental dynamism that hallows life arises from the rhythm produced by these two opposites, creation and death, expansion and contraction, each embedded in cycles great and small, cycles which are the fundamental pulse of life.

In–spirit. Each inhalation of our lives is a bringing in of the spirit, the breath, the divine urge.

Ex–spirit. The exhalation is our response, a giving back, a return. Each exhalation constitutes a personal response to the universe. Furthermore, with each expiration we may offer laughter or profanity, poetry or gossip, gratitude or propaganda, warmth or bigotry, music or sarcasm. Whatever flows across a person's tongue, however, is his or her song, the expression of his or her experience of life.

The other night I went with some teenage friends to see *Le Nozze di Figaro* by W. A. Mozart. Toward the end of the fourth act there exists one of the most sublime scenes in all opera. After three hours of breathtaking arias and breathless comedy in which roles are reversed and lovers get into the most awkward of situations, there arrives a moment when Count Almaviva recognizes how thoughtlessly arrogant he has been toward just about everyone, including his wife. Now, after four acts of almost continuous and often dizzying music and action—broken, of course, by the intervals between the acts—the orchestra is momentarily silent, the stage is still, all attention is focused on the Count. In this moment of poignant revelation it is possible to feel a collective inhalation from the audience as we watch the Count himself take a breath before singing one of the most lovely phrases in opera, a simple melody in which he graciously asks forgiveness from his wife, the Countess. It is only a short phrase, a simple avowal, after which his wife takes up the melody and tenderly responds. Nothing verbose, nothing grandiloquent, only a beautifully human interaction set afloat on the collective breath of an entire audience, orchestra and cast of singers. It is a confirmation of Mozart's genius that he fully understood, in some eighteenth-century Austrian manner, the importance of a breath at the most complicated moment of the plot's convolutions, a breath from which forgiveness, reconciliation and love may flow.

At the beginning of the third movement of Gustav Mahler's Sixth Symphony (the "Tragic") the requisite inhalation occurs not before the orchestra plays, but with the first two notes, the subsequent exhalation on the third and following notes gently opening onto an exquisite harmonic landscape. Throughout the remainder of this third movement there are many instances in which a person not only senses but knows the very breath of the music, as though the music were an animal, a human being, oneself.

Either way, whether in the moment of silence preceding the Count's request for forgiveness, or whether embedded within the sinews of the music itself, inspiration is an urge from the universe, the divine breath flowing into our bodies, our souls, becoming the genesis of gestures with which we touch the world.

Expiration, then, becomes our response.

The personal decision whether or not to be placed on a permanent ventilator has to be one of the most difficult a person may ever face, particularly in instances where, due to the degenerative nature of one's illness, there is little if any hope of ever again living without such mechanical assistance. While one may read of people who have lived for years on ventilators, and have lived happily, peacefully and successfully, there is nonetheless a powerful counter argument saying that one's decision to live on a ventilator will only increase the burdens of one's caregivers specifically, and of society generally. This, by the way, is not mere imagining. The naked truth is that life on a ventilator will undoubtedly increase the need for care, for assistance and for resources. And I am not speaking of an occasional communal stroll around the park in a wheelchair, my dears, but the constant suctioning of tubes, the vigilance of maintaining equipment, the fragility of ever changing concerns—for instance, when the electricity goes out in the middle of the night, most people roll over and go back to sleep. When the electricity fails in the home of someone on a ventilator, he dies, unless there is a back-up power source that can be accessed quickly.

Furthermore, the ability to extend one's life by artificial ventilation brings up inevitable philosophical questions—and theological ones, if a person is so inclined. There are also ethical implications arising from, among other things, the exorbitant resources, both human and financial, required for maintaining such a life—estimates range between $200,000 and $300,000 per year, expenses which are paid by the public, whether through higher insurance rates or higher taxes. With many able-bodied CEO's demanding greater profits at the expense of client care, or politicians voting for less government spending on social programs, a person facing such a future may readily feel that the most socially responsible thing to do would be to die sooner rather than later. After all, those funds could buy another bomb, you know, or a nice vacation home for the CEO, rather than support the life of someone idly sitting about in a wheelchair.

Under this prevailing ruling ethos, the question becomes: Is not the best choice simply to accept the natural course of things, the imminent stagnation not only of my lungs, but also my life, knowing that this outcome will place less stress on a social fabric which already balks at having to help others, particularly the indigent and infirm? Furthermore, and most importantly, one set of rules cannot be applied to me, and another to someone else. Whatever ethical reasoning is used for me and in my situation, must somehow be applicable to every human life on the planet. People may say, "Your life is worth extending, Zsolt, no matter the cost." If, however, we cannot say the same to each and every human being we encounter, the hypocrisy of such a statement is cruel in the extreme, even to myself. For, in an environment in which we provide for the saving of one life but not another, it is certain that somewhere someone is wishing for my death in order that a loved one may survive.

Thankfully, while it is vitally important that I consider today what my decision will ultimately be if ever I need to make such a choice, there are hours and days and months between now and then, and there are things I may do that will hopefully provide me with some breathing room, so to speak. One of those is to allow each breath to fulfill its natural course, even if its expiration be a stutteringly graceless response. Another is to find full breath within the shallows, each breath rising and coming to its completion regardless of its capacity. With these concepts I hope to feel each breath as an existence unto itself and at the same time part of a larger continuum. Fulfilled within its own context, each breath is and shall be sufficient, so long as it is a true response to the spirit that fills me with life.

Lao Tze says:

> *Whoever is stiff and inflexible is a disciple of death.*
> *Whoever is soft and yielding is a disciple of life.*

It is undeniable that the gradually increasing spasticity of my body aptly illustrates the first of the above lines. If I so choose, I can let the other aspects of my life follow suit, my song becoming ever more that of a disciple of death; or I may allow what remains of my life to become ever more soft and yielding, in order to counterbalance the powerful effects of the paralysis, and, by living such a discipline of life, eventually redefining and embracing the moment of death within a larger cycle, a greater breath.

Rising step by step out of the cold water, my hands gripping the railing, I am slowly making my way up the ramp toward where a lifeguard is waiting to help me. As the water molts from my flesh, and with each step I take into the non-buoyant realm of land, my muscles become ever more unwilling to bear my weight, my strength ebbing in the power of earth's gravitational field. Taking a moment to rest at the boundary where the water of the pool laps onto the tiles of the floor, here where the lifeguard has met me and is helping to hold me up, my legs give way, causing me to slump down onto the cold tiles, my spastic muscles contracting into a fetal position, an expectant position maintained momentarily with the full intention of standing up as soon as possible. As I lean against Matt's arm, one unresolved moment goes by, then another, and another, during which I am attempting to regulate my breathing. Huddled in this uncertain position, I am unable to find the rhythm of my breath, yet I remain intent on standing up and getting on with things, with living.

After a time, however, and ultimately relinquishing my grip on life, I faintly instruct Matt to lower me into a reclining position in order that I may breathe more easily. At this point, being ever further removed from the greater world, I can no longer be concerned with how he does it, trusting that he will do what he thinks best. Exhausted, I close my eyes, even as his colleague is laying towels over me, her kind hands trying to stretch my spastic legs into a more comfortable posture. My psyche, no longer capable of being stiff and inflexible, can only be soft and yielding, my body covered with supple towels, the water of the pool quietly lapping my back where it rises to rest against Matt's torso.

My eyes remain closed.

I hear only the vaguest of sounds, the voices of the nearby lifeguards floating about me inconsequentially.

I no longer know the world.

All that remains is the shallowest of breath.

Cradled in the soft fullness of its truth, I gradually succumb to life.

July 15, 2000

34. THE WATER DRAGON

And what about the ending that bears witness to the beginning?

Within this subtle turning, I once again discover the realm of water.

Perhaps it is because I live in a desert, high above the ocean, far from the intricate realms of wet marshes and humid jungles, the exhilarating cold of mountain lakes. Here in the high desert, water runs mostly unseen and untasted, subtly altering the landscape whenever we turn our eyes to gaze at astonishing flashes of lightning, powerful surges of electricity which illuminate monstrous, towering thunderheads.

ACT I

Scene 1:   In the cold, barren confine of the locker room I slowly remove first my waistcoat, then my shirt, handing them to a man who then takes my shoes and socks before assisting me with my trousers. Lifting me up from my wheelchair, he lowers me onto a bench.

Scene 2:   The sudden water of the shower is not the water of gods and goddesses, but of humankind. Even as it hits my naked body, its shallow purpose is unreasonable, as are the swimming trunks we pull up over the dripping hair of my pubic bone. Because, in truth, the deeper water which awaits me has no concern about the sweat of my glands or the shape of my body.

Scene 3:   With my washed, wet torso wrapped in a giant towel, I walk assisted and unsteadily toward the tongue of a ramp whose tiles are submerged in a mouth of warm water. The man who holds me firmly in his grasp is at once escort and messenger, the warmth of his limbs bringing me news of the water, as well as the stern knowledge that he can accompany me no farther than the border, the edge of the ramp where I lean for a moment against the railing, trying to catch my breath.

Scene 4:   He removes the towel from around my shoulders, then girds my

43

belly with a flotation belt, the only device I will be allowed to take with me. Still leaning against the railing, I look first into his eyes, then into the water. At this point the man carefully removes my eyeglasses, thereby depriving me of most of my sight. Lastly, he asks if I need anything more, then gives me a kiss.

Scene 5:   Turning to walk alone down the ramp, I am able to do so only by locking my arms and shuffling or swinging my non-supportive legs along beneath me. For the first few steps I can still sense the messenger behind me, prepared to catch me if necessary. As I gradually move into deeper water, I am increasingly aware of his diminishing ability to help me, placed as he is in a world of concrete and tile. There now comes a fulcrum—when the water level reaches my groin, my lower body totally submerged in warm water—which utterly defines the limit of the messenger's influence. I have already said goodbye to him. I have already struggled successfully to take the remaining steps without his assistance. Here, with my body balanced in this unaccountable moment, I will momentarily pass from one world to another.

Scene 6:   Taking a breath, I allow my arms to unlock, knowing that by doing so my legs will buckle beneath me, my body will falter. Needless to say, the initial sensation is of uncontrollable collapse, a plunge from which there is no turning back. This is immediately followed by a feeling of embrasure, of rapture, as my entire body, my entire life, succumbs to and is embraced by the sensuous body of warm water. A smile rises to my face, because, as my limbs float and move in the water, they are once again fluid and expressive. I am once again in the arms of a great mystery that wants only that the exuberant dragon in my heart whip its tail to and fro, its regal head gliding gracefully or dancing playfully atop the water, fire and steam issuing from its mouth, its nostrils.

Scene 7:   Looking toward the top of the ramp from which I have just come, I can tell that the messenger has departed, having brought me to a realm in which he now exists only within my heart.

INTERLUDE

Over the past months, I have learned much about water. I have learned, for example, that whenever I take a drink of water and some of it slips unwanted and inadvertently into my lungs, a process begins that can ultimately destroy me. I have learned that when the water in the pool is cold it can paralyze the muscles which control my lungs, bringing me closer than ever to the edge between now and then. Yet, I have also learned that in these harsher sentences of justice, the embrace of water, rather than the apparent nemesis it may appear to be, is—as is the man whose steady hands keep my naked body from slipping off the bench and crashing onto the locker room floor—a moment of profound meeting. Against and within this sometimes harsh encounter, existence is lovingly illuminated.

Here, amid the drought-brittled grasses hibernating in the heat of summer, water sears the imagination. Here, meandering among the rocks, sandy river beds abide the heat of the sun, ever prepared to embrace each brief flood delivered from within the clouded passions of gods intent on bringing us to a table replete with madness, ecstasy, and deliverance. Here, beyond one's flesh, there is no middle ground; the extremes remain eternally intact. Only in one's heart may they come together, and only if forged into a soft, white heat obtained from the rocks themselves, a heat which, when plunged into the sudden embrasure of water sends forth plumes of steam, a synthesized poetics of strength and laughter.

ACT II

Many stairs and far above the concrete floor there is a great surging of water. I stare at its ferocity, even as it leers back with a taunting sneer, daring me to go forth with my foolish plan. Together, Daniel and Matt have brought me, one stair at a time, up to yet another point of no return, here where the Water Dragon confronts a scrawny little disabled man who rather absurdly believes he is a Poet of Life. Following Matt's instructions to sit down, I can feel the lashing tongues of the Water Dragon snatching at my feet. Though only a short distance behind me, Daniel is now worlds away, clothed for a different kind of encounter. Matt the Lifeguard, on the other hand, is sitting down behind me, his right arm wrapping itself securely around my torso, the other holding onto the very edge of the cliff from which we will momentarily leap, as it were, into the fury of the Water Dragon's legendary and powerful maw. I hear myself thinking, *You must be mad, Zsolt. You can hardly walk; your breathing is as frail as the tail of a comet; and you've never in your life been down a water slide.* Yet, here I am, gazing into the mouth of a vast unknown beast, a place inside of myself that I know I have to enter.

I will admit that there was indeed a moment in this whole episode when the conniving Steward of Doubt almost convinced me that perhaps it would be best to not go forward; that the night and tomorrow and all the remaining days did not necessarily have to have meaning. It was a fleeting moment, however, squeezed out of existence by the secure feel of Matt's arm around me. While I did not trust the voice of the Steward of Doubt, I had no reason not to trust the arms of this Guardian of Life.

On the count of three, the two of us rushed as one into the lashing tongues of the Water Dragon, only to discover that they were laughing as boisterously as were Matt and I. Unstoppable, we sped down and around and down some more. With each whoosh of water I entered deeper into a world I am becoming ever more familiar with, a world in which I am kept alive by the arms of other human beings, even as Matt and I plunged into the pool itself, my body unable to do

45

anything but allow itself to be brought to the surface by a Messenger from God, a man whose beaming face told me everything about how we had together laughed with the tongues of dragons and in the process had become Heralds of Life.

July 24, 2000

40. ADVENTURES IN ENTOMOLOGY

The desiccated corpse of the centipede has disappeared, having been either stolen by the voracious wind or taken away piecemeal by a contingent of ants.

Furthermore, I regret to inform you that Harriet the Tarantula is gone.

The aforementioned centipede, having been caught beneath the bed by one of the cats and been mercilessly played with before succumbing to death—its mangled body then found by me and placed outside where it slowly shriveled from its former glorious size of fifteen centimeters to a meager eight—probably just blew away.

Harriet, on the other hand, and to the best of my knowledge, is alive and well.

At least she was when I last saw her.

Harriet and I met one day by the outhouse. I was just beginning what has become an ever more challenging six-legged, twenty meter shuffle with the support of my walker when I first spotted her. She, for her part, was dutifully engaged in an eight-legged, many kilometer migration, her black, fuzzy body steadily heading southeast.

In this part of the world one of the harbingers of autumn's cooler days and their inevitable decline into winter, is the tarantula migration. Driving home late at night, you will see them crossing the road in the bright glare of the headlights, their solitary and single-minded bodies intuitively programmed to trundle toward the safety of a gentler climate.

Shuffling alongside Harriet for a quarter of an hour, my pace not much faster than hers, I marveled at how she made use of her eight legs. I watched in amazement as she climbed over tall tufts of brittle grass. Though I suggested it would be easier were she to go around them, she insisted on showing me that she could do it, and did. After many little steps on her part, and quite a few shuffles on mine—along with generous pauses in order to focus on my breathing and to offer Harriet pieces of anthropocentric wisdom, which she graciously shrugged off—she and I found ourselves at the edge of the property, there where a barbed wire fence conveniently delineates my own physical limit. Crawling easily beneath it, Harriet stalwartly proceeded to saunter over the dry ground, heading southeast into the high desert. With the sun lowering in the west, and the clouds towering on the distant eastern horizon, I watched Harriet amble along for another five meters or so, her body becoming gradually intermixed with the shadows of the grasses, her nimble legs carrying her forward on a mysterious journey dictated by. . .

By what?

I haven't a clue, darling.

Ah, so much I do not know, and maybe it was this, this moment of gentle unknowing which caused me to wave my hand and say, "Goodbye, Harriet."

As autumn proceeds, I find it less necessary to use the "spider stick" in the outhouse, a stick with which I remove spider webs ingeniously built across the hole by black widow spiders. In these cooler days there are seldom webs needing to be cleared out, yet I find myself swirling the stick around as a precautionary measure, at least until the first true frost. I suppose I could purchase some kind of pesticide to spray into the deeply dug hole, some chemical that would rid the outhouse of every single one of its black widow spiders. But why bother when a stick will do the job without resorting to destroying the same arachnids who, after all, are quite helpful in controlling the fly population? Besides, I do find black widow spiders extraordinarily beautiful.

This past summer an indoor toilet was installed in the bathroom, a convenience which, believe it or not, I have yet to use. Sane people look a bit askance at me when I mention this, as though the only thing more stupid than committing suicide is to use an outhouse when there is an indoor flush toilet on the premises. Using the outhouse, however, challenges me to walk, and by doing so, gets me outside where I can enjoy the fabulous sunrises of dawn, and the slow descent of the crescent moon in the evening. With the assistance of my walker, I am still able to go these short distances and thereby participate in the ordinary, though mysterious, interplay of the natural world.

There has also been, in these last days of warmth, a burst of beetle activity. They are everywhere, and I must say—hopefully without too much sentimentality—that I find them charming as they trod about the landscape in their diligent meanderings. Indeed, I am quite fond of their easygoing approach to the rigors of survival. They are superb role models.

Sitting outside in the warmth of an afternoon, the angle of the sun's light having shifted towards autumn, I hear a riveting cacophony which signals the seasonal migration of birds. Scanning the sky with ears and eyes, I discover a ribbon of undulating dark flecks which seems to stretch into the horizon forever. Continually mesmerized by this recurrent phenomenon, I will sit, watching and listening, as the ribbon flutters across the deep, clear blue, until it flutters out of sight, the chatter of the birds gradually dying away. Generally there are one or two stragglers who come along behind, their single voices trying to catch up with the others.

Seeing them causes me to think of the term an exaltation of larks. I have often wondered how the word exaltation ever came to be used to describe a group of larks. And surely, a murder of crows demands the attention of my curiosity whenever I hear it used. I am also rather fond of a pod of whales, a murmuration of starlings, and a dalliance of Zsolts. For some reason this calls to mind the interesting fact that a butt is two hogsheads, and I am not making this up.

In his essay, "The Uses of Diversity," from his book, *The Common But Less Frequent Loon*, biologist Keith Stewart Thomson writes:

> We are all hypocrites about biodiversity. We campaign to save whales, join societies to protect birds and wild plants, and then ruthlessly exterminate cockroaches, black flies, poison ivy, crabgrass, and ragweed, to name just a few. We contribute a few dollars each to worthy groups and collectively spend billions a year on pesticides and herbicides to control our own little environments. Then we throw up our hands at the enormity of the problem of biodiversity world-wide. Who are we to pontificate about saving the redwoods when we have explicitly and implicitly decided to let so many other species go for our own immediate convenience and gain?

About once a week I am treated to the remarkable sight of a hawk soaring high above the landscape. Sometimes it is off in the distance, more often it is directly above me. Once, several years ago, while riding my motorbike, a hawk swooped down out of the sky, and settled into a flight pattern approximately two meters in front of me. For about a kilometer it stayed directly before me, as though guiding me. I was totally entranced not only by the nearness of the creature, but by some unspoken engagement with it. It is fascinating that in this age we tend to think of such intimate encounters as close to miraculous, though they were, in the past, what constituted the very fabric of existence.

Returning to the outhouse: If I do not disturb the web built across the hole by an industrious black widow spider, and then if I let a few drops of urine trickle through the web, the spider will momentarily come darting out, thinking that the drops of urine are flies, or some other such morsel. The spider being upside down, it is easy, particularly in the bright sun of midday, to see the brilliant crimson hourglass marking her belly. One must look quickly, however, because once disappointed in her quest for food, she quickly retreats out of sight, ever reclusive.

Sooner or later I will probably find myself, by necessity, using the indoor toilet and in the process using up valuable groundwater. Until then, however, I am quite content to meander the short distance to the outhouse, listening to the birds in the trees, maintaining a communal relationship with the black widow spiders, and even being visited by a curious lizard who perhaps perceives me as a big rock until I move slightly, causing him to scurry away.

I do occasionally find myself wondering where Harriet the Tarantula is, and whether she ever made it to her destination without the interference of somebody coming upon her and saying with disgust, "Oh ick!" before smashing her with a shovel.

Yet, I will never know if she successfully concluded her migration, and can only fondly recall our few moments together.

Ah, so much I do not know, and maybe it is this, this moment of utter unknowing which causes me to turn my gaze toward the horizon, there where the end of a ribbon of birds is undulating against a background of blue.

October 6, 2000

41. ROADBLOCKS

During my most recent appointment with my respiratory therapist I took the opportunity to ask some questions about life with a tracheostomy, questions such as, "Will I still be able to get into the water at the therapy pool?" To this particular question she had no specific answer, though she did explain how some of her patients on supplemental oxygen place their tanks in a crate beside the pool, and by using an extra long tube still manage to do their exercises. She then looked at me and said point blank, something to the effect of, "You know, Zsolt, people are going to start placing all sorts of road blocks and barriers in front of you. They'll tell you, 'Such and such a thing isn't possible.' Or, 'I've never heard of anybody doing what you want to do'." Her suggestion to me, in place of any concrete answers to my queries, was that I be diligent and persistent in my efforts to achieve whatever is important and meaningful to me, even if at first it seems beyond reach, or unsolvable.

Her words, coming out of nowhere—we were, after all, merely talking about the mechanics and logistics of trachs and portable ventilators—were a stark reminder to me, a reminder that not everyone, whether in the medical profession or the population at large, believes in redefining a patient's potential, let alone his or her essence. Nor do they believe that the inconceivable and the unapproachable might already exist within the limits of an ill person's life, and might, with enough imagination, perseverance and effort, come alive within those very limitations, and come alive with astonishing results.

A dear friend of mine is severely disabled, both physically and mentally, and has been since birth. During the first years of his life, the doctors pessimistically told his family that the only reasonable option they had was to place the boy in a state institution, because it was obvious he would never be anything more than a vegetable. His mother, however, flatly refused to agree to this and proceeded to embark on a parenting career for which she had no model. In those days the idea that people with severe disabilities could participate as full-fledged members of society was just beginning to emerge, particularly in this part of the world, therefore it was an unusual and remarkable step for this family to pursue the course it did.

I first met Matthew over fifteen years ago, when his family was in search of someone to assist with his care, essentially a relief person to give him baths, shave him, and feed him. Additionally, on doctor's orders, he was required to walk at least ten kilometers a day, split into two or three shifts. Though he was then almost twenty-one, he had only been walking for about six years, following a successful operation on his legs, yet he was still able to do so only with assistance. If someone did not hold on to him securely, he would fall over. I don't mean he would stumble, I mean he would topple over, and since he was incapable of diffusing the fall with his spastic hands and arms, he went down hard, taking the brunt of the fall on his face and head. Because of this, I was carefully instructed in the best method for holding him, practicing first by walking through his house several times before heading outside under the guidance of his mother. On the second day, having reassured her that I would do my best to keep him from falling, Matthew and I set off to traverse the streets of his neighborhood, following the routes which his mother and father had mapped out for him, patterns which seldom varied unless the weather were inclement, in which case I would drive him to the mall, where we would walk around and around and around until we had covered at least half of the day's requisite kilometers—in the meantime seeing enough tchotchkes to make a person nauseous.

One day, after I had grown accustomed to the routine, I looked at Matthew, who happens to be only a few years younger than myself, and said, "Okay, buddy, this whole city is yours, and there's no reason why we can't go anywhere we want. With ten kilometers we can go so many places, my friend."

And we did.

For years Matthew and I walked the streets. To keep us occupied, I would tell him stories about the adventures of a man named Isaac, who lived in a tree. Isaac was a fictional character I had created one day for Matthew's delight, and though I will never know for certain, Matthew seemed to find pleasure in Isaac's rather surreal escapades; though his pleasure may have had more to do with my own delight in telling the stories than in any intrinsic interest in Isaac as a character. Other times I would sing aloud, though I am not sure it counts as singing if the only words in the song are la-la-la. Not personally adept in popular Songology, I unashamedly made up tunes, or hummed "Mack the Knife," or attempted to intone the Brahms Violin Concerto all by myself, and was eternally discovering that Mimi had just succumbed to tuberculosis, my voice ringing out with those famous words directed to her distraught lover Rodolfo: *Corragio! Corragio!*

As Matthew and I wound our way through the year's cycles, I would find myself singing the "Dreidel Song," because it is the only song I know all the words to, other than the "Happy Birthday Song," though I can usually bumble my way through "God Save the Queen," often inadvertently substituting the word "perjury" for "victory," all in an attempt to maintain rhyme and meter. For some reason I have never been able to retain lyrics, though I can hum any number of tunes, and can even recreate complicated quartets, fugues, and sonatas using my notorious la-la-la system. Therefore you may picture us, the snow gently falling, walking along the streets, Matthew giggling his head off while I sang, "I have a little dreidel, I made it out of clay. . . " Truly, passers-by must have thought he and I lived together in a group home for the mentally challenged, a surmisal which, had I been informed of it, would not have annoyed me, because I had no pretensions of being, nor appearing to be, superior to Matthew. He was my buddy, we were friends. What other people thought? I don't care.

After several months of helping Matthew with his physical therapy, I began to realize that while he was unable to maintain balance unassisted, he did have what I came to call balance in motion. In other words, so long as he was walking forward he was capable of maintaining balance. As soon as he stopped, however, someone had to hold on to him, or else he would topple over. Furthermore, he could not walk backwards without assistance. With this realization in mind, I gradually began to allow him more and more freedom, first by loosening the regulation grip, then by placing myself in front of him, holding onto his hands, me walking backwards while he walked forwards. By using this configuration, if he stumbled or tripped he would fall toward me, and could easily be kept from total collapse with either a good hand-to-hand grip, or by embracing him in a bear hug. In this face-to-face, teeter-totter position, we walked many, many kilometers—I once calculated it to be thousands of kilometers over the years.

Gradually, as he gained confidence both in me and in his own body, I gently started to let go of his hands, always making sure mine were directly beneath his in case he himself needed to lean on them or I needed to steady him all of a sudden. This arrangement allowed him to walk unassisted for the first time in his life. Initially I only let go for a couple of steps, always being certain he was comfortable and confident; then as the weeks progressed I let him walk unassisted for longer distances. I suppose at this point I ought to confess that this was all done in direct contradiction of his parents' strict instructions. If they had known what Matthew and I were doing, they would have had a fit. Nonetheless, I also felt intuitively that if their son could gain the confidence and ability to walk unassisted, they would be overjoyed at his accomplishment, to see their "vegetable" walking on his own. You see, every day they prayed to Jesus, asking that their son be allowed to walk, that he be given the gift of speech and song, and that he wouldn't always have to wear a diaper.

One day I decided it was time for a full confession of our clandestine agenda. Toward the end of our walk that afternoon, as we came down the final stretch of tarmac, I gently let go of his hands and began counting how many steps Matthew could take by himself, urging him to go as far as he could before I finally took hold of his hands just before reaching his house. I cannot say he was exactly in a good mood by that point, but what an accomplishment!

Upon entering the kitchen where his mother was preparing dinner, I helped

Matthew sit down, then looked at his mother and asked, "Guess how many steps Matthew took by himself today?"

The look on her face told all. Obviously the news that he had been walking without someone holding securely onto him came as a shock. Nonetheless she took a breath and gamely answered, "Three."

I told her to guess higher.

"Seven."

I shook my head.

At this point she was definitely looking concerned.

Cutting short her agony, I said, "Matthew just walked three hundred and twenty steps all by himself."

Yet, and as I had expected, once the surprise—dare I say shock—of the news had settled, she was overjoyed that after twenty-one years her baby had walked all by himself.

I am quite accustomed to roadblocks.

Ever since I was a boy barriers have been put in front of me, barriers set into place by the status quo, by society or by individuals. Each of those barriers, if they prevented me or those around me from living with dignity, I have attempted either to hurdle, smash into pieces, take apart brick by brick or otherwise circumvent. I will admit that in my youth such seemingly precocious chutzpah probably stemmed less from any clearly defined sense of justice than from pure naivete, though, being a sensitive boy, the former was present from the beginning, hence my totally irrational responses to road kill. Rather, it simply did not occur to me that I could not fulfill the idealistic daydreams which flourished inside of my mind, the rich colors which burned in my soul. Consequently I was an extreme annoyance to many people who either said or would have liked to have said, "If you'd just be like everyone else, Zsolt, you'd make life a lot easier for yourself...and for us." They were more than correct, of course. Yet their words made little sense to me, particularly when they spoke in trite phrases such as, "Get real, Zsolt." They might just as well have told me the earth was flat. My response to either statement would have been more or less the same, "Say what?" With a perspective and an attitude like this, it was obvious to almost everyone that I would come to no good. And they were absolutely right. I have come to no good, if to be good means to toe the line and not to stand up against tyranny, if to be good means to stand aside while others suffer, if to be good is to judge any person's life less worthy than another's.

You see, after all is said and done, a good person would not have gone against the dictates of Matthew's parents. What it took for Matthew to be able to walk unassisted was a steady regimen of rebellious naughtiness. It took imagination and defiant chutzpah to show the world that my buddy could gain the confidence and the ability to walk by himself. Perhaps now you can understand why I will never be able to claim the mantle, the scepter, and the tiara of the good boy, the good man, the good citizen. Any such moniker ill fits my life, my actions, and my deeds; far more fitting that I be dubbed Zsolt the Naughty.

Over the four decades of my life, one of my greatest challenges has been to transform the simple naivete of an intensely dreamy boy into tensile courage and fluid strength. In this I was fortunate to grow up in the shadows of Mahatma Gandhi, Elie Wiesel, and Dr. Martin Luther King, Jr., among others. As a youth, I avidly read their lives and their words, while in the same years fervently playing the music of Beethoven and Bartók; delving into the scientific realms of Albert Einstein and Marie Curie; reading the words of Tolstoy, Dostoyevsky, Hardy and Virginia Woolf, as well as the poetry of Dylan Thomas, e. e. cummings, and Arthur Rimbaud. Furthermore, I came of age in a time when many individuals felt emboldened to question everything from the horrors of war to the injustices of racism and sexism, and conversely to take a stand for what they truly believed in, their defiant actions hearkening back to earlier years in the last century when suffragettes were willing to go to prison in order to force the issue of suffrage for women, when workers were uniting in efforts to create better working conditions and more liveable wages, actions hearkening back to the work of Harriet Tubman and the abolitionists, each of the above echoing the gesture of a Jewish kid named David who took up a stone and, using it with stunning expertise, killed the tyrant Goliath.

Within the then prevailing climate of questioning the establishment, whether it were the entire British Empire or the local School Board, my own opposition to what I considered to be an unjust status quo was undoubtedly less noticeable than it might otherwise have been. A generation earlier, in the midst of American McCarthyism, I would probably have been forced into an institution of one kind or another, for one reason or another, me and Janet Frame, me and Alan Turing. Not that in my own time there weren't people who fervently felt I would be less of a threat to society were I behind bars, or electrically shocked into compliancy. Yet, and contrary to the clucking soothsayers, I have made it through as far as this, though I am not certain how. I guess, when I think about it, and when all is summed and subtracted and taken into account, it comes down to chutzpah.

The truth of the matter remains that a person seldom gets to Goodness through being good, because the former is a gesture of fluidity, while the latter is a state of rigidity.

Gandhi, for instance, did all sorts of things he ought not have done, thereby annoying the hell out of the British.

And MLK...

You know, if these guys would just be like everyone else, if they would simply stop stirring things up, and would just sit down and shut up, everything would be fine, just fine, and we would have little need to call in the authorities.

In case you have forgotten, I will bring to your attention the fact that Mr.

Gandhi did sit down and shut up...

...right in the middle of the British Empire, so to speak. What a traffic jam he caused, what a traffic jam!

I ask you, where would we be without Rosa Parks taking an illegal seat on the bus?

Where would we be without St. Francis removing his fine clothing in the middle of the town of Assisi, in naked defiance of both paternal and civil authority?

Where would we be without those thousands of unnamed Wobblies demanding more humane working conditions...

...without Raoul Wallenberg literally standing up to the Nazis and freeing entire trainloads of Jews...

...without Hannah Szénes parachuting behind enemy lines when she could as easily have remained safely in Palestine?

To which questions many people will knowingly respond, "And look what happened to them, with their preposterous notions, their indignant chutzpah."

Mahatma Gandhi: assassinated.

Dr. Martin Luther King, Jr.: assassinated.

Raoul Wallenberg: disappeared under mysterious circumstances, never to be heard from again.

Hannah Szénes: captured and killed.

Francis of Assisi: dead at forty-five, having spent his final years nearly blind and in ill health. If the foolish bloke had merely kept his clothing on and done what his father had told him, he'd have lived to be at least forty-six.

Yes, it can be agreed upon, and sadly enough, that chutzpah does not always alleviate the suffering of humanity, nor does it even change the immediate reality of the world, yet it can show us the raw sources of dignity, and in the process it can often unmask injustices.

Some years ago, after crossing one of the many international borders I have crossed in my life, I was informed by the passport officer on the train that I was missing a visa which I ought to have obtained before entering the country. I tried to explain to him that I had been told I could get it directly from him, there aboard the train, but to no avail. The only way to fix the problem, he replied, was to return across the border and reenter via the nearby motorway, where there were governmental offices and personnel to deal with such issues. Therefore, and with little further recourse available to me, I was duly removed from the train, and told to wait in the security office. Under watchful eyes I sat and read for a while until the appropriate train came into the station, at which point two tall guards arrived to escort me to my wagon, which happened to be at the farthest end of the train. As we strolled along the platform, passengers leaned their heads out to watch as these two burly guards escorted some scrawny guy with a violin case slung over his shoulders. Once I was ensconced in my official wagon, the two of them obviously had to remain with me until the train departed. By this time, however, we were pretty good buddies and spent the remaining minutes speaking in proletarian Hungarian about books and writers. Soon enough the whistle blew, and the two guards cheerily shook my hand, telling me they hoped to one day read my books, waving goodbye as the train pulled out of the station.

A couple of minutes later I arrived on the other side of the border, where I now had no visa to legally reenter that country. Somehow I was able to explain this unusual situation, and was thereby hauled into a dingy office where everything would hopefully be sorted out, though, in typical bureaucratic fashion, not without the appropriate delays, the shuttling me back and forth from one disgruntled official to another, and the final payment of $30 in order to receive my visa and assure me a lift to the border crossing. None of this, by the way, seemed unreasonable by international political standards, and after several hours everything was tidied up. I was therefore placed into a vehicle with a driver and two security officials—one of whom had handled the final payment of money and taken care of the visa stamp—and driven to a rather desolate spot a couple of kilometers from the actual border crossing. I graciously said goodbye, fully prepared to walk the remaining distance. At this point, however, they told me I had to pay them $30. I explained to the man who had earlier taken my money, that not only had I already paid, but he was the one who had taken the money. This did not work, however, and they kept insisting I pay them $30.

Needless to say, the obvious injustice of this turn of events only incensed your Aunt Zsolt, and after a few minutes of attempting to reason with them, I rather perfunctorily gathered up my belongings, and got out of the car. The three of them also stepped out of the car, only they were armed and I wasn't. Dear me, what to do now? You will be glad to know that I did the only dignified thing possible and started walking away. I believe the legal term for this is escaping, further providing evidence that naughtiness seems to come naturally to me. Yes, there I was, in the middle of nowhere, defiantly striding away from three state-endorsed bullies, thinking to myself, *Why bother getting indignant about the injustice of the situation when there's nothing I can do about it anyway? All I had to do was hand over $30. Now they're going to come running after me, beat me up and haul me off to prison. Or, out of sheer spite, they're going to shoot me on the spot, and out here in the middle of nowhere, who'll ever know what happened?* By this point, they would certainly have had every right to shoot, backed up by one law or another. Besides, how easy it would have been for them to concoct any story they wanted in order to support their case. Because of this, each step I took brought with it images of my imminent demise, yet I would not turn back, nor would I run. I was certain of the dignity of my decision. Therefore, I refused to act like a fugitive. With each ensuing step, I found myself unharmed and alive. I was also gradually gaining distance. It was when I was still relatively near the car that I heard the doors slam shut. To this day I cannot believe I did not faint at that very moment, knowing for certain they were either going to drive up and arrest me, or simply do a hit and run out of spite. Yet, oddly enough, the car drove off in the opposite direction, bringing a modicum of relief to the situation, though no certain resolution. As I trod the remaining kilometers I hardly breathed the torrid afternoon air, continually alert for the return of the three men, who would surely be bringing the entire army with them. Near the border I joined up with the motor traffic which was slowly and innocuously passing between two of the world's nations.

It must have been an odd sight to the Hungarian Border Patrol to see this solitary, stubble-whiskered man stroll up with a violin case strapped over his shoulder. Knowing full well that I was entering illegally, and therefore would need to obtain an official visa, I singled out one of the guards and strode up to him in order to ask for assistance. I do not know if he was more surprised that I had arrived on foot, or that as soon as I reached him I collapsed in his arms. What else could I do? After the heat of the day, the lack of food and water, and the stress of wondering if I would be incarcerated or shot or both, I was suddenly incapable of taking another step in any direction. Even chutzpah has to rest now and then. Quite gallantly, the guard helped me to the appropriate office where a kindly, efficient woman was able to untangle the mess and get me the needed visa.

A short time later, with my papers officially tidied up, I returned to where the guard was patrolling, and thanked him for his assistance. He smiled and asked if I would play him a tune on the violin. Taking the instrument out of its case, I tightened the hair on the bow, tuned up the old fiddle, and proceeded to play him several songs, much to his delight and that of his colleagues.

Today, as the sun goes down, I hear the following words echoing in my mind:

"You know, Zsolt, people are going to start placing all sorts of road blocks and barriers in front of you..."

So what's new, my friend?

I ask you, what's new?

October 13, 2000

44. Tzaddik in a Santa Suit

At an altitude of 3,700 meters, atop a snowy mountain from which it is possible to see for hundreds of kilometers, I am sitting face to face with Death. Quite literally I am looking into the icy eyes of *La Muerte*. The only thing keeping me from slipping and tumbling headlong into her frozen maw is a tether being held by a masked, bearded man I have never seen before. The suicidal incline in front of me is sheer enough that from my vantage point I cannot even see its face, the face of *La Muerte*, Death.

As the winter season subtly begins to change, and as it becomes apparent that the sun is indeed returning, the marked difference in the quality of the sun's light is far more stunning, in its quiet way, than any garish display of lights seen during the month of December. Only the flaming of a candle can compare with this serene unfolding of the dark arms of winter to reveal an inner luminosity.

The winter air, cold to the touch, even brittle, seems capable of sending messages vast distances without hindrance. Indeed, it seems that at this rarefied moment more than any other, a person could deliver a word so far into the horizon that its echo would bring with it a future as clear as the brilliant unending sky. Furthermore, were we to delay for even a moment and not say the very words which are the essence of each one of us—whether expressed through our voices, our hands, our bodies—the future might never arrive, it might never arise from the depths of our hearts, ever turning, turning, turning.

Surely, then, we would be consumed by the silence of Death.

I am not a skier by any definition of the word, neither by habit nor inclination—though I have often thought it would be quite an enjoyable skill to be able to ski jump. Instead, my preferred winter sports, were I ever given the full opportunity to pursue any of them, would be figure skating and luge. I suppose, in a queer sort of way, that about sums up who I am.

No, I am not a skier, and at this point in my life, with my body in a state of neural degeneration, I would never have considered learning to ski had not my respiratory therapist urged me to look into a skiing program designed for people with disabilities. This seemed rather a curious, almost irresponsible suggestion, considering how the cold weather adversely affects my breathing, coupled with the gain in altitude and subsequent decline in oxygen levels necessary for there to be a slope steep enough to ski down. Nonetheless, she did not blink an eyelid, and while at the time I was barely acquainted with this woman, I was perceptive enough to notice that she was not inclined toward inappropriate teasing of people with disabilities. In other words, if she had not felt the program would be feasible for me, she would never have mentioned it.

Ever the fool, perhaps, I believed her, and forthwith sent in my application form and tuition. Several weeks later, after receiving a list of suggested gear from the program's director, I pulled out my old one-piece motorbike outfit—in truth, a red ski suit, though it was purchased some years ago for winter motorbiking—and my electric gloves, also purchased and used for wintertime commuting on my motorcycle.

In the intervening months since first signing up for the Adaptive Ski Program, I have had occasion to hear rumors about it from a variety of sources. Additionally I have also received a surprising gamut of responses concerning my own participation in it—everything from "Awesome," to "Sweet," to what can only be described as a mortified silence, as though I had finally admitted my Jovian birth. With each new piece of gossip, with each passing day my curiosity had only increased. What I had originally presumed would be a morning of schlepping me around on a snowy parking lot in some sort of techno-sled would apparently be much more than that, and certainly more involved, if the rumors were anywhere near the truth. Yet, even with increasingly unbelievable tidbits of news, it never once entered my mind that in registering for the Adaptive Ski Program I would end up face to face with *La Muerte*, Death.

20 January, 2001, 0840 hours. My buddy Matt and I pulled into a handicapped parking space at the local ski basin. This alone seemed remarkably incongruous, though oddly comforting, even welcoming in a manner not usually associated with something so prosaic as a parking space.

Snow everywhere and there I was in a wheelchair. Matt and I looked at one another and said simultaneously, "Where do we go from here?" It was rather as though we had just been given the first of Hercules' seven tasks, only to discover that we did not precisely understand the instructions, nor, by the way, did either one of us even vaguely resemble Hercules, unless he was once an otter. Having read the information I had received from the program director, it was clear we were to go to a building located east of the ski lodge. Well enough. But how? It was just our luck that Matt had forgotten to bring along his nifty two-person helicopter complete with wheelchair stowage.

'Tis certainly odd, though, how life unfolds, and with one step, one turn following another we discovered not only that they had built an elaborate set of ramps and walkways, but that the convoluted path had for the most part been cleared of snow and ice in preparation for the arrival of a variety of people with disabilities.

20 January, 2001, 0915 hours. By this time barely able to speak, due to the bitter cold, I was almost completely strapped and belted into a queer contraption resembling something designed for military evacuations from wintry war zones, sort of an aluminum-framed chair with two skis attached to it, called, appropriately enough, a bi-ski. (Evidently they were out of homo-skis.) My arms, for whatever use they would be to me, remained unbridled. Attached to each one of them was a short pole fitted with a miniature ski, neatly called an outrigger, or rigger. In effect I had become a one piece slalom machine comprised of various sizes of skis, though truth be told I probably looked more like a shalom machine, my face roguishly grinning peace and goodwill to any and all. Politely excusing himself, one of my instructors reached down between my thighs to search for a metal ring attached to a cord which he made certain was readily accessible, further admonishing me to make sure it always remained accessible. "That's in case the chair lift breaks down," he explained to me. "With this it'll be easier to airlift you out."

Or in the event of a broken neck, perhaps.

Nonetheless, things could easily have been worse, and now that I was totally strapped into this evacuation bi-ski I decided I might as well survey the situation at hand. Looking around me, I noticed that there were a few gentle embankments which I presumed we would be using to practice on; you know, executing a few preliminary exercises, a couple of pliés, some tendus, a somersault or two.

I couldn't have been more wrong if I had tried.

"Don't worry, I've got you," Bruce yelled, and in the next split second I was literally dashing toward the chair lift, being propelled from behind by a fiendish lunatic, after which it was only a matter of fleeting moments before I was airborne on the chair lift, still strapped into the bi-ski, the outriggers resting quietly on my lap, me and all my adaptive equipment securely nestled between Bruce and Eliot, two men I had met a mere ten minutes earlier, and who, were it to become necessary to identify them from a line-up of suspects, I could only do so by the lower half of each one's face—anything else of note being hidden beneath hats, mirrored sunglasses and ski clothes.

(A note to the fashion editor in you: Both Bruce and Eliot looked way more cool than I, who doubtless looked like an addled tzaddik in a Santa suit being hauled in for questioning about his insistent belief that we live in a universe comprised mostly of dark matter, a mysterious substance which may or may not consist of the echoes of Maria Callas' voice. Though, in case you are wondering about any sartorial delinquency on my part, I can assure you that underneath my red ski outfit I was dutifully wearing a string of pearls, one of my nicest sets, in fact. You know, just in case the chair lift broke down.)

As we slowly rode above the snow-dusted pine trees it dawned on me that there was probably not going to be a special Zsolt-only practice area at the top of this mountain, and the only way down was via the slopes gliding away beneath our slowly ascending chair lift, slopes on which skiers of varying skills were even now adroitly zooming toward the ski lodge. Actually, those slopes were not the only way down. There was, after all, still the option of being airlifted out in a state of paraplegia, my spinal cord having snapped in two upon impact with a much-too-friendly tree.

Rising still higher, the views becoming ever more spectacular, I was beginning to wonder how we would manage to alight from this graceful ride. Since my voice had frozen into the most undignified, guttural sounds imaginable, I was unable to inquire aloud and had to resort to assuming that upon arrival at the top of the mountain the keenly observant lift operator would stop the machinery and allow us to mosey off as need be.

Wrong again.

"I'll take him," Bruce called to Eliot, and before my tiny little brain even had the opportunity to ponder the mechanics of the situation I was flying down the exit ramp. I haven't a clue how he did it, but I was impressed. And safe.

"Don't worry. I've got you," he yelled to me.

Not that there was much I could do—being strapped in as I was—other than piss in my pants.

It was precisely at this point, now I mention it, that I really did need to piss and somehow managed to convey this necessity to them. Bruce and Eliot, having been forewarned that I would likely need to urinate at the most inopportune times, gamely sledded me off into the trees, tamping down some of the snow with their skis so that I would not sink in when they stood me up. After undoing all those straps and belts, they somehow managed to get me into a standing position, leaning me slightly forward so I would not piss on my ski suit. As you are well aware, the essential thing about urination is that a person has got to relax or it simply does not happen. There I was, at 3,700 meters, already exhausted, totally spastic from the bitter cold, being cantilevered out over my center of gravity by a complete stranger whose eyes I had never even seen, the little I knew about him having been garnered from the sound of his voice and from the strange kinetic relationship which ever again arises between a person with disabilities and his or her assistant. Was this enough information, however, to allow me to piss? As desperately as I needed to urinate, there was only one way it was going to happen...

Trust.

Over the years, and especially in the past months, I have become ever more aware that trust is not a fortress, and that it is more aptly described as a dance. Furthermore, and regardless of how one chooses to describe it, it is certainly not a lopsided or one-sided relationship, though it may appear to be so. Rather, it is a mutual exercise, one requiring the full participation of both parties. It is not, however, as tidy a process as the image of a well balanced teeter-totter may present, for it is not a stasis, but a fluidity, a broken symmetry which nonetheless creates equilibrium. And, as in dancing with a partner, one of the parties generally has to accept responsibility for initiating the momentum through which trust may be generated and may remain vital during even the most challenging of ensuing situations, even as the dance itself unfolds through the relative participation of both dancers. It may seem, from the outside, that in the case of someone with a disability, the initiator would necessarily be the caregiver, the person upon whom the disabled person is dependent. This, however, and while it may sometimes be the case, is not necessarily the norm, nor ought it to be. By first recognizing our responsibilities, then by opening our hearts, our souls, those of us with disabilities can readily become the initiators in the dance of life, a dance which is created by a fascinating give and take between leader and follower, the roles themselves ebbing and flowing, traversing presumed boundaries. By giving our trust, we make the relationship possible in the first place.

For me personally this momentum generally flows from an act of acceptance, oftentimes a deliberately conscious act, though as the months go by I find that the impetus proceeds less and less from a conscious effort, and is becoming more and more an inherent statement of who I am. It seems to me that this moment of acceptance—whether of myself, of my condition, of the situation at hand, or of the person who has for whatever reason been placed in the equation with me—is the key to building and then maintaining trust. While many people may see this act of acceptance as one of resignation, I have come to understand it from a much deeper and less egocentric perspective, as a gesture of participation, of movement, as an expression of the unnameable, the unchartable. Far from being a mere philosophical stance, a mere theological device, for me the act of acceptance is palpable, and it is for this reason that it is such a powerful fulcrum for trust.

After three highly successful runs, each more challenging than the last, Bruce tells Eliot that he thinks I am ready for *La Muerte*, Death. As we ride the chair lift for the fourth and final time of my first day of skiing, he points toward this particular slope, its steep face glowering ominously at me through a break in the trees. Even from the air I can see that it is much different than the slopes we have been on, most of which were beginner slopes. He politely refrains from telling me that *La Muerte* is a slope for experienced skiers only, and his boyish enthusiasm carries me forward into this insane venture. From my perspective I have no reason to question his judgment of the mountain's challenges, nor his confidence in our ability to fly. For an hour and a half he and Eliot have wisely, safely and joyfully managed to get me up and down this mountain three times, in the process teaching me the basic skills of how to maneuver and control the bi-ski contraption which has been securely strapped onto my butt and legs all morning. At the top of the mountain, as usual, one of them competently guides me off the chair lift and skis me down the ramp, steering me away from the general flow of skiers and toward a quiet, sparsely populated spot on the mountain, where I sit face to face with *La Muerte*, Death. After a few last-minute suggestions from Bruce and Eliot, along with an enthusiastic show of confidence in me, all is ready.

I take a moment to try and remember my final meal, but in vain.

I suddenly have an intense desire to smoke a cigarette, though I have never smoked in my life.

I pathetically wonder if my last comprehensible words were eloquent enough to be etched into the historical archives, and suddenly remember that my most recently uttered sentence was, "I gotta piss."

From the vantage point of my low-slung bi-ski, I cannot even see the slope which I will momentarily be skiing down. In other words, I haven't a clue about the shape of *La Muerte's* face, let alone the length of her hair, nor the color of her mouth, though it is possible to feel the chill of her breath, a chill which is easily differentiated from that of the prevailing winds. If only I could now report to you how I blithely joked about *La Muerte's* total lack of vocabulary, thus underscoring her obvious ineptitude. Yes, I would like to be able to tell you how I scornfully laughed at the silent threat of *La Muerte's* windblown song. But to be perfectly honest, I instead found myself questioning the very word of my being, questioning everything that life is putting me through. Not concrete questions, mind you, but more a wondering centered in the spirit, the essence of my existence. How is it that I am here, that I am sitting in a device designed to allow people with disabilities to ski down even the most treacherous of slopes? And more pursuant, how is it that I have come face to face with *La Muerte* on my first day of skiing?

I could easily have backed out of this venture. I could have told Bruce and Eliot to pull me back up the preparatory incline and take me down by another route.

But I didn't.

Not through any fear of humiliation. Nor through any sense of reckless bravado—somehow, when facing even the shadow of Death, bravado shrivels and fades into the illusion it truly is. Nor did I feel any sense of intimidation from Bruce and Eliot, that they would think less of me if I opted not to proceed. Indeed, they seemed to exude nothing if not sheer joy at being on the mountain, at being with me, and in helping a total stranger fly, regardless of which slope we descended.

Sitting at the top of that mountain, tethered to a man named Eliot—a man whose begoggled eyes I had never even seen, and whom I knew only from the shape of his lips, the color of his goatee, and the various words he had spoken throughout the morning—I went forward for no other reason than that I trusted him.

I faced *La Muerte*, I flew into her face, not defiantly, but respectfully, even circumspectfully, albeit clumsily and only barely in control of my bi-ski. Down I went, gravity carrying me into the maw of Death as I maneuvered myself left then right, creating arcs of swift, wobbly momentum. Toward the bottom of the slope

Eliot and I veered toward the side in order to come to a stop, to rest. Arriving a split second later, Bruce excitedly told me to turn my head and look up. There before me was the face of *La Muerte*, sheer as a cliff from this perspective, frigid as ever.

And yet...

Was it my imagination, or did I indeed detect a faint, icy smile on that face?

Yes, one must learn to trust even *La Muerte*, Death.

You may very well ask why a man would spend two hours strapped into a bi-ski when he knows it will take him another four or five days to recover from the experience, and that by the end of the ski season he might very well be in a state of worse physical deterioration because of the strenuous efforts required. Admittedly this is a tough question, and I am not sure I can put the answer into words, though, fearless as ever, I shall blunder ahead, yet another part of the adventure.

Foremost, perhaps, is the remarkably visceral sense of liberty, a fundamental realization of the amazing potential of what can be accomplished without full use of one's legs. Whereas for me this had previously been a mostly intellectual, philosophical proposition, it is now etched into the fibers of my body. Furthermore, while it is one thing to feel the freedom which my body is able to enjoy in the warm water of the therapy pool, it is quite another thing to be flying down the steep, snowy slope of a mountain in a contraption specially designed for people like me. It is beyond exhilarating; it is sweet, my friends, it is sweet as life.

As a result, I feel that, given enough resources, enough ingenuity, along with the right assistive technologies and the competent assistance of others, a person could do most anything without legs. Call up NASA. Tell them I am ready to go. Mars in 2020? Count me in.

Another realization coming out of this experience of learning to ski in a bi-ski is that my life simply is not the same as the lives of others. I know this sounds obvious—after all, is not each life different from all others?—yet there is often such a stress placed on the need for people with disabilities to be like everyone else, or to be treated like everyone else, as though the state of "normalcy" somehow reaps more benefits. Well, the truth is, living with a disability is not the same as not living with a disability. There is nothing in the world that can change this, and it is totally ludicrous to pretend otherwise. The lesson garnered from skiing down *La Muerte* is not that I am now no different than the other skiers, that in accomplishing this feat I have managed to return to some ill-defined normal, even non-disabled, state. No, I am skiing down a mountain not in spite of my disability, nor because I have somehow overcome it or suspended it, but because of it. You see, it is because of my disability that I had to sign up with the Adaptive Ski Program in the first place, rather than with some regular ski school; it is because of my disability that I had to be strapped into a bi-ski; it is because of my disability that I had to learn to trust Bruce and Eliot. It is also my disability that has given me the opportunity over time to accrue and hone the inner tools necessary for facing *La Muerte* on my first day of skiing. I ski as a man with a disability, not as a poor, pitiable bloke attempting through the use of technology to be normal.

Lastly, this experience has also heightened the importance of trust as a component in the lives of all of us, but particularly those of us living with disabilities; trust not only in the varying and often unknown skills and intentions of others, but trust in one's self, and ultimately, trust in Death, a fundamental trust from which we may spring full-throated, joy-hearted, and even recklessly into the fullness of Life, ever turning, turning, turning.

27 January, 2001, 1100 hours. The entire region is enveloped by a heavy snowstorm. Through the determination of a relay team of drivers and helpers, I am on top of a mountain where the intense wind is blowing the snow in dense and breathtakingly beautiful arabesques. I can barely contain my astonishment at being here, at being once again bundled up in my red ski suit and strapped into a bi-ski, for the moment securely braked by a man named Eliot. Though the storm is intense, I feel no fear, nor trepidation, nor even much cold, but rather a deep joy. Not mere happiness, but joy, a feeling of being utterly alive, though not necessarily invincible. It is almost incomprehensible to me that a person who depends exclusively on wheelchairs for extended mobility is now sitting on top of a mountain in a blizzard. Somehow, through the ingenuity of inventors and designers, through the organizational skills of program directors, and through the volunteering efforts of various individuals, people like me are given opportunities unheard of twenty years ago. Perhaps what I am feeling more than anything else is an intense gratitude for the accumulated efforts of these people, for the dramatic wind-driven snow, for this stunning adventure.

It is the last run of the day for me. It has now been decided that we will attempt more moguls. Still tethered to Eliot who is skiing behind me, I work my way through these treacherous mounds of snow feeling not so much a sense of confidence—as I haven't a clue what I am doing—as I do a sense of being totally absorbed and focused, elemental, challenged both psychologically and physically. All of a sudden, however, something does not feel right and before I can understand what is happening I have crashed, not just toppled, but really ploughed headfirst into the soft snow. Above me I can hear Eliot apologizing, telling me it was entirely his fault, that if he hadn't fumbled I would have been fine, and that I probably would have successfully completed the difficult run without mishap.

At a time like this a person could easily be disappointed.

One could be annoyed.

One could be angry and frustrated, lying there upside down, covered in snow, all because Eliot fumbled, and yet...

And yet...

I am not angry in the least.

I am laughing.

I am laughing, because it is the most incredible moment. Here I am, a guy who can barely even walk, and I am on a mountain in a blizzard, strapped into a bi-ski, my head covered in snow not because a mistake was made, but because two guys cared enough to wake up on their day off and risk the hazardous road conditions in order that a stranger might fly and soar and swoop and crash into a heap of laughter.

Here in the middle of a blizzard, in a deep powdery bed of snow, the tzaddik in a Santa suit is laughing his head off, his dervish heart ever turning, turning, turning...

February 2, 2001

45. Do

Spurred on by the suggestion of an e-mail acquaintance in India, I have been pondering a list of Do's and Don'ts applicable to my current state of being. While his concern was primarily for the practical aspects of living with a disability—for example: DO carry a cell phone, DON'T fall down, and DON'T stop breathing—I have broadened my scope to the more universal, and because of my personality, have focused specifically on the Do column rather than the Don't. Some of the following thoughts are applicable to any human being, while a few may only pertain to this quirky life of mine. Take what you want and discard the rest, making sure to leave the refuse in a place where the syllables may readily decompose and regenerate into vibrant words in the mouths of men and women you do know and also those you don't.

Do...

...wake up in the feathery, blithery morning
on these days of all days
to begin again the work of lighting thin candles
with which to guide the sleeping sun
and all its human progeny
across the blue burning sky.

...inhale what will not last
and exhale what has already succumbed,
leaving it to be carried away
in the honest fingers of the wind,
to be tossed against the white cliffs,
the red sea,
and all the violet clouds of remembering.

. . . taste the oily, salty, bitter olive
with the tongue's edge,
recognizing in its flesh
the beginning,
the end,
and every sorrow woven into the rapture of being.

. . . swing in the heartland of the body
toward a depth which may never arrive,
but will,
and because it will
the sun warms the wheeled chariot of the sky's heart.

. . . rest in the roundness of a pomegranate
abundant with its seeds of love
and the hidden fruit of contemplation
whose red juice dribbles down the stubbly chin
in an inescapable display of incompetence.

. . . acknowledge the biting despair
when the long-taloned sky clutches the battered body
and will not let go no matter the sincerity of the prayer,
the wealth of the tithe,
nor the birth of the prey itself.

. . . fill in the hours of the day
with voluptuous deeds which can be placed
anywhere muddy or green
desolate or despised,
there to shine unsigned,
unnamed,
and unashamed.

. . . allow the pain to be itself and none other,
holding it near that to suckle its milk
is to comprehend what is shared
and what must not be disdained
lest humility be made a refugee
from the very light it generates.

... gaze full-eyed upon the partial eclipse which appears
on a blank piece of white paper,
its image having traversed the heavens
before squeezing through a tiny pin-prick,
spreading awe and wonder into the blood of day.

... pursue the tail of the universe,
for in catching it between one's teeth
a circle is created without,
eternity within,
echoes of a vast and elegantly unruly knowledge.

... invite the essence to resume itself
burgeoning from out of the rotting decay of its former shape
to ripple across the watery flesh of time
toward unknown destinations,
lighting the dark moon
while shading the brilliant blue sun.

... turn again and again toward the birth of the universe,
its unfathomable truth,
its inveigling whispers,
as each of its magnificent cycles begins anew,
called into existence
within the waking of a feathery, blithery morning.

March 4, 2001

50. SECRETS OF SCYTHING

I first learned the secrets of scything from a weather-wizened man who lived with his wife high on the side of a mountain which looked out across a shimmering landscape that tumbled down from the nearby crest toward a far horizon which might have been the sea itself, might have been a distant planet. Having stopped by his golden field, a field which abutted the meager dirt road I was travelling by foot, a lonely path whence one could gaze out across the warm, refulgent afternoon of Buddha's boundless breath, I offered to assist him with his solitary reaping. Wary at first, probably stemming from the fact that we had in common a mere hundred or two Serbian words, he finally relented and handed me his scythe. It seemed a simple enough task, not even a motor to start, and I went at it zealously, as though I were a beast off its tether. I was young, after all, and it felt good, high above the distant valley, amidst the thick hay of a remote field far from everything, to feel my flesh sweating in the redolent heat of summer. The old man watched for a while, then explained to me rather emphatically, through words and gestures, that I was working too hard, I was trying too hard.

As in so much we learn in our lives, his apparently nonsensical admonition did not bear fruit for several years. On that summery afternoon, being strong and perseverant, I was able to finish mowing his entire field for him, for which I received a simple, hand-carved walking staff. Having downed a couple of glasses of vodka with him and his wife, I bid them good day and went pleasantly on my way. His words and gestures, however, stayed with me. Over the years, with each accruing opportunity to practice scything, I began to understand the meaning of his wisdom, a meaning which is sublimated in the very shape of the tool itself, a meaning which stretches back through generations of men and women who have swept their hand-hewn wooden snaths, their smithy-hammered metal scythes through tall, luxuriant grasses of fields and meadows, the surrounding landscape falling into patterns of gold which when gathered became fodder for animals cared for by those same hardened hands, which cannot but fail to speak in primordial verbs about the cycles of life.

NOTE: Beginning with this essay, I stopped using capital letters because it required more than one finger to type a letter, which became increasingly difficult. The editor and I have agreed to regularize capitalization to make life easier for you, gentle reader.

And then there is the oft told parable about the elephant and the blind men. This parable, to refresh your memory, is the story of three blind men who are each touching a different segment of an elephant. When asked to describe the elephant, the man touching the leg speaks of it as a building made of columns, while the opinion of the one touching the ear is that it must be a piece of heavy fabric, and the one touching the trunk suggests that it is a section of tubing from a spaceship—or whatever imaginative object the fabulist brews up. And whereas you and I may titter about the obvious mistakes of the misled blokes, and whereas we may want to call out from the audience to tell them they are each touching different parts of the same thing, namely an elephant, even we, finely settled in our subtle hubris, cannot see the entirety of the situation, because, allegorically speaking, we ourselves are the blind men, unable to know fully the universe, the world, the elephant, and one another. In the end, you see, only the elephant knows its elephantness in the deepest sense. Yes, throughout the entire farce, only the elephant fully understands its ineffably ambiguous relationship to Mother Nature.

Perhaps the parable's ubiquity throughout time and place stems from its catholic aptness. Certainly it has been a useful tool for me during these past months, helping me to realize that no matter what another person sees in terms of my disease, my abilities, or my life, past, present and future, they are in fact touching only a small part of my wholeness, my elephantness.

The truth of this became very apparent to me some months ago when, in the process of seeing a variety of doctors, each spoke of me as though he or she were perceiving an entirely different beast than were the others. Among the varied responses, one proclaimed with patronizing smugness that there is nothing to be done; another consolingly told me to prepare for the worst and beyond; and yet another gave only a dismissive shrug of baffled shoulders. Outside of the medical milieu, one person will view my condition as pitiful, a second as heroic, a third as ironic, a fourth as inspiring, ad infinitum, each person's view biased according to his or her own emotional state, personal history, and hard-won concepts of the human body. Some people, when their hand touches the chrome of my wheelchair, see a vortex of increasingly dismal dependence, while others comprehend a valuable tool which enables its user to continue living a vital and viable life. The broad range of these viewpoints, these objective definitions of my condition and my life, is utterly astonishing, to say the least, as it would be were we discussing you and your life. And while it can be agreed upon that everyone is trying his or her utmost to be helpful, the composite beast which they have managed to piece together—as though a committee were surveying the ethical pros and cons of legalizing itinerant circus performers—is truly mind boggling.

Let me now hasten to add, with all due respect to the lovely and loving people in my life, that they are not necessarily trying to piece together anything.

Rather it is I who have been doing the piecing together, having put myself in the precarious position of attempting to gather together these disparate prognoses, concerns and biases in order to somehow come up with a me. In other words, I have been grasping at a multitude of shifting shapes in front of me, rather than contemplating the truth which lies within my own phenomenal experience. Now, does this not strike you as a bit, well, shall I say, stupid, on my part? It finally did me. Yes, after months and months of listening to myriad and generally contradictory accounts of my life from others, of trying to piece together those motley phrases, gestures, and facial expressions, it has finally occurred to me what a ludicrous endeavor this is, as though I myself no longer have any connection to my own body, my own mind, my own soul and spirit.

After a time I came to realize that I was in grave danger of becoming nothing less than a conglomerate beast metamorphosed out of the fears, illusions and opinions of others, as though I were little more than a specimen in a textbook, rather than a thoughtful, intelligent, curiously dynamic human being, however imperfect he might be. Put another way, over a period of many months, I had essentially and imperceptibly begun to relinquish the essence, the source of my life to others, primarily the medical community and its assorted subsidiaries, bit by bit, moment by moment. Each presumably innocent and often unfounded bias of people who hardly knew me had become nothing less than an iron bar with which I had gradually constructed a haphazard cage of confining proportions, and while I could easily enough peer out between the bars, it became increasingly apparent that I could no longer fly, imprisoned as I was by the varied, often contradictory opinions, prognoses and admonitions of others, well intentioned as they were.

Once the realization of my enfetterment dawned on me, I was, to say the least, horrified. Put another way, I was shocked, simply shocked. Yet, I cannot deny that I ought to have known better, that I ought to have sensed something was amiss long before I actually did. In my defense, however, the enfetterment came on gradually, as the ague often does: all afternoon you feel things are not quite right, then awareness suddenly sets in. Enlightenment is perhaps too grandiose a term for something so mundane, yet it gets the point across, does it not? I suppose I may be comforted with the knowledge that I am not the only one in this predicament. Indeed, as I have come to learn, it seems to be almost pandemic, this mindless conforming to the opinions and judgments of those we consciously or unconsciously elevate into positions of power.

For those of us compromised by disease and/or disability, I feel that our naive, sometimes ridiculous conformation to whatever is told us by doctors without giving it much thought arises from finding ourselves living with an unfamiliar and unexpected vulnerability. We are often in pain. Perhaps we are disoriented. We are usually going through a variety of physical and psychological changes, making it quite easy for someone in a position of power to take possession of the situation, consciously or not, and possibly—at least in the medical profession—with the firm belief that he or she is acting in the client's best interest. Yet, while the initial impetus for the deterioration of a person's individual freedoms might arise through the words and actions of those who reside in positions of authority, the truth is that neither Doctors nor the Government nor the Almighty is fully responsible for wresting control of our lives from us. Rather—and this is a very important point to understand—it is we ourselves who thus empower them, relegating control of our lives to people we often do not even know. I find it fascinating how we will readily listen to all manner of artificially selected authorities—doctors, newscasters, and politicians, among others—yet we will deny our own deepest sense of Self, of Truth, of our own relationship with the mysterious spark of life within.

Creepy, isn't it?

To be sure, something had to be done, and getting my nails lacquered was not going to solve anything, though in hindsight it might have made me more presentable. Somehow I had to figure out how to wend my way out of the dark labyrinth into which I had wandered, how to free my self from the bonds of an ugly iron cage, to then return care of my body, my mind and my spirit to the mysterious unknown, the divine within.

As for solutions, I had already tried at the onset of symptoms simply to ignore them, pretending that tripping was a normal activity for any thirty-eight-year-old athletic male.

I had already tried fighting, as in, "You ain't gonna get me, you f-----g disease!"

I had tried effort with a capital E, as in, "If I do enough rounds of physical therapy and then I race here and there seeing this and that therapist before running off to see yet another doctor, I will simply wear out this disease."

And pleading prostration accomplished little more than smudging my frock, which, as you can imagine, was not a pleasant sight, my friend.

Needless to say, none of these avenues was working to bring about any kind of healing or reconciliation, let alone grace—though they certainly kept me occupied, and were, each in its own way, part of the trek.

No, ultimately for me the way out of the labyrinth was, and continues to be, one of surrender, which, oddly enough, brings us back to vulnerability, though vulnerability viewed from a very different perspective. You see, rather than use our vulnerability as a weapon against ourselves, I believe it is possible to utilize it as a wellspring from which we may draw deep sources of strength and from which we may discover endless clues about the mystery of life.

Each motion of the surrendered soul is a vessel of holiness and power.
—Martin Buber

'Tis a conundrum, to be sure, that…

    … the pathway to power is through surrender.
    … the pathway to wisdom is through innocence.
    … the pathway to strength is through suppleness.
    … the pathway to healing is through acceptance.
    … the pathway to grace is through darkness.
    … the pathway to courage is through vulnerability.
    … the pathway to scything is through effortlessness.

While scything is undoubtedly an act of physical labor, as opposed to one of pure thought, it is also true that if a person were to go about it the same way I did on that first brilliant afternoon near the top of a mountain, one would shortly be consumed by overwork and exhaustion as the day turned into a week which turned into a season which become a rather too brief life. Nonetheless, the hay, the grass, the grain must be reaped, so there is no possibility of simply reclining in the field, gazing up at the gradually changing cloudscape.

Yes, the weeds are there, the moment has come to mow them.

June, 1997. I take up the scythe, my own scythe. I stand in the midst of a high desert, here where the tall prairie grasses have long ago been grazed into scarcity and where the need to mow is more a matter of reducing the lusty, invasive weeds of summer. I grasp the snath lightly in my hands, I hold it in a position in which my arms are steady but not rigid. I begin to swing my torso gently back and forth, taking a small step with each sweep, first one foot then the other, the legs being slightly bent at the knees, allowing the shape and weight of the scythe to create an easy rhythm in my limbs. In this manner, being not a rigid, brittle stalk, but a supple, gentle one, it is possible to feel a sustaining pulse emerge from within the earth and rise up through my legs. With each sweep of the scythe I can hear the sharpened blade slicing through the weeds, the dusty plants falling into a pungent pattern on the ground. High above me the sun shines brightly. An almost spoken breeze billows through my shirt. In this timeless, rhythmic manner a person could mow for hours and days, a whole lifetime of mowing etched into the lines of the face, the hands, the soul.

You see, the task of scything, while it uses a rather intense and well-peened blade, is not one of conquering, of using brute force. Rather it is one of relinquishing the hard angularity of fear for the lithely curved life within. If you look at and touch the components of the tool itself, the snath and the scythe, you will find in them a remarkable extension of interior grace, as is the very act of scything, if done properly. And while it is undeniably exhausting work, one could say the same for the act of surrendering, of falling backwards into the white clouds of a blue sky. Nonetheless both, in their own way, arise from grace, leading toward a sustained fortitude of spirit.

Recently I came across an acquaintance of mine whom I had not seen in a long time. While I do not know this man very well, our relationship nevertheless goes back a surprising number of years. It was a lovely Thursday afternoon and my friend Courtenay had just wheeled me into a book shop and offered to serve me a cup of complimentary tea. At this moment my acquaintance happened to walk by and almost did not notice me. Even when he did it was with a bit of confusion, as he had not seen me for several years. He, of course, asked some routinely pertinent question which demanded a reply, a reply which I dutifully supplied with my weak voice, though to no communicative avail. Swiftly discerning the situation, and without any prompting from me, he knelt down in order to meet me at eye level and gently placed his hand over mine. For my own part I initially felt somewhat ill-at-ease because, as usual, there would be much explaining to do, and not only was my voice at a near standstill, I was also exhausted and simply had no desire to tell a long, complicated story. My acquaintance, however, bless his soul, seemed to intuit this. He asked another question, an easier one, to which I once more attempted an answer, but instead found myself giggling at the complete absurdity of my life, which then made him laugh, and after we had both giggled for a while he sputtered a benignly wise comment which was both nothingness and everness rolled into one, a comment which succeeded in inducing yet more laughter from the two of us. Most wonderfully for me, this man seemed to feel little compunction to judge my situation or to create my life for me, simply allowing the moment to be what it was, a moment which uncoiled into ripples in which we sat wordlessly in the midst of a busy world, all the while holding hands, before beginning to giggle again, and giggle again, and giggle again, surrendering to the infectious laughter which ever tumbles in great cycles within the Buddha's boundless belly.

You see, turning to words of Doris Lessing,

> *Laughter is a most powerful thing, and only the civilized, the liberated, the free person can laugh at herself, himself.*

Having in these past months gradually reclaimed my body, my life, my spirit, and having laid them humbly into the white clouds in the blue sky, I have rediscovered deep within me the power to giggle with grace, to laugh cradled in the Buddha's golden belly, surrendering my body to be my body and none other, my mind to be my mind and none other, my soul to be my soul, to be the freedom of a hawk uncaged.

Furthermore, as each life-giving breath tumbles down from the clouds I find my life imbued with the rhythms of a scythe sweeping softly through luxuriant grasses, the landscape falling into such lovely patterns high on the edge of a mountain, here where I have rolled my wheelchair and whence I may gaze out across a serenely unfolding landscape. Oh that we may come to inhabit, each in his or her own way, the words Virginia Woolf once wrote about the dead Rupert Brooke,

> ... that he still goes on being his self, since none of those who knew him can forget him; and it must be a wonderful self when no two people remember the same thing, but all are agreed that he was wonderful.

But wait, my friend! As is often the case, there remains one small but significant chapter in the story of the old man.

As I set out that afternoon to walk away from his field the old peasant firmly exhorted me to return down the mountain the way I had come up, that I ought not continue on the dusty path leading toward the other side of the mountain. When I asked him why, he vividly explained to me that the people who lived on the other side of the mountain were thieves, murderers, and monsters. You must turn around, he stated again and again. And, truth be told, he almost had me convinced. After all, the sun was beginning to lower and the path I was on would only take me into more remote regions, down into a densely forested swath of the mountain, far from the outside world. Something, however, encouraged me to pursue my journey, to put aside his fears and look at my own. I therefore assured him I would be safe, and waved goodbye.

Soon thereafter the narrow dirt pathway began its descent into a thick of trees even as the sun settled closer to the earth's far horizon, now hidden from view. With each accumulating step I descended deeper into forest, deeper into darkness, into solitude and remoteness. And where would these thieves, murderers and monsters be lurking, I wondered, and what would they look like when I finally encountered them?

To make a long story short, they looked like many another Muslim in that region.

You see, the people I was warned about, the people I came face to face with on the other side of the mountain were not thieves, murderers and monsters—not any more so than you or I—they were simply different, with different habits, different beliefs, different attitudes, people who warmly welcomed me into their homes, inviting me to sit down on the floor where we partook of the traditional communal pot of food, each of us dipping into it with his or her spoon. They were a people who made room in their humble homes for me to sleep, people who laughed and loved, and who willingly shared their lives with a complete stranger. If this is the definition of a thief, a murderer, and a monster, then I want more than anything else to grow up to be a thief, a murderer, and a monster.

Had I listened to everything the old man on the mountain told me, I would have succumbed to living out his life, an extension of his fears, his ignorance, his bigotry, rather than experiencing the vibrancy of my own journey. Yes, it is true that in listening to his words I learned some of the secrets of scything, but it is also true that had I believed everything he said I would never have had the opportunity to sup and sleep and laugh with the monsters on the other side of the mountain.

The words of others, when we take them for our own, become like the bars of a cage detaining us from the journey we must embark upon else find ourselves eviscerated, emptied, hollow. Eventually, when we have erected enough of these iron bars, we find that we are not merely caged but have in fact become entombed in our own darkness. Is it not enough that we have already been blessed each with his or her own fears? Ultimately it is these, rather than the fears of others, which must accompany us on our journeys.

Our lives are our own, not the figment of someone else's narrow vision.

Our bodies are our own, not the fragmented opinions of others.

Additionally, it is always our choice whether or not we become imprisoned by the ignorance, the arrogance, the bitterness, or the bigotry of other people.

While I can still feel the imprint of the iron bars on my flesh and can still smell the stifling constriction of the labyrinth recently departed, I have nevertheless surrendered to the wings of the hawk, to the golden clouds in the Buddha's laughing belly, and I have not once looked back, choosing instead to gaze out across a serenely unfolding landscape which is none other than my own body, my own spirit, my own life, nestled as it is within the divine breath of the Unknown.

June 6, 2001

51. HANDS

Standing above me, a man turns a lever which activates a hydraulic lift. Slowly, as slowly as water turns to air, I rise up out of the warm water, gradually rising from a realm of fluid arabesques to one of concrete angularity. Slowly, as slowly as air turns to metal, the chair I am sitting in swings around to its original position, here beside my waiting wheelchair. I, however, remain afloat upon a sky of water, weak and exhausted, my eyes closed, my flesh finely resonating with an eternity which will remain forever unvoiced. Indeed, I have no sense of before and after; I have no sense of forward and backward, of near and far.

As I inhale this moment of unboundedness, the tender lowering of a man's hand on my shoulder brings me news of the essential mystery of life, a loving gesture of such immense grace that there is no word for it.

In the landscape which surrounds this house one can walk for many kilometers before encountering any surface water; there are no running rivers, no fish-laden lakes, no plummeting waterfalls. True, on the abutting ranch land there do exist occasional watering spots for the cattle, the water either pumped from below ground by windmills or gathered into man-made dams during summer rainstorms. It is, of course, during the awakening aftermaths of just such tempests that variously sized puddles, some as large as ponds, appear in the anachronistic dirt roads which transect this uneven landscape. Nonetheless, this is a realm of desert, waterless and enigmatic. The rain, when it does come, generally swoops in across the sere land, great walls and columns of falling water marching across the desert, departing as recklessly as it arrived, an arrival which is traditionally stunning and therefore transformatively destructive, ever reforging the apparently solid landmass, this haunting environment which at first glance seems to harbor little in the way of wildlife, though upon closer examination it is possible to notice an occasional antelope, the barking of coyotes, the usual horned toads, several kinds of snakes and lizards, along with rabbits in manic abundance, assorted mice, thoughtful beetles, roaming tarantulas, varieties of bugs and arachnids, as well as avians ranging in size from hummingbirds to vultures and hawks, all of them the intriguing denizens of this harsh desert.

Yes, in the late afternoon the rain arrives.

The dark clouds roll across the unprotected land.

Ferocious bursts of thunder call us to witness.

Jabs of lightning illuminate not only the interiors of those ominously dark clouds but also the finely textured landscapes of our mortalities.

To be outside amid such a swift thrust of the hand of nature is nothing if not a magnification of life, at once terrifying and rapturous, fraught and immense.

And as quickly as the sword is thrust it is removed, leaving the body of earth drenched in sudden water, its shoulders garlanded in rainbows intense enough to light the way toward eternity, if only we were capable of holding such glorious light in our hearts.

Then, in an almost miraculous display of nature's abundant diversity, one hears from across the simple, torrented land the sound of frogs singing.

Yes, frogs.

Not a little ribbet here and there, but a resounding panoply, a golden horde of frogs sprung from the hot, dry earth, taking full advantage of the sudden wetness to sing and mate, before singing some more and mating some more, their voices unfolding in rich waves across the sighing land.

By morning their ecstatic voices will be stilled, their bodies having burrowed back into the earth to await the next swift deluge.

Sitting here pondering the obvious though rather unfortunate observation that the human hand is generally taken for granted by most of us, I envision the hands of the almost blind Edgar Degas, rough hands covered in pigment, their idiosyncratic gestures applying the ground pastels onto large pieces of blank paper or canvas in sensuous swaths of pattern, creating in his later years a striking portfolio of female figures.

I am further reminded of how the late eighteenth-century composer and keyboardist Hélène Montgeroult, aged twenty-eight, was condemned to die at the guillotine, her severe sentence reduced only upon her improvised performance, following months of imprisonment, of the "Marseillaise" on a harpsichord carried into the crowded courtroom, a performance which roused the attendant mob to a state of fervent singing.

I ponder the shape of Walt Whitman's hands as they once tended the wounded and dying young men of the American Civil War, and am also reminded of those innocent survivors of recent African conflicts whose hands were mercilessly hacked off with swift blows of machete blades.

I think also of the hands of a young man carefully refurbishing a 1987 Mustang GT convertible, interior and exterior—400 horsepower engine, racing suspension, upholstery, wiring, and all manner of things I know so little about.

Furthermore, I find myself gazing at my own hands, how they have always had an improper propensity to dance, to tell stories which stretch back in time toward a prehistory indiscernible by any other manner; these same hands that have grasped the axe and brought it skillfully down onto logs of pine and oak, splitting them into flames which echo across a quiet hour before turning into smoke which rises peacefully into the winter air; these hands that now have a tendency to curl in upon themselves or to spastically contort into the frozen gestures of bas-relief sculptures ornamenting ancient temples, the very contortion of the fingers eloquently expressing not only the story of the birth of Sri Rama, but also the tale of a degeneration of nerves deep within my brain.

You see, upon closer examination, it is a delusion that we communicate predominantly with the voice.

As the thirteenth-century Sufi poet Rumi reminds us,

> *A mouth is not for talking.*
> *A mouth is for tasting this Sweetness.*

With the mouth we taste the sweet nearness of the divine; through the hands, the body we are ever communicating it. This, in direct contradiction of what we have been taught, and also of the socio-cultural edifices we are continually erecting, but which little serve to deepen our taste of the earth, of one another, and of the universe.

This past spring I found myself in need of an additional volunteer caregiver, a situation complicated by the recent deterioration in my physical condition, meaning that I have to be increasingly more particular about those who assist me. After searching fruitlessly for many weeks I was one day conversing with a guy whom I had recently met at the sports complex where I do my physical therapy. Since he was inquiring about my team of helpers, there seemed little harm in asking him if he would be willing to assist me with my water therapy regimen, to which he readily agreed, with the understanding that he would first need to obtain permission from his employer to miss those hours of work.

Several weeks later, at nine o'clock on a Tuesday morning early in the month of June, a twenty-eight-year-old auto mechanic named Eli, father of three and devout Christian, strolled into the high-ceilinged chamber which houses the therapy pool.

Over the past several years as my friend Jeremy has generously assisted me in numerous ways, he and I have had the fortunate opportunity to exchange a veritable encyclopedia of words, whether in the locker room of the pool, in the cab of his old red pickup truck, in the men's room at the cinema, or over a pint of ale, and while my role as an active perpetrator of such verbal vandalism continues to diminish with each passing month, his capacities remain verily untarnished. On the other hand, as of the beginning of June the amount of words Eli and I had exchanged since first meeting would readily have fit onto a single sheet of paper, and would have consisted predominantly of the following words in various reconfigurations: hello, how, are, you, I'm, late, for, work, and, I, am, going, to, the, pool, so, have, a, nice, day—not exactly revealing of either of our souls, one must admit.

Yet here he is, standing at the edge of the pool, prepared to do what he does not know, his face breaking into a comfortable smile as I glance up from the water. In spite of what he does not know, however, Eli is certainly intelligent enough to have realized that he will not be able to rely on me for much in the way of verbal leadership and must himself forge a path within these first moments, a path which leads from a superficial acquaintance toward a deeper intimacy demanding from each of us a most daring plunge into the unknown, the vulnerable, the place of meeting.

Additionally, whatever this man has not told me about himself, whatever I do not know of his life, his soul, his compassion—which, after all, is most everything —will of necessity be unerringly and precisely conveyed to me during the next hour, as his essence is undeniably expressed to me through hands that steady me, hands that comfort me, fingers that adjust the cuff of the sphygmomanometer, through a body which lifts me, holds me, catches me.

In order to better understand the fragility of this situation let us look at it in more depth:

It is nine o'clock on a Tuesday morning. I have just completed an hour of water therapy and exercises. Within the cyclical framework of my week, this is probably the occasion on which I am most vulnerable, most exhausted, and least capable of doing things for myself, let alone articulating my needs. It is a scenario which would truly challenge many of the guys who have capably assisted me in the past, indeed I would not even entrust some of them with such a situation on their first day, yet...

...into this state of intense need walks a man more or less unknown to me, a guy who has never before done anything quite like this, who has no training for it other than a few pertinent suggestions from Jeremy, and who is probably so conscientiously nervous about doing a decent job that he might actually be more hindrance than help. Additionally, he has only ever experienced me sitting peacefully in a wheelchair in the lobby of the sports complex: At this point, at nine o'clock on a June morning, he has no clue how unnervingly extreme a paroxysmal seizure can be; he likely has no clue what it is like to have a person slip out of his arms and crash to the floor; he does not even know where the brakes are positioned on my wheelchair; and he certainly hasn't a clue what the next hour is going to bring.

Nor do I.

There is surrounding each one of us a certain point in three-dimensional space which correlates to this very moment, to a time which is now, and is the time being. How far from the body this point lies is entirely dependent upon the trajectory of each person's life and may incorporate many diverse factors, none of which need concern us here. What is of interest is that most of us unconsciously cultivate and maintain the illusion that so long as others remain beyond that perimeter, they—and we—can be said to exist in the present moment, much as puppets in a puppet theater act out their well-ordered actions in a space bounded by a before and an after, by a proscenium, a space we can easily identify as now, a particular point on a paper graph of space-time.

The question naturally arises, what happens when another person's hand confronts that perimeter, that point on the paper graph which surrounds me? Furthermore, what ensues when said hand breaks through that supposedly secure piece of paper, destroying the fragile security of that nebulous perimeter? Well, to be sure, a very odd sequence of events is set into motion; namely my culturally constructed now begins to disintegrate and time itself begins unravelling toward some preliterate, even preverbal state of being, toward the moment when the hand of another makes contact with my body, thus breaching the walls of eternity. While it may be noted that this manifestation of infinity is constantly flowing and ebbing within the intercourses of our daily lives, generally speaking it is almost impossible to comprehend the depth of eternity when the gesture of contact is brief, or is habitual, therefore ritualized, such as a welcoming hug, a parting kiss, a pat on the back, a confidential whisper.

It is quite another matter, however, and consequently more difficult to deflect the truth of the Self, when my naked body lurches forward in a sudden spasm and a man's hand bursts through the thin paper of that superficial perimeter, his palm slamming against my chest, shoving me back against the wall, both of us drenched with water raining down unceasingly from the shower.

If ever there were a time and place where the universe were unbounded, this is it.

Additionally, it is an altogether different matter to find oneself, by necessity or choice, dwelling in a realm wherein every defining action, every communication must exist within the aforementioned perimeter, rather than without, each moment intimately expanding ever deeper into eternity, not merely a tantalizing droplet of eternity, as one might experience with a hug or a whisper to the ear, but a veritable river of unboundedness, a dissolution of time itself, of all concepts of now, of right or wrong, of the very construct of beingness.

Yes, we want so much to tell our stories primarily through the voice, which we have been led to believe is a grand culmination of evolutionary ingenuity, or is a unique gift from the gods, but which is indeed little more than noisy chatter. Does our hesitancy to communicate with the hands, the lips, the body stem from an uncertainty about whether the truer stories of our hands will be sufficient, and will they be understood; worse, might they indeed reveal some infinite truth, that a person must therefore be mindlessly spewing out endless chains of words in order to deflect the thoughts of others from what is ultimately a person's deepest commitment to the universe?

Simply stated, our hands disclose our essences. While our spoken words may serve to augment, distort, embellish, or confound the expressions of our hands, they cannot destroy the essential truth bound within the touch of the hand, the sinews of the body.

Hanuman the Monkey, Son of the Wind, was born wearing small golden earrings which were invisible to everyone except an unspecified person who would remain unidentified to Hanuman until the two actually encountered one another—some special person who would one day be revealed to him and would thereafter be a true comrade.

Years later, as Sri Rama of Ayodhya climbed Rishyamukha Hill alongside his faithful brother Lakshmana, he came across what appeared to be a poor woodcutter. Noticing the earrings which he alone could perceive, Sri Rama immediately recognized Hanuman and called him by his true name, at which Hanuman resumed his original form, that of a monkey, Son of the Wind.

Thus began one of the deepest, most selfless friendships of all time.

Each one of us is metaphorically wearing the golden earrings of Hanuman the Monkey, though they hang not from our ears nor upon our arrogantly superficial words. Rather they are embedded in our hands. These earrings—however they be crafted upon our birth, or forged through our living—are furthermore generally unseen by the hordes of people through which we meander during the days of our lives. Nonetheless, when the hand of a comrade comes to rest upon our faces, our shoulders, our thighs, we know immediately his essence, regardless of whatever clever disguise he has donned, intentionally or not. For this reason it matters not what a person wears, or how she speaks, or the color of her skin. Ultimately the earrings of Hanuman will disclose the gift of grace; the touch of the hand will tell of love better than any verb, any noun, or any grammar.

Earlier when I described Eli as a devout Christian, a father of three, and an auto mechanic, it is undeniable that you immediately found yourself forming an opinion of him, favorable or not, as you would were I to tell you that Jeremy is a bicycle mechanic and a full-blooded ale devourer who married his wife in Las Vegas, Nevada, on Halloween, a member of the wedding party dressed as a giant rabbit.

These words, however—and your interpretations of them—must remain forever meaningless, mere illusions.

It is only through the touch of Eli's hands securely holding me in the midst of a violent paroxysmal seizure, only through the gestures of Jeremy's arms as he competently cradles my body and maneuvers my limbs through the warm water during my physical therapy, that their selves are fully expressed and revealed. Only then can the true Self discard the clothing of words and know of itself.

Today an unusually low sky brings with it a gentle rain.

In front of me, as slowly as metal turns to water, the motorcar rises above the concrete pad of a garage, the motorcar's bulk hoisted up by two hydraulic forks supporting the vehicle on either side.

When the sedan on the lift is sufficiently high, Eli confidently drives his 1987 Mustang GT convertible underneath it before unlatching the canvas roof, opening it through and across the aromas of oil and metal, gradually revealing to me the underbelly of the car poised directly above us.

. . . Because it is raining outside.

. . . Because he needs to lift my wheelchair out of the back seat.

. . . Because he is going to fix the wheelchair's safety belt.

. . . Because an hour earlier, in the midst of a rather violent paroxysm, my contorted body had ripped the belt from its grommet.

It is for this reason that Eli has driven us beneath the other car, to gain access to the wheelchair without getting me wet with rain, in order to fix the severed safety belt—my empty wheelchair looking so insignificant in the vast chamber of this huge garage.

One of his comrades jokingly asks him if he is planning to turbo-charge the wheelchair.

Eli retorts that it'll be the fastest wheelchair in the state.

But it won't be, because those are only words.

No matter.

As I turn my silent gaze from the dented, corroded underbelly of the sedan hovering above me toward where Eli's hands are expertly repairing not only the safety belt but also replacing some lost screws on the armrests, I am once again astounded at what our hands tell of our souls.

Ever more I find myself knowing the world not through its voices but through its hands, as they bless me and hold me, as they do for me things I can no longer do, as they dance around and upon me, explaining to me more than all the libraries of earth, more than the word of God, more than what we have been told is life and death.

I am also filled with an awareness that spoken words cannot of themselves sustain nor support life; furthermore that our existences can unfold only through the touch of the wind's fingers on our flesh, the rain's prayers on our lips, our deepest stories being expressed through the nearness of Jeremy's compassionate arms, through the hand of Eli reaching over to reassure us, his smile brought low and near with the gentle rain as he and his comrade close the canvas roof of the convertible, latching it securely before we each depart into the future.

Perhaps after all is said and deconstructed, analyzed and pondered, orated and refuted, after we have finally freed ourselves of those seemingly imperishable words, and in particular the words which once so defined us, we find ourselves, much to our surprise, in an unfathomable state of grace, and haven't a clue how to speak of it, how to express the scent of rain on our flesh, how to write of the silent gestures of love, how to translate the essential mystery as told through the touch of another's hand, how to speak of grace without destroying it.

Because, in the end, it refuses to be spoken of.

It is dark.

My body is lying on the highway.

Someone is removing my motorcycle helmet; a kind motorist is speaking to me, foggily explaining that she is a nurse.

From somewhere in the darkness comes the sound of a policeman's voice asking questions which for one reason or another I cannot answer, because the universe has become very small. I am not even sure my eyes are open and whether I am seeing what I am hearing or hearing what I am seeing.

At this moment I become aware of a different voice, that of a man who is answering the officer's questions, telling the other disembodied voices that the accident was his fault, that he hadn't noticed me.

Of all the voices this one is nearest, and as I force my eyes partially open I gradually realize that it is his arms and his lap which are cradling my head, my shoulders.

Even in my semiconscious state I find this action of his so honorable that I feel I must respond. Yes, I must find a way to tell him that such actions as his exist in a realm beyond blame, beyond names, beyond words.

Not knowing what else to do I reach my hand toward his face and run my fingers through his short hair, my hand then falling against his shoulder as I slip back into unconsciousness.

I did not die that night.

If I had, however, I feel certain that this stranger could have told those who know me that I had died in peace. Yes, in the aftermath of a violent collision I had died in peace.

A few weeks later, having mostly recuperated from this accident, I was in the local feed store. The owner—who also happens to be the chief of the volunteer fire department—after helping me with my purchase, said in his laconic way, "I can't believe you're still alive after that accident."

Since we know one another only on the most peripheral of terms, I wondered aloud how he had learned about the collision.

He looked at me, smiled gently, and responded, "It was me driving the ambulance."

The immediacy, the intimacy of a rainstorm arriving across the desert brings life near and close and fervently illumined by uncompromising strokes of lightning.

The gift of rain, wordless and pre-rational, floods the flesh of earth, creating out of the intensity of its nearness the songs of frogs.

Yes, and as a glorious rainbow bursts into existence among the clouds above me, I am once again reminded of the ever-recurrent mystery, namely, as I wrote in "Isaiah's Fugue" that...

...as much as he meant to me there exists no word to describe what we were to each other...

July 25, 2001

53. ISAAC AND LORENZO

In a long poetic work called simply *Mathnawi*, meaning couplets, the thirteenth-century Sufi poet Jelaluddin Rumi writes,

> *A True Human Being is never what he or she appears to be. Rub your eyes and look again.*

So be it, in the sacred hours embedded in the high holy days stretching from Rosh Hashanah to Yom Kippur, the violinist Isaac Stern has died, blessed be his name.

As a child I had the temerity to secretly and unilaterally write a letter seeking to interview the great violinist. Why this chutzpah, I do not know. It certainly was not with any intent to further my brilliant career as a violinist. While I did indeed play the violin, it was not my primary instrument, nor did I harbor any delusions about the securely mediocre talent I displayed. I was also not a budding journalist, and neither at that point nor at any subsequent juncture have I yearned for a career in journalism. Yet, for whatever reason I was inspired to request an interview with the violinist, it was nonetheless granted me, and by such a path I one day found myself sitting in a posh hotel suite with maestro Stern.

There were four of us present that day. Besides maestro Stern and myself there were my mother—I can hardly think of a better person to accompany me to an interview with one of the world's finest musicians—and a journalist, a bona fide journalist. For my part, I had dutifully brought along a notepad, a pencil and some questions to put forth in my squeaky, fairy tale voice. Following the appropriate introductions the journalist graciously ceded to me to begin, at which point I innocently asked maestro Stern a question which was undoubtedly of earth-shattering importance to a young lad, such as, "When is your birthday?"

Or, "Do you like flying in airplanes?"

Or, "What's your favorite pizza topping?"

To which question, whichever one it was, maestro Stern summarily replied that if I wanted such topical information concerning his biography it could easily be found in any number of resources; in essence, we were there to discuss more important issues. He was not cruel in his condemnation of my meager question, just straightforward about the intention of his life. At which point the interview slid into the more capable hands of the journalist, while I listened intently, trying to think of what could possibly be more important than a person's birthday or one's favorite pizza topping. In subdued and hopefully unnoticed desperation I scanned my list of questions, searching for one that might fit into maestro Stern's category of important issues, and could do little better than, "Do you play any instrument other than the violin?"—a question which, by the way, did elicit a smiling response, something akin to, "No, the fiddle's hard enough for me."

Needless to say, I was somewhat abashed by his ready dismissal of my meager and admittedly topical questions. How was I to know what to ask, I thought to myself. But, to be certain, he was absolutely correct, as would be expected of such a fine human being. His disdain for the superficial, along with his desire to move directly to the issues underlying the life of music and the music of life, while at first disconcerting and challenging for a boy, were in the end powerfully instructive.

In the Qur'an it is written,

> *Wheresoever you turn, there is the face of God.* (2:115)

As simple as these nine words may strike us, they are more easily written than seen, more easily spoken than heard, more easily published than tasted, more easily forgotten than lived.

I first met Lorenzo a couple of years ago.

Sitting outside one of my local haunts, leaning on my walking stick, gazing at the lustrous blue sky, I greeted him as he wandered down the street toward me. A homeless man in his late forties or early fifties, he forthwith came to sit beside me, opening a cheap beer he had just purchased from the proceeds of his panhandling. As we sat conversing, or rather as I listened to his litany of woes, I had ample opportunity to observe how he would expertly wind the conversation toward the primary question of his existence, namely, "Can you spare a dime?" Each time he approached the question, however, he would look at me, at my walking stick, at my odd assortment of clothing, then shrug his shoulders.

Whenever he spoke ponderously of his woes, I found myself replying, "Could be worse, my friend." This, not in order to diminish or discount his experiences, but as a kind of recognition of our mutually challenging human existences. For some reason he found this phrase quite pithy, laughing good-naturedly before returning to his own private Woeville, expressed with almost biblical fortitude. After fifteen or twenty minutes of chit-chat, during which time I had the chance to inquire about his name, his birthday, and how old he was—though not his favorite pizza topping—he tossed the empty beer can in a shopping bag and rose from the bench to continue on his way, even then struggling unsuccessfully to voice his need for spare change.

I still do not know why he ultimately couldn't bring himself to ask for a handout. As I have since learned, he is certainly not shy about asking for money, and indeed can be utterly blatant about it. Over time I have had ample opportunity to watch him ask for money from every person he has encountered in my presence, regardless of age, gender, or class. Yet, curiously enough, he has never once asked me for money. Had he, I would have gladly helped him out with whatever spare change was in my pockets.

Thereafter, for a year or more, Lorenzo and I would often encounter one another, always by chance, since there was no other way for our lives to intersect. For his part he would invariably expound upon the woes of his life; for mine I would invariably tell him it could be worse, to which he would reply with a burst of guffaws and a hearty nodding of his head. During our visits it was ever fascinating to watch him maneuver his soliloquy toward that vital question, "Can you spare a dime?" Then as usual he would glance toward me, who after a time had become dependent on using a walker for ambulation, and go silent, the question remaining unspoken. Perhaps he could not quite figure me out, could not find a category into which I neatly fit. Perhaps in his perception of the situation I was a brother, another guy struggling on the streets, since, like him, I would appear out of nowhere in the middle of the day and was seldom in a hurry, quite unlike any normal person. It would not have been the first time I was mistaken for a homeless person. If this were the case, it would perhaps in his assessment be poor form to ask me for money.

I do not truly know.

Over time his attempts to pursue tactics or to formulate arguments in order to get a handout diminished. Instead, we would just hang out together, his woes verily unmitigated, his sudden laughter laying as heartily on the tongue as mine. If our relationship brought him no monetary recompense, the companionship we shared was evidently sufficient enough impetus to encourage him to sit beside me, ever divulging the day's lamentations. Indeed, whenever he perceived me from a distance he would always make sure to wend his way toward where I was sitting. If he were accompanied by any of his street buddies he would be certain to introduce them to me with a certain proprietary propriety. His buddies and I would then shake hands as though we were observing protocol at an important ambassadorial event. Inevitably this would be followed by laughter spilling forth from toothless mouths, scarred faces, oily hair, grimy clothing, misshapen shoes. Thereafter, whenever they encountered me wandering the streets with my walker, those same buddies would shake my hand or give me a hug, rarely if ever asking me for money, as though they had agreed to a code of honor spelled out by Lorenzo, or perhaps simply by the queerness of life.

As far as the biographical details of my life, the topical information, Lorenzo knows nothing about me, not even my name, either because his personality is by nature so self-absorbed that it does not occur to him to ask, or because the few things I have told him do not resonate with him and therefore have not stayed with him.

A couple of weeks ago, after a period of many months during which I had not seen Lorenzo, he came upon me sitting in my wheelchair, gazing as usual at the intense blue sky. At first he seemed confused by the wheelchair, as are many others when they have not seen me for a while, and was apparently thinking it best to simply ignore me and pass by. Sensing his uncertainty, I waved my hand.

"Do you remember me?" he asked in his gruff voice as he came closer.

I motioned him to step nearer, that I could speak into his ear, a gesture which seemed only to further discombobulate him. Nonetheless he came near enough that I was able to pull his shoulder toward me and whisper hoarsely into his ear, "Of course I remember you, Lorenzo."

I had to repeat my words, since he could not understand them the first time, after which he unceremoniously plunked himself down on a bench situated a meter or two in front of me. Sitting there, he looked at me, just looked at me. Then, true to form, he expressed some woe to which, even at that short distance, I could only reply with a gesture of my hands and a smile of my face. This caused him to go silent again, perhaps the only time I have ever seen him thoughtful. In this particular situation the only method I had of truly communicating with him was to fully meet his gaze and to open my heart large enough that it could encompass both of us—any other solution necessitated a retreat from the truth.

For a minute or so the two of us looked intently at one another. He seemed somehow deeply moved. For the first time since I had met Lorenzo, I saw his eyes truly looking at me, encountering mine in the mutual realm of suffering inherent in all our lives.

Finally, and uncharacteristically, he stood up from the bench and left without a word.

Over time I have become accustomed to the responses I customarily get from people when they have not seen me for a while, responses which tend to be full of overemphasized pity or of syrupy gushing usually expressed in overly loud tones as though I've gone deaf or lost my senses, either of which is within the realm of reason, as it were. Indeed, I experienced this latter type of response not too long ago when a woman whom I had not seen in years, obviously taken aback by my condition, started clearly enunciating her words, speaking more loudly than would normally be the case, and repeating important words as though I would not otherwise be able to comprehend their meaning. In addition to these two types of response, each perfectly valid, there is also the ever popular, "You look great, Zsolt!"—to which I often feel like responding, "You would look pretty cute yourself in a wheelchair."

Lorenzo's response to the change in my condition is the only one I can recall that was almost purely one of compassion in its fundamental sense. There we were, two guys who are daily faced with the tough challenges of survival gazing open-eyed at one another, our lives stripped of everything except this gaze of compassion, of knowing one another so intently, so nonpersonally, so intimately.

The other day, as one of my friends was positioning her car in a parking lot in order to provide me access to the passenger's seat, Lorenzo and one of his buddies appeared unexpectedly from behind a wide pillar. Upon noticing me sitting in my wheelchair, Lorenzo immediately strode up to give me a skinny bear hug. In his usual woeful, jovial way, he heartily introduced me to his nephew, Phillip, as though we were strangers. Phillip grinned generously and told Lorenzo, "I know this guy. This is the guy who always smiles and waves."

When I was younger I had fervent hopes that I would be the guy who wrote brilliant novels, or the guy who developed a revolutionary cosmological theory, or the guy who saved hundreds of lives in a flood. As it turns out, I am the guy who always smiles and waves. So be it, Phillip. I hereby humbly and gratefully accept my moniker, so bestowed upon me with your own warm smile dressed as it is in the clothing of the street.

Lorenzo then asked me what I was doing. I pulled his head close to mine, his deeply furrowed skin weathered into a tough leather the deep color of chestnut shells, and spoke into his ear, my face brushed by his thick, unwashed hair. I told him my friend was taking me to the mountains to see the autumn colors. With this news of my imminent departure and the obvious appearance of a white vehicle pulling alongside us, Lorenzo became fired with purpose, with a mission. Suddenly he became Mr. Stage Director peremptorily prancing about.

"Help him in, Phillip! We gotta help him into the car."

With this sudden flutter of activity he began opening the back door of the car, as though it were a cab. I tugged on his arm and pointed to the front door.

"It's the front door he wants, Phillip, the front door. There, now open the door and help him in. We gotta help him into the car. Take care of him, don't let him fall."

Like a well-rehearsed actor, Phillip opened the door and confidently took his position before hoisting me up and gently transferring me onto the passenger seat. When my friend could not figure out how to collapse the wheelchair, Phillip took the situation in hand and expertly closed it up before helping her to stow it in the back of the car, all the while Lorenzo fluttering about directorially with a cigarette dangling out of his mouth, and, by the way, not missing an opportunity to ask my friend if she had any spare change.

Once the wheelchair was properly stowed, Phillip and Lorenzo came around to the open window to say goodbye, each reaching his hands inside the car to hold mine, not merely a shaking of hands, but a sincere holding of life between us, as Lorenzo, in a voice made gruff by years of smoking and years of living on the streets, said to me through a billowing puff of smoke, "You'll always have a place in my heart, man."

Then he emphatically patted his chest just to make sure I understood.

September 30, 2001

55. FIGGY CHARM

Charm, of course, conquers us utterly, gloriously. Less well known, perhaps, is that lack of charm, in its way, defeats us insidiously, ignominiously.

In her wittily insightful pillow book, the tenth-century Japanese court lady Sei Shōnagon expressed the following sentiment:

> *A preacher ought to be good-looking. For, if we are properly to understand his worthy sentiments, we must keep our eyes on him while he speaks; should we look away, we may forget to listen. Accordingly an ugly preacher may well be the source of sin.*

One could easily substitute charm for good-looking and achieve much the same sentiment, maybe even more so. But then, perhaps this is precisely what Sei Shōnagon meant. Since I am reading her words in a twentieth-century translation which uses as its impetus a text that is a thousand years old, it may well be that she was trying to express a subtly different concept, one which only vaguely resembles what a person would now translate as good-looking. Nonetheless, there is something in her sentiment to which we can attest even from this distance, a certain ineffable quality most of us sense time and again, a quality which if we were pushed to define it, might be expressed as charm.

And then there are these lines from an even older text, the Katha Upanishad:

> *The adorable one who is seated*
> *in the heart rules the breath of life.*

The first time I read this fragment, nestled as it is among many another exquisite thought, I found it captivating. I do wonder, however, if indeed I am intended to find it charming, and whether read in the original Sanskrit the words would have this same affect on me. Nonetheless, being a wholly delightful phrase as it stands, it is worthy of pause, of a catch in the heart, and an opening toward the bittersweet nectar of the universe.

Ah, charm.
The eyes,
the smile,
the elegant gesture,
the resolute laugh,
the fervent belief,
the thoughtful gleam,
the crossing of one's legs,
the uncrossing of one's legs,
the eloquent phrase,
the awkward word,
the turn of the head,
the lack of pretense,
the glint of superiority,
and the breath of dignity,
the posture of grace,
the giggle,
the delight,
the mystery,
the dimples,
the wink,
the light,
and also the shadow which hints at the substance,
the inherent humility,
the divine strength,
the articulate fingers,
the silent thought,
the cantankerous insistence on living,
the fearlessness,
the untamed,
the gentle,
the poised,
the fractious,
and the composed,
the sweet,
the delicious,
the sacred,
the heretical,
the thigh,
the lips,
the unmitigated mystery,
the sublime,

the iridescent affability,
the succulent,
the tender,
the giddy,
the sheen of knowing,
the surrender to not knowing,
the whisper,
the encounter,
the ordinary made exquisite,
and the profound made present,
the insatiable flight,
the utter imperturbability,
the eyelashes,
the turn of the head,
the sincerest of goodbyes,
all conspiring to charm us,
to conquer us,
utterly,
gloriously.

I remember as a teenager going for a job interview with a modeling agency. As soon as I walked into her office wearing what I hoped was a stunning outfit pieced together from the bowels of various thrift shops, the director looked at me, made a highly dramatic flourish with her arms, and loudly exclaimed, "You've got bones!"

On that day so long ago I first learned that I've got bones.

And evidently bones are good.

In fact, they must be great, else she would not have been nearly as excited as she was.

Yet, from my depraved and completely fringe perspective bones alone do not suffice. While we might readily gaze for a while at the good-looking preacher suggested by Sei Shōnagon in her pillow book, most of us would soon weary were it not for a certain something else, an alluring if indefinable quality. Conversely, I think we can all imagine situations where the person in our midst, whether she be a cherished friend or a complete stranger, is not especially good-looking, and may not even have bones, but is nonetheless totally enticing, captivating, and compelling to the point we want nothing more than to spend the entire afternoon in her company.

The effusion of this quality, by the way, is not limited to Homo sapiens. In light of this, certain dogs are so consummately charming in their demeanor that I find myself utterly enchanted, enamored, while many another dog is simply annoying in the extreme.

And, though by my mention of it you shall now have solid confessional evidence of my eccentric fatuousness, I do find chipmunks utterly charming.

As is a young man proudly growing his first moustache.

So too giggling children.

Even more so giggling adults.

And an unfamiliar four-year-old girl who, after noticing me whispering *Hello* to her, bravely leaves her mother's orbit in order to cautiously step up to my wheelchair and surreptitiously whisper, *Who are you?*

And cats asleep on their backs.

And an old man telling me about his mischievous youth with a glint in his eye betraying that he would do it all again, given the chance.

And two girls exuberantly gossiping in Spanish as they run gaily toward the open door of a church.

And beetles crawling across the lumpy earth beneath the sky's irrepressible beauty.

And the singular taste of fresh figs.

And young people yearning to make the world a better place, even though their dreams may one day falter and their ideas prove futile.

And old people yearning to make the world a better place, even though their dreams may one day falter and their ideas prove futile.

And anyone willing to open his or her mind to difficult and complex questions.

And the kiss of wonder.

As well as the rising of the crescent moon.

And the incomprehensible migrations of birds.

And Michelangelo's painting of the Lybian Sibyl on the ceiling of the Sistine Chapel.

And lizards.

And crickets.

And crisp white tablecloths neatly laid.

And elegant daffodils heralding the spring.

And someone confessing that she utterly adores life.

And someone else graciously accepting the hand of death.

And these poetic words of Jorge Luis Borges:

> *You will never recapture what the Persian*
> *said in his language woven with birds and roses,*
> *when, in the sunset, before the light disperses,*
> *you wish to give words to unforgettable things.*

Ah, the autumn leaves, floating down from unreachable heights, blown in on a hortatory gust, or swept beneath the metal belly of a swiftly moving vehicle, these curled leaves coming at last to rest far from the sky in an undisturbed nook of the earth.

Who among us is not somehow stirred by the falling leaves of autumn, the flamboyant display of their sudden colors, after months of seemingly imperturbable green, followed by the accompanying turn of the earth to reveal an exotic face, comforting in its own way, and almost knowable, nearly approachable?

Which one of us is not somehow captivated by certain seasonal aromas in the air, their pungency informing us of a change, of a slowing down of nature's song as portions of it return to the earth, there to rest beneath the lowering blanket of white snow?

And which one of us does not taste the bittersweet nectar implicit in the charming gestures which surround us at every turn, their meanings somehow more potent during times of transition, from one season to another, for instance, or from the word on the page to the call of the night owl?

Now at the end of a day in town, one which has been especially strenuous for both of us, Hart arrives to take me home. Having transferred from my wheelchair into the passenger seat, I lean back, taking a couple of deep, diaphragmatic breaths as I do, my eyes glancing down at the emergency brake lever to notice a small plastic basket full of plump, fresh figs. I try not to become interested in them, partly because I am almost too weary for excitement, and partly because the figs may be there for some as yet undisclosed reason, a reason, moreover, little relevant to me. For instance, perhaps they are intended as a gift for one of Hart's colleagues.

Perhaps, in the autumnal twilight, they are merely an illusion.

Having expertly stowed the wheelchair, Hart climbs into the driver's seat, hands me the figs and says, "I thought I ought to do something nice." Now, why he should say this, I do not know, because he is always doing nice things, not just for me, but in one way or another for many people in the community.

Obviously he knows how much I enjoy fresh figs, else he would not have bothered purchasing them; also how seldom I get an opportunity to partake of them.

It is also true that he himself has little interest in figs, fresh or dried. In other words, the entire little basketful is for me, ten or so of these succulent, plump, enigmatic fruits.

He smiles.

I gaze at a small plastic basket filled with the fruit of a harvest season drawing to a close.

Curious how these rotund morsels have travelled what to a piece of fruit must be vast distances in order to be here in my thin hands.

As we drive first toward the last remnants of the setting sun, then veer left for the homeward journey, I hold the figs in my lap, tenderly cradling in my heart the unforgettable days of my life.

Fresh figs.

How simply charming.

One might even say adorable.

October 11, 2001

57. TEA AND STONES

A cup of tea sits on the wooden table.

A cup of tea, slightly bitter, pungently stout, almost earthen in the revealing light of the sun.

A cup of tea cradled in my bony hands, the warmth of the ceramic a solace, my lips pressing against the rim of life, its rich liquid flowing over my tongue, its subtle yet complex aromas rising into my face, my closed eyes, a realm where the darkness sparkles, the light undulates, and where visions are born of the wind's fleeting words.

Where the intern looks earnestly at me, saying, "It may be that for you every moment must be a meditation; the rest of your life, each breath, each movement, even while you are asleep, is a meditation."

The words of this man, being at once a verdict, a prophecy and a blessing, now re-emerge from the depths of a cup of tea, a comfort.

Yes, as severe a verdict as his words are, and as challenging as their fulfillment will be—for to live and breathe at the same time can be a most elusive vocation—they are a comfort.

As I carefully set the cup down onto the table, my fingers contract into gnarled claws holding onto branches of trees which long ago entered the gardens of human mythology. There they withered and died, before being gathered up by the strong arms of a peasant woman who bundled them into fagots in preparation for the trek toward home, where the burning branches entered the language of legends in the eyes and minds of children staring into the liquid flames.

Where the taste of the tea hovers, slightly bitter on the back of the tongue, the earth made sweet with a touch of milk.

On the floor beside my armchair the old cat takes a step and falters, his
    unsteady hind legs collapsing beneath him, each moment of his failing
    life ebbing naturally within the rising and falling of his breath, as though
    the cat has readily understood and embodied the intern's words, as
    though the intern had spoken to him rather than to me.

Yet the intern does not know about the gray-and-white cat.

He has never seen this fifteen-year-old cat, though he has probably surmised
    the animal's existence from the omnipresent hairs clinging to my
    clothing as he rolls up my pant leg or unbuttons my shirt before
    inserting a needle into my flesh.

He does, however, know that breathing is one of the challenges facing me,
    therefore he has suggested I find a small stone to place in my
    bellybutton, securing it with a sash, as a reminder to breathe deeply,
    perhaps as a memento as well, a memento of one's original turning.

A stone dropped into my swirling tea.

A stone to remind me of the White Cliffs of Dover.

A stone to tell me the earth is round, as round as is my belly when I fully
    extend it, filling an entire lifetime with sumptuous air, the blue sky of my
    lungs balanced upon the round earth of my belly.

Or a flat stone, as flat as is my belly when I exhale, forcing the air out of my
    lungs and into an atmosphere where it will duly intersperse with the
    clouds to become what it never could have had it remained attached to
    the stones of my living.

A river stone, perhaps, brought up from the depths of a reclusive Serbian river,
    my naked body glistening in the hot sunlight.

A lunar stone dropped into my eyes by the ominous figure of an owl, dark
    against dark, flying a couple of meters overhead, the great whooshing of
    its wings causing surgent waves to ripple through my nocturnal blood.

A stone turned into roundness by evenings of waltzing, by years of pirouetting,
    of executing tremendous spinning leaps over the heads of those who
    would attempt to silence the sapphires in my eyes, each successful

landing bringing poise to a stone balanced serenely on the edge
of a knife.

A stone which over incomprehensible eons has become transfigured into clay
before being shaped into a cup cradled by fingers which, in the
inimitable way of each person's love, will continue to express the
language of life until those same fingers are indistinguishable from the
branch itself, magnificent flames rising from the bones, a final breath
reaching toward the sky even as the ashes are subsumed by the earth's
stones, by the clay, the silt, the loam which will become ever and again
life.

At once sacred and profane, the cup of tea is nestled in my hands, the hands of
a holy fool in whose heart life is continuously distilled into essential
embers which are then fanned by the breath into flames, transforming
the humble stone of the belly into molten rivers the color of blood,
flowing as they do throughout the valleys and crevices of language.

Language not as words, but language as the feel of the sun's tongue on the
flesh, the aroma of freshly brewed ale, the taste of sweat, each an
impression and an expression of a journey, sometimes harsh, often
exalted, through the skies, the oceans, the blood of life.

And as the breath ever more embodies the language of the mind, of the heart
and of the spirit, there is quietly less distinction between the gesture and
the noun, between the kiss and the verb.

It is the sacred become simple; the profane become hallowed.

It is the moment when, helping me to dress, the intern hands me my
shawl and says,
    Your tallith.

Then he hands me my small woolen cap and says,
    Your yarmulke.

Then he passes me my triple strand of faux pearls, pauses a moment for
dramatic effect, then proclaims,
    Your schmaltz.

At which wonderful wit the flames of life rise through my heart, transfiguring
my breath into joyous giggles that intertwine with the laughter of the

intern, laughter which ripples toward the fecund skies, there where it will gather into drops of rain falling gently into a cup of tea, a cup of tea placed upon a wooden table somewhere on the far side of the earth, the tea's aromatic darkness awaiting the opening of eyes, the eyes of an elderly man, perhaps, or maybe a young girl, yes, a young girl who has just understood the utter uniqueness, the loneliness, the immensity, of her visions, her life.

My own eyes smiling, I take a sip of tea, watching the flaming, blood-red sun plunge through a thousand thousand skies into the cool roundness of the earth, into the porcelain stone of the past, even as I turn to witness the full and milky moon rising on the prophetic, bittersweet breath, a comfort.

November 4, 2001

58. THE MAGIC THRESHOLD

—For My Brother, Craig

Let us be perfectly clear about one thing: It was not ME who jumped out of a perfectly good airplane at an altitude of 4,000 meters above sea level. It was the OTHER GUY who jumped out of the gaping hatch of the airplane.

As fate would have it, however, I happened to be attached to him.

And for the record—thus absolving me of all pertinent lunacy—this whacko scheme of leaping from an airplane was not my idea to begin with. The onus for its genesis lies with one of my medical interns, whose brilliant plan was then enthusiastically seconded by another.

So it is that I find myself ensconced in my wheelchair inside a hangar used to train people to jump willingly out of airplanes. It is here in this spacious chamber where my official jump buddy, with assistance from my brother, has already snugly tightened the harness, one strap around each of my thighs and through my crotch, several other straps bound over my shoulders and around my chest. With the entire harness pulled, looped, cinched, and buckled, I am little more than another scrawny turkey ready for basting. As though this were not enough bondage, however, my jump buddy is now tying a looped belt around my knees, which he then proceeds to bind with several rounds of duct tape—this so that while floating down through the atmosphere he will be able to pull my knees upward, firmly securing them in order that my legs will not smash into the ground upon landing. As an added precaution he then tapes my ankles together with duct tape.

You see, ultimately he is the one who will be doing the work of jumping out of the airplane, of managing the parachute, and of landing us safely on the ground. Me, I am more or less a trussed teddy bear attached to his chest.

Outside the hangar the sky is stunningly clear, a threshold of ungraspable proportions.

Here inside, bound and harnessed, I await an experience I cannot even begin to comprehend. A voice over the loudspeaker informs us that we will be departing in ten minutes. For the others this announcement likely makes them feel as though they are in an airport—which they are, small as it is—but for me the announcement suddenly and unexpectedly takes me back many years, to a life of sitting in theater dressing rooms, my makeup carefully applied, my costume snugly fitted, my limbs warmed up, a voice calling out over the intercom, *Ten minutes to curtain!*

Similarly, I am now snugly harnessed, industrially duct-taped, and nattily fitted out with aeronautical hat, goggles and gloves, awaiting the imminent rising of a curtain which stretches into eternity.

In the focused preparations following the announcement, my jump buddy asks me if I am scared. Strangely, I am not, partly because I have no idea what I have gotten myself into, and partly because I am still sitting in my wheelchair, bound to the earth by the force of gravity, bound to myself by the force of duct tape. At this point the only thing I could possibly be afraid of is falling out of my wheelchair when no one is around to undo the tape and help me up. Believe me, a tied-up teddy bear lying helplessly on his back is not a pretty sight.

When the final boarding call rings throughout the hangar, the difference between my past and my present becomes strikingly evident. Then, in those glorious days, I would have flitted toward the stage wings with strength and poise woven into my muscles and tendons from years of rigorous training, a training which had given me the agility to become airborne with the merest spring of the legs, to fly through the beams of the brilliant stage lights, to spin and turn and glide, to balance as though suspended by the fingers of a god—my body strong and lithe, a young tiger. Now, however, with the grace and strength of those years relentlessly migrating away from my muscles and tendons to become centered in my heart, I am by necessity wheeled out to the waiting airplane—a trussed teddy bear.

There will be about fifteen of us jumping today, most of them experienced skydivers, some of them already inside the aircraft from which they reach down to gather my shoulders, a couple of guys on the ground lifting my legs, thus hoisting me up into the small aircraft. In this manner the teddy bear has just completed the first leg of his airborne mission. Yes, for my part I am incapable of doing anything but attempting to maintain my balance while the others settle me into position straddling a narrow bench before securing the safety belt, my jump buddy seated immediately behind me. Because of my unique situation, which might be described as helpless, though not hopeless, my spot on the bench is directly next to the hatch—truly, if I were to fall forward toward the right, I would topple out of the airplane. In place of regular seats, there are two benches running parallel with the body of the aircraft, each newly arriving skydiver sliding backwards onto it, the convexity of his body fitting neatly into the concavity of the one behind him, a stack of bowls laid on its side.

After positioning me, the boarding ladder outside is replaced and the remaining jumpers eagerly scramble up into the small aircraft's belly, each scooting backwards along the bench until all fifteen are securely in place, some of them friends or acquaintances, others employees of the skydiving company—not one of them known to me before this weekend, most of them seen for the first time within the last quarter of an hour. As has often been the case, my life is once again in the hands of complete strangers.

Within moments the ladder is removed one final time, the clear Plexiglas hatch confidently pulled down into position.

We have arrived for departure.

Prior to boarding, while still on the ground, I had available to me a portable electronic word processor which allowed me to communicate my needs, questions and quips. As soon as I was lifted up into the airplane, however, I lost any and all ability to communicate, other than to respond to simple yes/no questions. Because of this, it had been prearranged with my jump buddy to confirm with me when we neared altitude whether or not I still wanted to plummet to earth. Beyond this it was a matter of trust, of releasing any intellectual or psychological desires to control the unfolding situation.

As the aircraft begins to taxi toward the runway, I look around at the guys in front of me and to my side, different colors, different ages. The men visible to me are obviously veteran skydivers, their faces exuding both the truth of excitement and the essence of raw reality, an essence rarely seen on the faces of most people. Yes, these guys are fully aware of what is happening, whereas I must appear to them to be some idiotic dunderhead, mute, wild-eyed and mostly immobile in my trussed state. Nevertheless, they completely accept my presence in their midst.

As so often throughout my life I find myself in a situation in which each passing moment destroys the boundaries that tend to create strife among human beings, for as the airplane lifts away from the earth, we become with each successive gain in altitude a single entity, an entity comprised of units, for sure, but a whole beast nonetheless, exuding clumsy yet lofty hopes. Egos begin to dissipate, humanity begins to emerge.

The atmosphere inside the aircraft is both serious and jocular. One of the skydivers has glued a stuffed lizard onto his helmet. This flight, we soon find out, will be the lizard's debut jump.

As we quickly gain altitude, I must remind myself to breathe, for if anything it will be pulmonary arrest, not smashing into the ground, that will be my undoing in this adventure. Yes, my ability to continue breathing is, in the final analysis, the great variable. Will I be able to breathe at 4,000 meters? Will I be able to control my breathing during free fall, as my body plummets toward the earth's surface at a speed of 200 kilometers per hour? Not one of us knows the answer to these questions, myself included.

With the continuing climb in altitude the air naturally gets colder and colder. At 3,300 meters one of the guys helps to put on my helmet and goggles. As arranged, my jump buddy asks me if I still want to jump. I nod my head. To my right the Plexiglas hatch is rattling. Through its scratched surface I have a spectacular view of the land falling ever and away into tiny landmarks of houses, roads, lakes, and hills.

How he knows when, I do not know, but the foremost guy on my left suddenly leaps toward the hatch and thrusts it upward, thus opening a gaping hole in the side of the airplane. Before I can fully grasp this rather striking development he is standing on the edge of the threshold, turning around and falling backwards. At the same time his friend is leaping forwards out of the hatch, his timing allowing the two of them to hold hands as I watch them plummet toward the earth and out of view.

My face must have a look of utter astonishment on it. Certainly my mind is reeling as several of the other guys casually and eagerly leap out of the airplane in fleet succession, their bodies unattached to anything, their limbs plunging toward the unknown.

I find myself wanting to call out after them, to tell them they forgot their parachutes, as though I had expected them to step out of the airplane holding parasols. I am certainly smart enough to realize they must get beyond the airplane's milieu before opening their parachutes, and also that there is such a thing as free fall. Nevertheless it is too queer to see these guys falling out of view, their spread-eagled limbs so unequipped for flight.

This was all the time I had for astonishment, however, because I myself am suddenly falling, the cold air rushing into my face. Truly, I have no idea how I went from sitting calmly in an airplane to whooshing madly toward planet earth. I do not even know how my jump buddy got me through the hatch, it happened so fast in those moments during which I was mesmerized by the disappearing bodies of several young men and a very calm lizard. Since my jump buddy and I were next to the hatch all he had to do was more or less stand up and step out. Regardless, those couple of seconds simply do not exist in my memory.

What had been a window, a hatch, an opening was in fact a magic threshold. To step or leap through it was to become something extraordinary, to become mythical, the experience of the threshold itself remaining forever unknowable by the intellect.

Framed windows,
coal dusted adits,
orifices,
porous skin,
visionary wormholes,
the cervix,
this moment,
and the surface of water,
are each in and of themselves thresholds.

All are veils between the known and the unknown, between the womb and life, between life and death, arrival and departure, closing and opening.

Furthermore, each threshold is, in essence, a moment of vulnerability, some astounding us by the radical extremity of their transformative natures, while others may be spoken of as an emergence into the within. Many thresholds are so pedestrian as to dissipate unrealized unless an effort on our part hallows them.

Regardless, to be held, in our vulnerability, by the very substance of the threshold, to be wrapped in its voice, surrounded by the unknown, is to be transfigured by the scent of the breath, the feel of it on one's flesh.

It is 3:00 A.M. on a brisk but not cold November morning. Planet earth is bursting through scattered particles remaining from the journey of a now distant comet, particles left behind during an orbit which occurred in the middle of the eighteenth century C.E. Bundled up in sweaters, robes and blankets I gaze at a moonless, cloudless expanse stretching unimaginable distances away from my life and into the pulsing chambers of my heart. As our hurtling planet slams into the comet's debris, the dark sky above me is punctuated by meteors darting this way and that, some brilliant, others faint; some brief, others stretching a moment longer, long enough indeed to enter one's vision never again to depart.

Within a week I too would be tumbling through earth's mostly unclouded atmosphere, a dark spot against an enigmatic blue background.

Uncertain of my ability to pull the rip-cord, I had readily relinquished control of it to my jump buddy. When after some moments of free fall he does pull it there comes an accompanying jerking and jarring as the parachute catches the air, slowing our descent. Yet, before I can even string together a mental complaint about this rough transition, a positively beatific serenity envelopes us, a calm that is as surprising in its way as was the sudden painful rush of air encountered upon first falling from the open hatch of the airplane.

Nonetheless, this is no time for mere daydreaming. As soon as the parachute has opened, my jump buddy begins the task of threading a cord through the loop belted around my knees preparatory to pulling them up into a fetal position, firmly securing the cord in order to free his hands for landing. Meanwhile I am concentrating on inhaling and exhaling, an accomplishment that would make my respiratory therapist proud. The most unexpected thing, however, is not what is happening, rather what is not happening, namely that I am not giggling. It had been accepted wisdom among those who know me that I would probably giggle and laugh all the way down, therefore the absence of any laughter piques my attention. Not overly concerned, however, I presume that once I am on the ground my body will find the capacity to giggle, to laugh.

Inevitably, gradually, the earth rises to meet us, each object growing larger with the passing moments. There in the landing field I espy a skydiver who has already landed, and over there another, his brightly colored canopy fluttering to a standstill against the autumn grass. Not knowing what to expect for a landing, I can assure you I was not expecting it to be as smooth as it ultimately is. With my knees secured into position and my toes pointed upward, my jump buddy safely and competently brings us in for a landing which is so gentle I might have thought we had landed in a feather bed were we not bathed in raw, strikingly blue sunlight.

As people run to help unbind me, my mind is telling me to assist them, but my body is bound to itself. Helplessly I watch as people go about disconnecting and unharnessing me, tearing off the strips of duct tape. They move so quickly that I can hardly make sense of their movements. I am not even sure who is who, though I am able to catch a glimpse of my brother as he helps the others lift me into my wheelchair.

And the expected giggles? They never did arise. Not because they did not exist. They were certainly there, bubbling away. The reason they could not exist outside the chambers of my heart was because my body had shut down all muscular activity not related to the shallow breathing which had sustained me through the thin atmosphere. Even after the harness had been loosened and removed, my thoracic muscles were more or less immobilized. In those minutes after landing I felt more paralyzed and helpless than at any time during the past several years. Even the grin on my face felt frozen into place.

It is a week since my successful skydiving adventure, the certificate announcing its completion placed at home beside the computer.

Back to my usual routine, I am immersed in the warm water of the pool. At the end of a long therapy session, as my professional aide is getting ready to set me into the hydraulic chair lift, my body unexpectedly goes into a paroxysmal spasm. After it subsides the alarmed aide manages to get me into the chair and secure the safety belt.

With my body exhausted, contracted, bound to itself, I close my eyes on the world. Unable to communicate, I feel utterly isolated. Not alone, but isolated. It does not help that the aide, well meaning as he is, is not adept at handling this kind of situation. Additionally the unfamiliar lifeguard—apparently a nice person—is quite naturally looking to the aide for guidance. It is one of those stagnant situations in which it is not so much that things are going badly as that they are not going well. In the midst of this, unable to intervene, I feel completely vulnerable.

I also hear, in the midst of this stagnation, a splash—not an uncommon sound in a swimming pool.

A moment later I feel a hand on my thigh, the unexpectedness of it causing my body to spasm again, my eyes to jerk violently open.

Of all the thousands of people who might have jumped into the water to greet me at this difficult moment, it is a minor miracle that the man standing in front of me is Brian. If anyone is capable of breaking the stalemate of the situation, this is the man. If anyone is capable of reaching through the threshold of isolation, it is this young guy who is firmly holding my shoulder, stabilizing my body as the spasms subside.

At this moment I am no longer listening to anything being said by the aide and the lifeguard above me.

I no longer even see the greater world.

For everything has narrowed into this small space in which I am watching Brian's right hand.

Not his voice, but his hand, as his fingers ask me if I am all right.

I gaze in disbelief at his strong, smiling eyes.

Slowly, gratefully, I raise my left hand to reply, water dripping from my fingers as they form the letters.

Where others feared to cross the threshold, Brian has courageously broken through, his body literally shattering the surface of the glistening water.

Where others see only a body in danger, he is fully aware of the spirit within that body, a spirit he is determined to reach, not only with his hands but with his eyes. As I sit awaiting the rising of the hydraulic lift, peering out of a spastic, voiceless body, I see him looking intently back at me, his eyes fiercely focused on the fire within me.

We are where two tigers have met.

Intellectually, I gained little from my skydiving experience that could not have been obtained from driving to the top of a tall mountain, or seeing a film taken by a skydiver. Because of this I felt little sense of profundity in its immediate aftermath. Indeed, my jump seemed little more than yet another successful achievement, an accomplishment to add to one's portfolio. In the intervening time, however, I have realized that a very deep and exquisite transformation occurred as I fell through the hatch and floated into the sky, a transformation which baffles the intellect, the eyes, though they by necessity participated in it. It was, for lack of better words, a transformation of the body and the spirit, as though my spirit at once accepted the bound condition of my body for what it is while also soaring free of it.

Existing within and without at once.

It is as though after four decades of life I have accrued an intimation of how not only to cross a threshold, nor even a series of thresholds, but also how to dwell within the threshold, to live the threshold, there where the voice of eternity rises and falls at once.

Yes, if I am to meet life face to face it behooves me to accept its contradictory nature, to be and not be at once, to wither and grow at the same time, to destroy and create within the same breath.

Having secured me safely in my wheelchair, Brian continues to use his hands and eyes to speak to me, soundlessly questioning me.

"Are you okay, Zsolt?"

"Do you feel ill?"

"Do you have a headache?"

"Is there anything you need?"

Each query elicits a response from my hand, slow and weary. Yet I am utterly relieved to be able to communicate.

In this way, for this moment, Brian and I exist within the threshold.

Seen from without we may appear to be merely two guys gesticulating at one another.

In truth we are two tigers perched in a window, the universe above us and below us at once, an unutterable place of being.

"Is there anything else I can do for you?" he signs with his hands.

I tell him "No," then immediately rescind my answer, closing my eyes in order to think more clearly. For if I do indeed need something, anything, this is the time to ask for it.

And, truth be told, there are so many things I need.

Yet, taking a deep breath, I relinquish any control I had presumed was mine, allowing myself simply to teeter on the threshold of being.

I open my eyes, and with my left hand, tell him, "No."

Then, in the last moment before falling to earth, he puts his paws around my torso, holding me—a blessing.

What we think we need we seldom receive, but what we receive in its stead is nothing short of miraculous.

December 6, 2001

61. The Parable of Gimpley Everest

There was, in those days now gone, a ruddy-toed bloke by the name of Gimpley Everest. Unfortunately for him, while the forename of Gimpley is a virile and archaically distinguished nomen of great consequence, within several weeks of the child's birth it had quickly disintegrated into the rather unaesthetically shortened form of Gimp.

As the history of this ruddy-toed fellow is picaresque to a disproportionate degree, we shall not intrude at the beginning of the chronology, but rather at the point when our protagonist by circumstances beyond his control began to resemble his name. It is often said that we grow into likenesses of our names, and this adage was never more true than in the case of Gimp.

Now, while Gimp was throughout his life an especially active person, and even something of a daredevil, thus contradicting the definitive nature of his shortened name, though pertinently exemplifying the challenging heights of his surname, there came a point in midlife when things began to go awry, when he began to trip and stumble inextricably, when the most ordinary activities became a challenge for him, when dishes and pencils would fall uncontrollably out of his hands. For a man such as Gimp, who had been especially agile, strong and fleet, this turn of events was disconcerting to say the least. Within the span of a few months he was obliged to lay aside many of his favorite athletic activities—dancing, bullfighting, bicycling, jousting, motorcycling, marathon balderdashing, tournament insulting, mud-wrestling, and jogging. Thankfully, with the use of a walking stick he was still able to wobble among the glories of nature; additionally, the gentlemanly but presently disreputable sport of ruminating remains with him to this day, as does the ancient discipline of meditating.

Not a man to give up easily, Gimp accoutered himself with appropriate assistive technologies, took life as it was, for what it was, and made the best of the situation.

He gamely proceeded to study and master the entirety of Johann Sebastian Bach's *Goldberg Variations*—a clavier composition consisting of an aria followed by thirty variations.

He simultaneously set about writing a novel whose first sentence is over 16,000 words long—yes, the first sentence.

With the valiant aid of others, and allied with his usual pluck, he learned how to ski without use of his legs. He made regular treks to the hitherto unfamiliar world of the swimming pool. He involved himself in excursions of varying complexities. He even jumped out of an airplane.

Furthermore, having had to relinquish any immediate hope of learning to speak another foreign language, he readily accepted an opportunity to study sign language.

Over many months, unawares and imperceptibly, he had become none other than Super Gimp, part of a loose guild of like-minded and like-titled persons.

Truly a worthy distinction which can be bestowed only by the universe.

It must be clarified, however, that within the Supergimp Guild there are various classifications of supergimps. Some members, having lost use of a limb or a sense, or having sustained spinal chord injuries might be thought of as supergimps with potential. In other words, their skiing techniques will likely improve year after year, until the usual concerns of ageing step in to alter the potential. These men and women remain, like the endearing and enduring violinist Itzhak Perlman, capable of virtuosic feats, supersonic careers.

On the other hand, there are some supergimps who are confronted with the challenges of continuously deteriorating bodies, thus they cannot presume to achieve an ever more commanding skiing technique year after year. They cannot presume to build a virtuosic career through their dwindling prowess on the violin.

Balanced precariously between these two subgroups, Gimp's record on the roster of the Supergimp Guild was nonetheless impeccably versatile. Therefore he would watch with sadness but without any sense of personal threat as other members' names were eventually withdrawn from the roll due either to their decreasing capabilities to maintain a competent level of supergimpiness, or due to death. This, he felt, would never happen to him, or leastwise at such a distant remove that it need not concern him now, nor interfere with his nascent plans to sail solo around the world in a pickle barrel while reciting the complete works of Shakespeare in the most eloquent sign language imaginable.

Envision then, if you will, a day full of potential, a right proper supergimp day. Imagine the sun rising, full and noteworthy. Imagine our protagonist, no longer merely Gimp, but knighted with the title of Super Gimp, eagerly plotting out the route of his forthcoming traversal around the globe, conscientiously researching the best pickle barrel for the rigorous journey, daily practicing his sign language version of Shakespeare. Imagine potential spelled with a capital P.

Now bestir yourself to envision our middle-aged Super Gimp, not young, not old, sitting in his wheelchair at a cafe, grasping his grilled salamander and stinky Stilton sandwich preparatory to lifting it to his mouth—in much the same manner, I might add, that he had eaten sandwiches for four decades. Imagine his consternation, even surprise, at how heavy two pieces of bread, a couple of salamander legs and some stinky cheese could be.

113

"What ho!" he exclaimed inwardly.

"How odd, how positively, irreconcilably queer," our protagonist mumbled to himself.

It was one thing to not have full use of his legs.

And not having a voice was one thing.

And not having full capacity to breathe was one thing.

And those dwindling arms were one thing.

But struggling to lift a sandwich? This was altogether another matter, not so much in and of itself, but because it was the precisely measured arc that completed a circle of inner comprehension. Yes, it was at that mathematically revelatory moment when Gimp realized without a doubt that his name had been erased from the roster of the Supergimp Guild. No need to go look, for he knew deep inside himself that between the names of the illustrious Pat Eagerthrasher and the resilient Udu Everlasting-Glory there would forevermore be a blank spot where once resided the name of Gimpley Everest.

Letting the sandwich lie limp on its plate, Gimp stared at the wall of the restaurant. All around him people chattered and spoke loudly. The staff bustled easily from table to table to kitchen and back. Diners ate without knowing they were eating. Every limb, every mouth, every word moved quickly, with unabashed frenzy. Here, however, in Gimp's body, all was slow and quiet, to the point of contemplation. At that moment Gimp was confronted with a harsh truth—there would be no solo traversal of the globe in a pickle barrel, no matter the quality of the pickle barrel or the size of the globe. There would not be a pelagic recitation in sign language of the complete works of Shakespeare, merely snippets and fragments, brittle letters falling from his fingers, more likely in a bathtub than on the high seas.

Most of those cleverly designed assistive devices constructed and marketed in order to help supergimps achieve astounding feats on mountainsides and in basketball courts would now be of little avail to Gimp. In comparison to those feats that define supergimpitude, successfully lifting one's sandwich is a pallid accomplishment. And while there would undoubtedly still be moments of unquestionable supergimpiness ahead of him, they would likely be too sparse and possibly too insignificant to count toward the rigorous obligations imposed by the Supergimp Guild.

Mustering his resolve, Gimp slowly, laboriously finished his grilled salamander and stinky Stilton sandwich, then signaled to the waitress to help wheel him down the cafe's wheelchair ramp, a ramp which for many months now he had no longer had the strength to manage by himself. As usual and per his gesticulated instructions, she deposited him in the middle of the street, where it was easier for him to propel himself than on the uneven sidewalks. The speeding trucks and cars did not unnerve him; vulnerability was nothing new to Gimp. Indeed, over time he had grown quite accustomed to wandering among motorized lions and tigers and bears on the asphalt arenas of life. Besides, there was the immediate task at hand, namely the excruciatingly hard work of wheeling himself along, stopping every few meters to rest, to breathe, to contemplate.

To contemplate what?

That there is an enormous difference between being disabled and being ill.

That while an ailing person may be or become disabled, not everyone who is disabled is ill nor enfeebled.

That chronic or terminal illness means the eventual loss of abilities, whether that be eyesight as in the case of diabetes, loss of physical or mental control, or merely the bedridden nature of hospice.

Subtle points, to be sure, but for Gimp, on the day in question, they were salient points whose fine distinction delineated each breath, each painfully burning muscle of a body that could no longer be defined as only disabled.

These wending thoughts eventually brought him to another line of inner discourse.

Ultimately, he noted to himself and not for the first time, it was about utility, regardless whether a person were disabled, ill, or both. In most if not all human cultures each person is evaluated and valued for his or her usefulness. As with most cultural institutions the Supergimp Guild mirrored this valuation. Even supergimps who were not able to work were valued for their exemplary stories, tales of how each had overcome overwhelming obstacles. We watch respectfully as amputees play basketball in wheelchairs, their game serving as a model of the indomitable human spirit. Furthermore, in some societies the disabled or ill person may be venerated for his or her accumulated wisdom.

Conversely—and Gimp understood this quite well—the schizophrenic, unemployed guy tottering on the street corner reeking of alcohol serves little purpose and is roundly, flatly dismissed by the majority. Of what value then is the woman resting in a coma for twenty-two years, her comatose state brought on by an invasive parasite in her blood?

Like it or not, the line of human worth is indelibly drawn in stone, perhaps embedded in our biology. And without a doubt, supergimpitude was on one side of the line, while mere gimpiness, though often quite near the line, was definitely on the other side. It didn't take a genius to notice the innuendoes coming from those who are securely placed on the worthy side of the line. It did not take a genius to observe the attitudes held by most toward those who do not somehow produce or provide. Indeed, these haughty attitudes, though ingeniously veiled by patriotism, moral superiority, social welfare, religious dogma, and even on occasion pseudoscientific theory—remember eugenics?—leave little question as to the underlying and undying message.

Membership in the Supergimp Guild was not merely about tackling and rising above one's disabilities, it was a matter of worthiness, of utility, and ultimately of life and death.

When confronted with caring for the aforementioned woman who had never in twenty-two years awoken from her comatose existence, how are we to define human worth?

Stopping in the middle of the street to catch his breath and rest his aching arms, Gimp looked upward to where a flock of pigeons was taking flight above a rooftop.

Even as his heart soared, as his soul sang, Gimp felt a feebleness creeping through his limbs, the seat, armrests and footrests of a wheelchair supporting a faltering, unproductive body.

"Yes," he murmured to the disappearing pigeons, "how are we to define human worth?"

It is generally at this point in the telling of a parable that the storyteller sums up the tale, creates a moral, and provides a sense of completion, of resolution, often one of inspiration, edification or encouragement.

In the context of the above tale, however, there are no tidy answers to the question provoked by the tale itself.

As creator of the fictitious Supergimp Guild I have struggled in vain to find an apt resolution to Gimpley Everest's question, a fair and equitable resolution that would leave each of us wiser and more compassionate. Therefore, and not without regret and some sense of failure, I must leave you, individual reader, to ponder the question for yourself, to seek wisdom not from the words of the parable, but in the convoluted labyrinths of your own quest.

On the day you yourself come across Gimpley Everest—formerly known as Super Gimp—arduously endeavoring to lift his sandwich or wearily resting in the middle of a busy street, you will have to confront your own preconceived valuation of the worthiness of human lives. The challenge, of course, will be to attempt an answer that diminishes none of us. When that day comes, will you also, as have so many billions of people before you, be soundly defeated by the question?

Godspeed, my friend.

January 18, 2002

62. SANCTUARIES

The walls of a room.
A clothed bed.
One's body.

Each of these, for the terminally or chronically ill, or for the severely disabled person, constitutes more than a noun, more than an objective space. Each, in its subtle and enigmatic shadows, is a sanctuary within which each sound, each touch calls us to witness, here amid the ever-changing light infusing the windows, the walls, the linens, and the flesh.

(Having found the correct address on Calle Grillo—Cricket Street—I had long ago alit from my bicycle in order to search for the side door I was instructed to use. His was a small house, humble in appearance, just waking from a long, snowy winter. Indeed, it was so small that the two doors were quite near to one another, the entire structure easily fitting into one of the curved blue fingers of Shiva's dancing body.

I no longer recall whether there was a note tacked on the door, as there would be in later years for others, or if the unseen man simply called out to me when I knocked, telling me to let myself in. Regardless, I opened the quiet, early morning door, a door leading directly into this stranger's bedroom, a cozy room filled for the most part by a large water bed occupied by a tall, handsome man, a black sleeping mask stretched over his eyes.

The necessity of letting oneself into Juan's humble home arose from the fact that it was simply too cumbersome for him to answer the door by himself, at least in a timely manner. To do so he would have had to haul his uncooperative limbs out of bed and into his wheelchair; he would probably have had to make a dire stop at the toilet, hopefully not falling onto the floor in the process, before wheeling himself toward a doorknob which he might not have had the strength or coordination to turn once he got there. The whole process could easily have taken thirty minutes or more. Better to let oneself in, thus becoming enveloped by the placid aromas of Juan's sleep, the fragrances of his lanky body; thereby becoming infused with complex odors just stirring out of a nocturnal recumbency which on that particular morning spoke less of the receding winter and more of a mustering spring.

This, then, was the beginning. How many mornings Juan and I spent together I cannot now tabulate. Over the ensuing years the tasks presented us by the act of living became more varied and innumerable than either of us could have predicted, the accumulation of stories beyond recounting.

One day, while still living in that small house, Juan requested I write to the Hemlock Society, an organization which provides information and support to people, whether ill or elderly, who feel they would rather end their own lives in a timely manner than to burden friends, family or society with the duties of caring for a terminally ill comrade. Several weeks later a packet of information arrived.

Sometime after this, it became apparent from the deterioration of his condition that if Juan did indeed desire to end his own life without the aid of another person, the decision would have to be made and carried out soon. Therefore, and not without some hesitancy, I broached the subject one fine morning, certainly not because I had any interest in him actually killing himself, nor because I was intent on egotistically and patronizingly dissuading him—one of the cornerstones of our relationship, after all, was a deep respect for one another's choices, one another's beliefs. I merely began to speak of it because it was part of his actuality, his truth. For me to fear the issues arising from this aspect of his journey would have been tantamount to seeing him not as a human being struggling with life and death issues, but merely as some totem object; an object, furthermore, that could then be denied, ignored, coerced or manipulated.

In the end, after much contemplation and peer counselling, Juan made the decision to place his life in the hands of the divine as he understood it.

And there it resided, ever more luminous, until the day he died.)

To fully enter the dwelling place of the terminally ill or severely disabled person— in other words, to leave behind us that which was to be and accept that which is, to inhale the fragrances of this fragile, unchartable moment—is to admit and to accept one's fundamental humanity.

It is equally true that to stand literally or figuratively at the door and peer in, thus objectifying the man or woman in the bed, the wheelchair, not only leeches the blood, the marrow from the thing observed, but also from the observer.

The chthonic sanctuaries of the room, the bed and the body, in order to be fully elucidated, fully sensed, cannot be realized as mere object, but must instead be dynamically witnessed and hallowed as relation.

In objectifying the sanctuary, the once potent gesture of compassion is brought to stasis, a situation inevitably leading to stress, strife, and the breakdown of the sanctity of life itself.

(Already enveloped by a complex aroma of urine and feces, of disinfectants and food, an aroma which belonged to no one single person, I stepped out of the lift, my motorcycle helmet cradled in the crook of my arm. Walking past the nurses' station, I made my way to Juan's room, an institutional room bereft of even the slight accouterments of his humble house...

This space in which all of Juan's belongings, other than a few photos on the wall, were locked away in a metal cabinet, an attempt to keep them safe from pilfering by the nursing home staff, the key to the cabinet hanging from Juan's long neck.

Nonetheless, despite its minimal size, its paucity of architectural delight, this was still, in the deepest sense, a sacred sanctuary of human life, filled as it was with Juan's magnanimous spirit.

Within minutes of my regular Tuesday morning arrival one of the nurse's aides would bring in Juan's breakfast tray. For whatever reason, the aides never questioned why I invariably and without explanation took the plastic tray from their hands and proceeded to feed Juan myself. Doubtless they appreciated having one less chore to include in their hectic duties, as these kind-hearted men and women bustled off to deliver the remainder of the generally unappetizing breakfast trays, and to hand-feed the more incapacitated residents.

Thus left alone, the two of us within a dismally supplied sanctuary to which he and I flowingly, endlessly, fearlessly contributed rays of light—he the blue, I the red, he the yellow, I the purple, these oddly shaped panes of stained glass which, when seen from even a short distance resolved into nothing less than the petals of a rose window, a finely crafted mandala of color and light—we slowly, steadily scooped pathways through little mounds of ground up food of indistinguishable origins. We painstakingly wended our way through dialogues constructed one letter at a time, dialogues that barely had enough momentum to stay aloft, and only managed to do so through sheer will and patience, as we characteristically smiled at our laughable mistakes, starting anew, rekindling again and again a riant, affectionate fire within the sanctuaries of room and bed and body, where one is ever allowed to begin again, to regenerate one's compassion for the other, provided one has the humility to simply, utterly be.

At the end of each visit, when it came time to say goodbye, I would kiss Juan's forehead, gather up my motorcycle helmet, tell him I loved him, then re-enter the outer world, transfigured.

For truly, once a person has been humbly gathered within the living sanctuary of another human being—in the process expanding one's own pulsing heart to envelop the sanctity of another—one ever carries a glimmer of reflected light within one's own heart, a shimmering spectrum which cannot but filter through one's own thews.)

Every gesture, each thought, every word, and all the myriad waste products we produce alter the environments which we encounter and which we inhabit, from the body itself to the entire ecosystem of the planet.

How is it then that we have each come to objectify our own actions, thoughts, beliefs, that we so readily and willingly divorce our selves from the greater momentum called life?

For we cannot fundamentally remain apart and alive at once.

Nowhere is this more evident, more crucial, than in the room, the bed, and the body of the terminally ill or the severely disabled person.

To remain human—and humane—within that sanctuary, wherein the most meager of thoughts and gestures expands exponentially, we must destroy ourselves as objects in order to expand into a relation with life.

In order to not create strife and the eventual breakdown of the sanctity of life, we must destroy our propensity for objectifying the sanctuary, a propensity that easily allows us to force our hard, limited egos upon its sometimes fragile, oftentimes enigmatic structure, a structure of richly oneiric dimensions.

The result of objectifying another is a closed, stultified heart.

The legacy of an expansive heart is life witnessed in all its dynamic relationship.

(It was a Tuesday morning, as usual.

And as usual, I stepped from the opening doors of the gurney-length lift, striding habitually past the nurses' station. As I turned into Juan's room, I immediately knew something was wrong. It was not so much that Juan wasn't there—after all, the nurse's aides could have scurried him off for a shower—it was that Juan was not there. You see, the room was completely devoid of his presence, down to the immaculately made bed, flat as death. Bewildered, I checked the room number in case I had made a mistake. I had not. At that moment an uncomfortable feeling welled up inside of me. Eleven years after first letting myself into Juan's humble home on Calle Grillo, I simply could not imagine not having him in my life.

Enquiring at the nurses' station, I learned that he had been in the hospital over the weekend, very near death, and had just returned. The nurse pointed me in the direction of his new room, his new bed.

Stepping from the wide hallway into a darkened room, it was clear to me that Juan's sanctuary was now no larger than himself. Even the cold metal bed seemed no part of it. Yet, in the queer way of the sanctuary, the boundaries were nevertheless fluid enough to admit the spirit of another.

I took a deep breath, gazing to where my buddy lay, his eyes closed, his veins hooked up to various apparatus.

A body.

But a body only if that was how I chose to see him, if I chose to stand apart, staring uncomfortably through a portal into the land of death, refusing to step within and bear witness.

Because this was more than an object...

It was Juan's body, ever and again a sanctuary for the remarkable spark that is life.

A body I had lifted naked out of the bathtub in his cozy home.

A body I had often fed with small spoonfuls of puréed food as he sat up in his institutional bed.

A body whose arms I had held aloft during horrific fits of choking.

Yes, he of the blue light and the yellow light.

Removing my motorcycle gear, I said nothing to disturb the delicate dialogue between breathing and dying, but instead ran my fingers through his stubbly hair. Truly, there was no need to say anything—Juan always knew it was me, whether or not I said a word. Anyway, there would be little value in empty, nervous chatter during the next five hours as I first crouched at the side of his bed, holding his hand, then, after a nurse's aide brought me a chair to sit in, cradling his arm in my lap, gently stroking Juan's exhausted body.

Within the sanctity of the sanctuary there is little need for words.

In the sanctuary we are brought to the most fundamental aspects of language—

we listen,

we feel,

we taste,

we inhale,

we sense,

we breathe,

and we witness.)

It took seven of us on an afternoon early in the year 2002, but we did it, we made the windows and walls of the cathedral quake, the music resounding through every corner of that lofty space.

Yes, seven of us.

To begin with, it was I who asked Pete to make the arrangements.

And it was Pete who called Father Jerome for permission.

Then it was Father Jerome who told Anita in the parish office that we did indeed have permission for this uncertain venture.

And it was Anita who told Deacon Bill we were on our way.

It was Deacon Bill who unlocked the organ so that Leanna could set the printed music on the music stand.

And it was Leanna who started searching for the power switch that nine-year-old Drew eventually found.

Then it was Drew who watched as his father, known to the rest of us as Pete, transferred me from my wheelchair to the organ bench, slowly swivelling me around to face three gleaming manuals of black and white keys. It was Pete who stood behind me that I could lean against his torso, his arms wrapped securely around my chest in order to support me.

After a few minutes of getting acquainted with the instrument panel of this particular pipe organ, I began by playing a restrained piece of music, after which I opened every pipe to full capacity and took a breath before lowering my bony fingers onto the stately C minor chord that opens Johann Sebastian Bach's Second Partita for keyboard. I am not sure Bach ever meant for that chord to shake massive stone walls, sending shivers through the spines of mere mortals, but so it had happened, every pipe blasting forth, a magnificent, awing resonance that was followed by hundreds of slowly accumulating notes originally entwined in an eighteenth-century soundscape now erupting in a twenty-first-century afternoon.

Truly, we cannot remain apart and alive at once.

And though it took seven of us, we did it.

For several unbounded moments we filled the eternal vastness with music.

After thirty minutes of Herculean effort, the final octaves of an E minor fugue echo from the stone walls of the cathedral, the reverberant tones fading into a near silence in which I collapse against Pete's shoulder, laboring to inhale and exhale.

As Pete lifts the quaking walls of my body back into my wheelchair I notice the afternoon sunlight streaming through the colored panes of the rose window set high above the choir loft.

From afar, light, having pierced the walls of the room, the sheets of the bed and the skin of the body, enters the chambers of the heart, a most humble dwelling place. It cannot tarry there, however, and remain alive. From within, it must reach forth, pulsating through one's hands, shimmering through one's eyes, in witness of the ever-evolving, dynamical relationship of the universe.

From the small printed notes of the music of Bach, to the strong arms of Pete, to the prismatic light pouring through the petals of a rose window, to the unfathomable blue sky opening above us as I am wheeled out of the now quiet cathedral, we are each of us sanctuaries within sanctuaries within sanctuaries, in undeniable, living relation one to the other.

(When Juan eventually died at the age of thirty-eight, with his resilient mother at his side, he had lived most of his adult life with multiple sclerosis. In the end, and inhabiting little more than an emaciated body, he was yet a sanctuary of unbounded dimensions, of timelessness and light, wisdom and grace, which he shared with the world simply by being alive, his essence calling us to witness each sound, each touch, amid the ever-changing light infusing the window of the room, the linens of the bed, and the flesh of the body.)

January 24, 2002

Quito, Ecuador, 1970s.

Briggs Geister.

Colorado, 1980s.

Briggs Geister.

Colorado, 1980s.

Santa Fe, New Mexico, 1980s.

Boston, Massachusetts, 1980s.

Santa Fé, New Mexico, 1990s.

Santa Fé, New Mexico, 1990s.

Santa Fé, New Mexico, 2003.

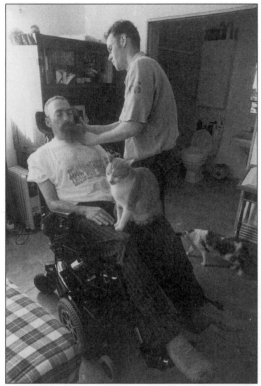

Santa Fé, New Mexico, 2003.

Santa Fé, New Mexico, 2003.

Santa Fé, Summer 2003.

64. THE EQUATION

And now to write about topics more prosaic, namely eight men in a locker room and...decubitus ulcers.

To begin with, the eight guys referred to are not the local version of the vice squad, nor will you ever find them in the locker room all at once, for they are the volunteers who currently assist me at the pool and who have each been finely trained to help me with my water therapy regimen. Because of their importance in my life and my health care, it has recently occurred to me that you might enjoy a portrait, as it were, of these men and therefore I will, in the hopes of neither insulting nor embarrassing, attempt to limn them, creating a group portrait pasted together from individual snapshots.

In terms of age, they range from late twenties to late forties, though in the past I have had pool buddies as young as sixteen and as old as fifty-five.

Of these current volunteers, seven of them live with a spouse, four with children.

Occupationally they come from a variety of fields: accounting, architecture, graphic arts, auto mechanics, custom bicycle manufacture, construction, and civil engineering.

All eight have a good sense of humor—some more traditional, others verging on the pathological.

Theologically, this lot ranges from hard-core Christian to hard-core atheist, while in the past the team has also included Jews and Buddhists.

Some of the guys are fuzzy chested, some not; some have skinny arms, while others are more muscular.

In height they range from medium to tall, mostly the latter.

The routine at the pool and in the locker room is the same with me for each of the eight men—the same therapy, the same bathing, the same care. Yet, because of the inherent diversity within the human family, each man brings to that routine certain quirks and idiosyncrasies.

Following is a brief sketch of my week with them...

MONDAY

This shift is alternately covered by Eli and Eliot, two men who are similar in

123

height and build. Additionally, both of them have dark hair interlaced with distinguished hints of silver, less so on Eli, who is after all the youngest of the eight men. As far as facial hair, Eli has an ever changing assortment of fashionable styles, while Eliot sports a respectable goatee and moustache. On the calendar, a week separates the birthdays of these two men, though they were in fact born a decade apart. Eli has three children—two girls and a boy—with a fourth on the way; Eliot has a one-year-old baby girl. Eli's sense of humor is perversely whacko; he is also an ardent and studious Christian. Eliot is an accomplished telemark skier, and is one of the guys who has assisted me in the Adaptive Ski Program, which is where he and I met.

TUESDAY

Courtenay and Pete share this shift—the 1959 shift, since all three of us were born in that year: Courtenay in May, I in October, and Pete in December. Both men are clean-shaven, and of medium brown hair color. Courtenay has one son, Pete two. Courtenay and his son are avid fly fishermen. Pete has a marvelous aptitude for reaching out to other guys and encouraging them to participate in my care—this, for instance, is how Phillip and Hugh each came to be part of the team. Whereas most of us are reluctant to ask our friends and acquaintances to volunteer on behalf of someone whom they hardly know or may not even have met, Pete has no such qualms. He is the kind of person who sees a need, notices a community full of guys who are fully capable of helping, and puts the two together.

THURSDAY

This is Hugh and Joseph's shift, who share the common aspect of being the guys I least knew when they first showed up to volunteer. Indeed, I had only the briefest of introductions to Joseph, about fifteen seconds, prior to later inquiring of his wife whether he would be inclined to help me. With Hugh it may have amounted to as much as sixty seconds—he had noticed me with Pete at other times and merely came over to ask if I had seen him that day. Later Pete encouraged him to volunteer. Dark-haired, Joseph currently has the fullest beard of the lot, tending toward the prophetic, or perhaps the insane, depending upon your vantage point. He is also the eldest of the lot. About Hugh I know only the slimmest of facts, to wit, his name, his surname, his birthday, and that he has never been married, which is even less than I know about Phillip.

FRIDAY

Both of them fair-haired and clean-shaven, Jeremy and Phillip are respectively my longest-term pool buddy and one of my newest—only Hugh has started more recently. As far as I know, Phillip has the distinction of being the only gay man who has ever helped me at the pool on an ongoing basis. As mentioned above, he came to begin helping me at the behest of Pete, and therefore I am still getting to know him. Once a teenage bomb builder, Jeremy is the man who on occasion describes himself as "unflappable" and it may be this trait which partly explains why he has weathered myriad changes throughout three dedicated years of regularly assisting me in the locker room, in addition to helping me in a variety of other ways. His is a sense of humor which is nothing if not irreverent.

I recently read an essay written by a nurse in which she expressed the opinion that the sick are not easy to love, a statement which some might find offensive, because we want so fervently to believe that the sick are lovable, even sweet, wise and saintly. Yet she is correct, and her words are especially appropriate in reference to the chronically or terminally ill. The dying, with malodorous bodies, unrelenting neediness, and quirky emotions, living with discomfort, pain and unpredictability, are not easy to love. This is not the same, however, as saying they are unlovable or that we do not love them. Nevertheless, who among us, when in the constant thrall of caring for them, cannot lay claim during moments of tension and exhaustion to wishing the dying person gone from our lives, if even momentarily—the stench, the moodiness, the stress, the strange world they inhabit which we ludicrously and rather desperately insist is this world but is in truth something of which we are not a part. We often claim that our feelings are in the loved one's best interest, that his or her suffering will be over, but the deeper truth of our thoughts arises precisely from what that nurse wrote: the sick are not easy to love.

My first encounter with decubitus ulcers—also known as bedsores or pressure sores—came when I was a strapping lad doing voluntary work in the geriatrics unit at Charing Cross Hospital, London. One Sunday afternoon I was patiently listening to an old woman propped up by bed pillows tell me of her bygone past, her demeanor utterly dignified in spite of the jet black wig dangling off the side of her head exposing thin wisps of weary, whitish hair; when a dashing young intern came in to ask me to assist him with cleaning and dressing a decubitus ulcer. I rather naively agreed, not knowing what to expect, nor even what he was referring to. Consequently we entered a large ward filled with approximately twelve beds, each one occupied by an elderly woman, some recovering, others dying. The spring sunlight shining through the windows was robust and even rapturous after a dark, rainy winter. Following the doctor to a bed nearer the windows than not, I watched as he removed the soiled dressing from the thigh of an emaciated, subdued woman. Whatever I was expecting, it was not what was revealed by the uncompromising sunlight—a gaping sore approximately eight centimeters across, a well of sickly red muscle at the bottom of which was exposed the glistening white bone. The intern was naturally quite composed and professional, explaining to me how the decubitus ulcer had come about, beginning with lack of attentive care at home leading initially to skin deterioration before disintegrating into an open sore, and how the hospital staff was attempting to treat one this severe. The aged woman remained unresponsive while I held her leg steady, and I must admit I have no idea what her face looked like, my entire focus being centered on the gaping sore in her thigh.

During my years of working with the disabled and dying, I necessarily had further encounters with decubitus ulcers, whether through the omnipresent preventative measures of proper skin maintenance—cleanliness, changing of the body position, gentle massage, cushioning of bony protuberances, airing of the skin and careful monitoring—or in the cleansing and dressing of such ulcers when they did occur, a sometimes desperate attempt to keep them from becoming as deep and wide and potentially life-threatening as the one I had seen on the old woman's thigh. It may be noted here that pressure sores are not an inevitable consequence of being wheelchair- or bed-bound. With proper skin care allied with appropriate equipment and vigilant monitoring, a person need never have a full-blown decubitus ulcer. On the other hand, even with diligent care they can progress with sickening alacrity once the skin begins to deteriorate.

Last month I was evaluated for a powerchair—otherwise known as an electric or motorized wheelchair. When we got to the topic of seat cushions, the man asked me if I was having problems with pressure sores. "Any redness on your butt?" he asked in that point blank manner necessary in such situations lest we wander from lucidity. Using my speaking laptop computer, I made some electronically-voiced jest about not being able to see my butt, to which he politely smiled while remaining firmly in control of a situation which is not a laughing matter. Recalling to mind the ulcer I had seen twenty-seven years earlier, I had to admit to him that I had not really been paying attention to whether or not I was incurring any early signs of skin breakdown, the precursor to a fully defined decubitus ulcer. In my mind, this had been something I would deal with down the road, if at all, a road that had once upon a time seemed plenty long enough, the horizon distant both in time and worry. Thus as I looked in turn at the faces of three relatively healthy individuals huddled around me in the corner of a small warehouse full of medical equipment, I came to the rather unsettling realization that my world was not the same as those of the evaluator, the aide, and the occupational therapist who were all participating in this meeting, as though I were an entirely different species altogether.

Furthermore, it is a life which is undoubtedly not the same as any of the lives of my eight pool buddies—all of them obviously able-bodied, a number of them very athletic—they who would now have yet more responsibilities placed upon them, a kind of care that would by its nature have to be thorough, complicated and intimate. I admit that it was not easy to inform these already dedicated, generous men that they would now have to make sure my butt, back, and crotch were thoroughly clean and dry, paying especial attention to any red patches that might be precursors to yet worse. Thankfully, since the timing of this care occurs when I have just come out of the pool, it is not a messy business, and is merely about good skin maintenance—cleaning off the chlorine; thoroughly drying the skin, particularly in areas prone to skin breakdown; gently massaging the skin and muscles to encourage blood circulation, along with diligent monitoring.

Allied with a disciplined regimen of home-based physical therapy, weekly acupuncture treatments and daily meditation, my regular visits to the pool have been an invaluable part of my health maintenance program. I have always felt that no matter how my disease progressed or how disabled I became, it was imperative that I find a way to be in the water, even if that were just to float around with assistance, a resolution which has been sustainable only through the assistance of many volunteer men over the years. Such resolve is easily enough maintained when a person is still somewhat healthy and relatively capable. As it is, and to be quite honest, I am finding the process ever more arduous, both logistically and physically, though not any less rewarding. Furthermore, not only is it more challenging for me, it has also become much more complicated for my volunteers than I had ever envisioned. Without a doubt it would be easier on all involved were I simply to stop going to the pool. It would certainly free these men to do other things. These concerns of mine, however, though they are meant to take into consideration the lives and feelings of those involved, are in the final analysis purely selfish. The questions—How exhausted am I by the exertion? How annoyed am I that the logistics break down on a regular basis? And why do I feel a twinge of shame asking guys to participate in a relationship that is doomed from the start to be unequal, unreciprocal?—do not take into consideration the thoughts and feelings of the volunteers themselves, let alone the larger context of the community.

It is three years since Jeremy first accompanied me to the swimming pool, three years during which, at least in my mind, I felt I was somewhat capable of maintaining a measure of equality within my relationships with my volunteer caregivers, some semblance of reciprocity—an occasional gift, witty conversation, a hearty physical effort on my part to make their tasks easier. Only now must I finally admit and accept that the relationship is no longer, if ever it were, equal or symmetrical. In truth, my relationships with these men are decidedly and ever more unequal; a broken symmetry, as it were. There is absolutely no way in which I will ever be able to reimburse them for their effort and time; there is no manner in which I can reciprocate their generosity with anything approaching an equal dealing.

Yet the equation is not as simplistic as my narrow ego would perhaps understand it. You see, my situation is not merely a matter of elementary addition or subtraction. It is more akin to an algebraic function in which the search for x may involve many variables, a complicated maze of computations, and in the end an answer that itself may make little sense. We only know it is correct because of the subtle laws of mathematics. When I search beyond the simplistic and venture into the complex, I find that the underlying equation has ultimately very little of me in it. I, it is discovered, am a minor integer nestled in a corner of the square root of a locker room. The larger equation, and our solving it for x, takes us far beyond the flesh, far beyond my ass, so to speak, into the lives of eight remarkable men and beyond.

Here I can do little better than to quote from a letter recently sent to me by one of my pool buddies, in response to a letter I had written delineating the need for a change in our routine in order to incorporate better skin care,

> ...Please don't hesitate to bring up any other needs you might have that we can help out with. I think there is more good coming out of this than you know. For example: at least once a week I will meet someone that has seen me at the pool helping you and they ask about you. This interaction creates an awareness, not only of you, but of all people that have problems. It also creates an awareness that it is everyday people (like the Z Team) that help solve the problems and help take care of each other. With this heightened awareness, I would bet that the people we cross paths with, open up a little and maybe make life easier for someone they know and can help.

In the midst of a busy locker room, in front of a row of sinks where on one side of me a fully naked man with a towel draped casually over his right shoulder is shaving, while on the other a kid is rinsing his hands after using the urinal, I am lying down in my reclining wheelchair, the legrests raised, as a man helps to roll me on my side in order to better clean, dry, and massage areas prone to pressure sores. Situated thus, what do other guys see as they walk past? Do they see me as a man whose so-called IQ is situated in the top one percentile of the population? Do they see in me a guy who once upon a time could surge through the frenzy of dizzyingly intricate and fast Hungarian couple dances and Bulgarian line dances with facility? Do they see the hands of a capable musician, or a mind of unbridled imagination? Of course not. They see an ass; a butt being tended by a kind-hearted comrade, the bare skin being kept healthy and free from the onset of debilitating decubitus ulcers. A couple of years ago it would probably have annoyed me to think that people perceived me as but an ass. Yet the dignity of life lies not in our possessions, our accomplishments, nor our superiority one over another, but in the most vulnerable, intimate sharing that arises when we embrace both life and death, graciously accepting its very unequal dealings.

As I lie on my side facing the sinks, my field of view limited to the plumbing beneath, I hear a hearty voice bellowing through the hard interior of the windowless, echoing locker room,

"Hey, how's my buddy?"

Though I cannot see the speaker, nor tell precisely where he is—nor do I even recognize the voice—I nevertheless sense that the man is speaking to me. Yet it is impossible for me to respond with my voice; nor may I signal to him with my arms, which are warmly folded up in a towel, my hands resting by my chin. I cannot even interact using a glint of my eyes, a smile of my forehead, incapacitated as I am, only my backside communicating with the world, when suddenly a hairy, robust arm reaches down beside the sink to grab my hand where it is poking out of the towel by my chin. I can see nothing of this man except a hand, a forearm, and I am unable to shift my head in order to catch sight of the rest of him. All I have is the suddenness of one human hand in another, then a thumbs up, a hearty pat on the shoulder and the man is gone, whoever he was. Still to this day I have no idea the identity of that man, one of many who daily pass through the concrete and metal locker room, many of whom either gape at me or avert their eyes, some of whom wave to me, others embracing me in arms of many colors, against torsos wet, bare, panting, sweaty, shirted, and/or laughing.

I fear that in my attempts neither to insult nor embarrass my volunteers in the above portrayal, I have actually not done full justice to them, for the essence of these relationships is much more exquisite than I have managed to describe. In solving for x, then in trying to explicate the process in nonmathematical terms, most of us are left grasping for the right words. In trying to express what it is that separates these men from the mundane, that each may be considered a real mensch, I find myself in much the same quandary. Perhaps the reason for this lies in the aforementioned thought of the nurse, that the sick are not easy to love.

To care for the infirm, the dying, isn't merely about kindness.

Or goodness.

Nor is it about one's own redemption.

And it certainly cannot effectively be about personal agendas and familial obligations.

You see, these guys who assist me in the pool and the locker room on a regular basis, who care for me at my most fragile and vulnerable moments, who are my link to the world during those times when I am especially challenged physically, are necessarily they who most profoundly witness my frustrations and struggles, my confusions and fears, along with the deterioration of my body, even, potentially, my skin. It is they, furthermore, who must respond. Yes, the relationship is undeniably not equal, as the brunt of my complicated needs, when I am with these guys, falls fully on their shoulders, needs that are by their nature emotionally, psychologically, and physically intimate.

Yet, while it can be said that the sick are not easy to love, it is also true that it is only through the intimacy of a love that has no need to plead for reciprocity, nor to demand acknowledgement, that we may find the courage to care deeply for the sick and the dying.

This then is the harmony within this unequal relationship, and as with any broken symmetry, the very act of having once broken it spawns something quite extraordinary, quite beyond the prosaic.

In the final analysis, after much pondering and many logistical computations, after my skin is thoroughly dried and massaged, as the pearls are once again being draped around my neck, I discover that in solving the equation of eight men in a locker room, x, the unknown, is none other than love.

This is fortunate, for it is also the only thing I have to offer in return.

April 14, 2002

65. MAX

This essay consists almost entirely of a personal letter, followed by some additional commentary. The letter was sent to an e-mail correspondent of mine, a woman who has primary lateral sclerosis, an upper motor neuron disease which, while affecting her whole body, has most notably restricted her ability to speak. In order to communicate with others she currently has to write down her thoughts on a special slate or piece of paper. Because of this disability—indeed it was our mutual speech challenges that initially brought us together via a third party—she has expressed interest in a new assistive technology in my life, namely a laptop computer which acts as a voice transducer, and which I have named Max. Max came to me in February, the result of months of researching various options, and of generous financial contributions from more than a hundred individuals across the continent.

Dear Barb,

In response to your interest in my laptop communication device—which, by the way, I have dubbed Max—I cannot pretend that he is a worthy substitute for the finesse and versatility which characterize the human voice. To wit, Max is lethargic in general, awkward in large ensembles, and occasionally a complete dunderhead—rather like myself, I suppose. Having said as much, I should hasten to assure you that Max in his own unassuming way is an enormous help with communication; a blessing, in fact. To imagine my life without his humble little body sitting on my lap monotonously, laboriously, electronically cooing into the ears of listeners is not a pleasant thought. During those times when he must by necessity be separated from me, such as when I am in the swimming pool, I find myself in the position of being completely cut off from verbally communicating with the world.

Physically he is quite compact, muscular, one might say, and comes with a protective carrying case and shoulder strap. I suppose for anyone with normal arm strength he would not be considered heavy, making him as portable as a medium sized handbag filled with lipsticks and concealed weapons.

Internally Max has been ingeniously programmed to predict word sequence, the screen displaying a set of options from which I may choose. This is very helpful, cutting down on the amount of effort it takes to input my thoughts. You can also change his voice quality, selecting from four male and four female voices, as well as a child's voice. During the first days Max was with me, while searching for a voice choice that people could most easily understand, I wandered between Dennis, Wendy, and Paul, ultimately settling on the latter. I also had to try different tempi in order to find one that was most pellucid—if I so choose I can have him speak up to six hundred words a minute, which is definitely beyond gibberish.

While the unemotional quality of his voice does not allow for expressing the nuances of our emotional selves, on the positive side, the listener cannot tell from the electronic voice whether one is a bit irate, a tad sad, or simply being ironic, thus any emotional content he or she interprets from Max's electronic voice will be purely a projection on the part of the listener. Vice versa, there are times when I am feeling quite emotional about a situation, and were I myself to speak, would likely create more harm than good, whereas Max simply states the words, the facts, as it were, and the listener does with them what he or she will. Allied to this is the necessary slowing down of my side of the conversation. While this can be infuriating, I also find that it allows me plenty of time to choose my words, truly allowing me to think before I speak. This has saved me many times from blurting out some regrettable notion that would have been better left unsaid.

It is possible to add words to the computer's dictionary, to alter pronunciation of any word, and to create phrases that are cued by simple abbreviations, this latter feature further cutting down on the amount of effort needed to communicate. There is also an arrangement of shortcut phrase buttons that I have yet to figure out fully.

In addition to the speech program, the computer also comes with word processing, calendar, calculator and e-mail programs, plus others I do not even know how to use. It can also be connected to your personal computer and to telephone lines.

Personally I feel it is vital for the user to have decent spelling skills to use the speech program most effectively. For using the computer in general, it is valuable to have basic computer skills, which you obviously have since you communicate with me via e-mail.

The screen itself is virtually impossible to read outdoors in sunlight, though this can be somewhat alleviated by moving into the shade. It is also possible to adjust the brightness of the screen slightly. This is helpful if, for instance, you were using it at night while riding in someone else's vehicle, a dimmer screen being perhaps less distracting for the driver. Speaking of motorcars, I myself find it difficult to use Max in a moving vehicle, due to weakness in my arms, which you may or may not experience.

While it was not my idea to give my device a name, it has proven to be good advice, as it ensures consistency in how people refer to it, thus removing a lot of confusion, such as, "Which assistive device does Zsolt need?" Or, "Which computer are we referring to?" Such questions are irrelevant when we speak simply of Max.

It is possible to enter messages by typing on Max's reduced keyboard, or, and this is what I prefer, using the touch-sensitive screen, which has various configurations of the alphabet from which to select, depending on one's physical abilities and thought processes. Max is versatile enough that he can also be modified for scanning technologies in case I eventually lose my finger function.

Max is a hungry little guy, and needs to be recharged each night, though seldom throughout the day, unless you are in the habit of incessantly chattering aloud to yourself or tend to engage in lengthy conversations with the deceased.

Because of the quality of the small speaker supplied with the device, Max is not very useful in a crowded or noisy environment, though listeners can always read directly from the screen in such conditions. Also, I have found that for true conversation or dialogue, he is most valuable one-on-one. If a third party is introduced, either the two of them will tend to carry the conversation, or it will split into various fragmented conversations. In such a case, it is helpful if one of the third parties has the grace to become a listener, only occasionally participating in the dialogue.

As with so much that you and I are experiencing, Barb, the response from the general community is quite mixed, at times hilarious, at times exasperating; sometimes poignant, and sometimes utterly pathetic—for instance, a man once asked me to turn Max off because he found it embarrassing.

Certainly one of the challenges in having Max as a transducer of my thoughts is that there is no longer any verbal eloquence in my dialogues with others, and few opportunities for witty repartee. This, by the by, is not entirely Max's fault, for while he may be slow, it is most often the listeners themselves who destroy any opportunity for eloquence or wit, either because they are too harried to allow it to unfold, or because they haven't the inclination to suspend life within a time-frame that allows their thoughts to be stretched and held and caressed long enough for lovely webs of meaning to take shape. As an illustration of the opposite phenomenon, my current acupuncture intern very kindly and patiently creates an open, serene environment in which our dialogues may unfold. Thus we have some surprisingly poignant and often hilarious dialogues.

Barb, if you do get a device like Max, you may discover like me that listeners will maneuver themselves, often quite ludicrously, in order to impatiently read the tiny screen rather than waiting for you to enter your thoughts for Max to iterate. This in itself is neither here nor there, and might even be helpful, as for instance in a noisy environment. However, I have had people who then begin repeating each word as I enter it into the computer, as though I myself were incapable of reading, or had no idea what my own thoughts were, the echoing voice being highly intrusive, if not outright insulting. More common, and thus more annoying, is when the listener, having thus maneuvered himself into a position from which he may read the narrow screen, has the audacity to finish off my sentences for me after I have only partially entered my thoughts. Personally I find this to be very disruptive—particularly when the listener guesses incorrectly—and only occasionally helpful. Certainly there may be said to be some advantage to this particular habit, in that it might save the pitiable, voiceless person from having to finish his or her sentence. It can also, however, be highly disempowering for that same individual, who might like to feel he or she is *not* some pitiable, voiceless person, but rather a cognitive human being who happens to use an alternative form of communication. Additionally, if people already know what I am going to say, why should I even bother trying to communicate my thoughts in my choice of words at the pace in which I am capable using the technology available to me? I find that rather than encouraging dialogue, this manner of interaction merely stifles it, thus I gradually begin to avoid meaningful conversation with such individuals. If they prefer to say everything, then they can just carry on a monologue. I'll gladly listen in.

I do not know what your experiences have been, Barb, when it comes to people not allowing you to express yourself using your special slate, but I will share a few abstract examples from mine...

1. Even with Max on my lap I find that people will ask me a question, then answer it themselves when it becomes apparent that it will take more time than anticipated to wait for my answer.

2. A third party asks me a question, and the person accompanying me answers it, often inaccurately, without referring to me.

3. A questioner turns to the person accompanying me and using the third person singular asks a question about me, and instead of directing the interrogator to communicate directly with me, my escort answers the question, often inaccurately.

We may no longer have voices, Barb, and our assistive technologies may be slow, cumbersome, and difficult to understand, but I do not believe either of us needs to be treated as though we were incapable of cognition, of having thoughts and opinions about our health care, about our futures, about life itself.

On the brighter side, there are those who are quite comfortable with Max's pace, who are more than willing to sit quietly while I enter my thoughts, and who are able to hold their own thoughts until I have completed my data input and given Max the opportunity to share those thoughts. There are also those who are not afraid of insisting that the greater world make the time and effort to communicate with me. I recall a day at the pool when I was with my buddy Pete. A stranger started speaking to Pete about me as though I were incapable of communicating. Pete, bless his heart, in his usual casual manner, said, "Talk to him yourself; he's not stupid."

Recently I had a visit from my editor, our first tête-à-tête meeting, in fact.

After about an hour of dialogue using Max as my transducer, he said, "I rather like this method of communication—it is much more thoughtful and spacious," or something to that effect, the important point being that he was able to take a novel situation, an even potentially hazardous one, and find within its boundaries a reason for it to exist of its own vector and on its own terms, terms which, while they may be initially delineated by my loss of voice and the subsequent introduction of Max, are nonetheless created anew with each person as he or she comes into contact with me.

I have always felt it imperative that we allow the disabled and the dying to speak for themselves, Barb. In light of this, anything that you and I can do for ourselves to facilitate our own involvement in communicating our needs and desires is worthwhile. I cannot be emphatic enough in this. Language, along with its underlying cognition, is one of the factors which makes of Homo sapiens a unique creature. For this reason, I highly encourage you to look into the assistive communication technologies available, especially if you are having increased difficulties using your hands to write down your thoughts for others.

Please let me know if I have addressed all your concerns or may in any other way be of assistance.

With love to you and your family,

Zsolt

Ensuring that the voices of the disabled and the dying are heard is of great importance to me for two reasons. First, I feel that language in all its mysterious forms—words, music, dance, painting, gesture—is the blood, the sap of the human soul. Second, in my work with the disabled and the dying I had often to witness instances in which well-meaning and not-so-well-meaning people literally hijacked language from individuals incapacitated by disability, disease or ageing. The appropriation of language from any individual is nothing less than heinous.

To put it bluntly, we must allow those who are disabled, ill and/or dying to speak for themselves, whether through assistive technologies, gnarled speech, or blinks of the eyelids. When we are willing to do so, our role then becomes one of assisting those people to express themselves, rather than one of presumptuously deciding their thoughts, dreams, and desires for them.

On a more personal level, I ask of everyone, please stop silencing the only vocality which remains to me, awkward and clumsy as it may be. Please stop dismissing the only means I have for expressing my needs and desires verbally. If you feel confident that you are not culpable in this matter, I congratulate you, while also encouraging you nevertheless to reevaluate your body language, your listening skills and the sincerity of your patience. Each of us can become better listeners, better communicators, myself included. Furthermore, if you feel you have the inner strength and the courage to do so, I ask you to please begin encouraging others to truly listen to the voices of the disabled and the dying, in whatever form those voices must be manifested.

You see, once we have appropriated the voice of a disabled man or a dying woman, communication is shattered and in order to reconstruct a trusting dialogue we will have to work very, very hard. If that person happens to be someone we care deeply about—a spouse, a friend, a parent—then there ought be that much more impetus for us to take the time to listen, to make an effort to acquire additional skills, whether that be a calming meditation, more appropriate body language, or the presence of sincere compassion, in order to ensure that the voice of our beloved is allowed space and time in which it may express itself.

I do not know how else to say it—

Slow down,
take a deep breath,
be thoughtful in your expressions,
fill your lungs with air,
discover a patience borne upon the strength of love,
feel the exhaling breath flow across your lips,
and listen.

Put your face against the face, the torso of your beloved;
listen to the language of her unique breath rising and falling.

Hear the song of his disabled body,
experience the stories in her dying eyes,
be touched by the visions of his flesh.

Celebrate the ways in which that individual can still communicate, then encourage others to also take time to listen to your beloved's voice, however it may be expressed, a voice which, in the end, is one of the infinite voices of the Beloved.

April 26, 2002

66. LIFE OF A HOLY FOOL

A friend tells me I should write a screenplay based on my sundry experiences, her reasoning being that if I do not, somebody else likely will, a task only a madman could relish; and while I may be suitably daft for the job, it is also true that I haven't the requisite skills for such a project.

Be this as it may, were a film to be made of even a segment of my life, the soundtrack would have to be packaged as a boxed set, nay, a suitcase of compact discs. Yes, the actual film itself would run little more than five stunningly action-packed minutes consisting of some giggles, a motorcycle crash or two, a fall from an airplane, some fancy footwork and a few tears, followed quite naturally by the credits, most of them for costuming and wiggery.

But the soundtrack!

The soundtrack, my friend...

Two hundred and thirteen hours of music to discombobulate, annoy, and intimidate the pusillanimous, the flaccid, and the dull. Yes, a lifetime of the world's most heart-thundering, mind-berserking, soul-soaring music squeezed onto a little more than two hundred compact discs—not recommended for use as a self-defense mechanism—ranging from the poignant joy of klezmer to the rarefied panpipes of the Andes; from the scintillations of sitar and tabla to the smoky intensity of tangos and milongas; from passionate flamenco to the haunting voice of a solitary shepherd; from the percussive power of the piano literature to the flamboyance of swing; from mediaeval settings of the Catholic mass evolving into the splendid polyphonic strata of the European Renaissance and through to the worldwide efflorescence of opera and onward toward the electronic and aleatoric sonic explorations of the twentieth century—to cite but a few examples.

With a bit of reflection it becomes rather obvious that the problem with portraying any one life is that there are so many lives within it, at least as many lives as there are people who have witnessed that purported singularity of a life. Were we to take any individual—your glorious self for instance—and gather together a dozen others who feel they know that person reasonably well, we would quickly discover that they speak not of one individual, but of twelve. You see, one of your acquaintances will solemnly aver that you would never harm a living thing, not even a mosquito; the next will eagerly disclose that you discipline your children with unfettered gusto, gleefully thwacking them with beribboned fairy wands and shiny plastic play swords. One tells us that you were always snickering at puerile and insipid office jokes; another that you were the most humorlessly efficient of co-workers. As we proceed to interview those twelve acquaintances of yours, you become ever more sundered into a dozen characters, each caricature spectrally sharing traits with the others, though also rather disconcertingly unlike them, as though we were gazing into a kaleidoscope within which it is possible to observe how the colors relate, as do the shapes, but the pattern itself is slightly and eerily distorted from facet to facet of the mirrored image. This naturally begs the question, "Who are you, my worthy friend?" Furthermore, which of the various though similar facets are we to believe is the inerrant you? Are you the upstanding citizen, the previously institutionalized maniac, or the presumed imbecile each of us is taken for on occasion? I suppose the answer is to be, none and all. None, because the perceptions from the twelve people are in fact not you; they remain the views and therefore the property of the individuals expressing those views. All, because each of those views has some basis in the world observed, namely, in this instance, you—whatever that means and whoever the hell you are.

A dear friend of mine is a highly successful young man. With persistent effort, he has strived throughout his school years to hone his natural talents and intelligence, and has thereby succeeded in gaining well-earned and well-deserved entry into some of the nation's finest universities. Such strenuous effort to succeed, however, can often be overwhelming, particularly for an adolescent. He once told me that whenever he begins to feel the strain of his chosen path he says to himself, "Fuck this, I'm going to grow up to be like my Aunt Zsolt." He then admitted he had no real concept of what that would entail, but merely thinking the thought allowed him to release some of the stress, to refresh his energies and to proceed anew on the path that is his, which in the end suits him very well. While I cannot say he would not look cute in pearls and also quite dashingly handsome astride a motorcycle, it would be incongruous with his personality and his dreams.

But what does it mean, ". . .to grow up to be like my Aunt Zsolt"? As you can imagine, my friend has quite a few options. He can grow up to be ignorant, maudlin, spontaneous and arrogant, for example. Or patient, humble and evil. Or brilliantly unlucky and elegantly insane. Of course, in spite of his occasional outbursts to the contrary, he will grow up to be none other than himself, his life woven from its own initial complexities, tattered by the blades and subterfuges of its own nemeses, eventually to ravel and decay of its own dying. My descriptions of him in the preceding paragraph—successful, persistent, intelligent, cute, and handsome—must remain only that, my descriptions, my perceptions.

Yet, as inconsistent as our views of one another inevitably are, we are to be grateful that no life is inconsistent within itself, regardless its incomprehensibly diverse or even contradictory trajectories, regardless the unavoidably disjointed perceptions of others.

If one imagines words as the warp of my life, music can then be considered its sumptuous weft, and dance the rhythmic pulsing of the weaving shuttle, the momentum of the body which creates the patterns, the arabesques of an ever-accumulating design. What then, one may ask, are the metaphorical wools, the silks and the cottons, the fundamental fibers of the tapestry? To which question I answer,

curiosity,

yearning,

rapture,

and awe.

Additionally, woven in among these intrinsic fibers are to be found ancient strands of gold and the glint of plastic sequins, along with the shimmering of glass beads, faceted rhinestones, and faux pearls, that mine is indeed a motley history easily condemned, lampooned, mocked, pilloried, and found utterly guilty of gross discrepancies and indecorous imperfections; even, befittingly, the pleasure of non-being.

As a child I was magnanimously told I could pursue any life I wanted, within limits, of course, it being fairly obvious to most that a shorty like me was never going to play professional basketball—which is not to say I was unprepared, outfitted as I was in patent leather stiletto heels. Needless to say, I do not think anyone expected me to take the aforementioned injunction to the extremes I have, that for me it became not merely any life I wanted, but any lives. Indeed, as several people have recently brought to my attention, in half of a life I have managed to live more lives than most people will live in one life—a conundrum only a mathematician could find appealing, or the holy fool. Consequently, while my journey may indeed be inspiring to some, it seems only to confound and discombobulate others.

True, as discussed above, the life of any given individual is by default an enigma to even the closest of comrades. Nonetheless, many people apparently pursue lives of such similitude, even when separated by culture, time and/or distance, that they are able to maintain some semblance of black or white—each person, each entity can then be categorized as either a this or a that, with me or against me, and never a *thisthat*. By contrast, some citizens—perhaps your neighbors or even you yourself—are gray, gray, gray and yet again a thousand thousand scintillating shades of gray. Therefore, in answer to the question, "Are you a this or a that?" such individuals must be forever shrugging their shoulders, smiling disconcertingly as they attempt to translate their *thisthatnesses* into black or white terms, at which they often fail quite miserably, much to the disgust of the mono-hued, unifacial interrogator, who then cries out in exasperation, "If you are not a this, then you must be a that—you cannot be at once smart and stupid!"

Need I say more?

Probably not, though it is worth pointing out that in speaking of grayness I am not referring to a flaccid, impotent, indecisive state. Rather it may be understood as a dynamic river flowing between two embankments, one of black, the other of white; a river of constantly shifting shades of gray, each ripple, each wave a subtle color not previously encountered, a new cadence, a delight, an unexpected spray of water, a laceration. To dwell in grayness is to chart a course into the midst of the unknown.

To taste the sweet kosher wine is to be once again small beside my mother as
    she and I long ago wandered the aisles of the liquor store in search of
    that same crimson wine,
is to be carefully removing tiny goblets of etched glass from a sacrosanct
    cabinet,
is to be pouring a measure of the thick red liquid into each one,
is to tumble momentarily backwards into a life which from its first flutterings of
    tellurian memory was neither black nor white, but overflowed with a
    multitude of striking images and exotic aromas, a diversity of
    landscapes overlaid with an abundance of sensual music,
years of a life which, like the square piece of paper in the hands of a Japanese
    man, were folded and pleated such that they no longer remained red-
    sided and white-sided, but emerged instead as a gracefully sharp-winged
    crane,
the kind-eyed man who spoke no English smiling at my childish attempts to
    replicate one of the traditional arts of his people,
his tutelage nevertheless abiding with me throughout the remaining thirty-seven
    years of my life, as I myself have enduringly fashioned thousands of
    origami cranes folded from squares of beautiful papers and scrap papers
    and even the mercantile brown of crumpled paper bags,
wordless cranes crafted by my long narrow fingers and proffered to remote
    villagers gathering me into their humble homes,
paper cranes made for the eager eyes of children sitting on crowded trains
    migrating across shifting landscapes, or presented to stranded boys and
    girls burdened with the ennui of waiting in the echoing expanses of
    airports,
that the gift of the Japanese man's hands, coming as it once did from a distant
    land, has been sown time and again among young and old across three
    other continents,
my own hands becoming apertures through which the cranes may ever and again
    take flight into the eyes of the other within,
these hands, these windows of expression shaped and framed by a rich
    compendium of musical gestures spanning more than a thousand years,

gestures shaped by rhythms and melodies resonating throughout the ceremonies, traditions and compositions of a variegated spectrum of humanity,

a common wealth of music ever rising from a melding of the heart and the mind,

its pulses expressed through the hands and fingers, the mouths and lips of a veritable menagerie of human beings,

rhythms and melodies that compel the body to motion, the grace of the ballerina as well as the ecstatic dances of Chasidim, of dervishes, and of diverse folk who have ever and again folded their bodies around assorted configurations of clarinets, drums, ouds, saxophones, dudelsacks, violins and voices,

transfiguring themselves into mythic versions of great-winged cranes and dignified antelope, powerful bison and cunning coyotes,

whose fervent dancing has been one of the pathways by which humanity has attempted to bridge the known and the unknown,

with feet on the earth and souls spiraling toward the heavens,

ecstatic moments piercing the fortified walls of an inner realm whose spectral boundaries may only be breached by a spark that has no flame yet which illumines the entire universe,

a spark of the mind, of the blood, of the heart, that the foundation of each life is at once a thought and a gesture, a word and a melody from which the soul is woven into a canopy,

a shawl of iridescent light mantling a fourteen-year-old boy as I long ago sat before an older friend,

a Buddhist monk who listened with patient kindness to my endlessly babbling story, its plot suddenly broken in mid-sentence as I once upon a time gazed into his gentle eyes,

a brief moment during which I rather quaintly discovered that within him dwelt a spark of myself,

while my own juvenile exuberance expressed an aspect of this other human being,

a thread of quiet human joy bonding us one to the other, to life and humanity, to the indescribable sky above as well as the wooden floor upon which we sat amid the witnessing shafts of sunlight,

our faces bearing an inexpressible delight in living, an irrepressible impulse toward life shared also by my mother as she would place thin slices of caramelized Norwegian cheese onto broken shards of matzo while blithely listening to people being endlessly, cruelly murdered—

villainously shot,

strangled,

poisoned,

and drowned—

in the passionate throes of grand opera,

even as she sat perusing harmless cookery books in search of recipes for meals
of vaguely Chinese origin and faux Italian richness, of Central European
heartiness and Mexican piquancy, of humble wholesomeness and meager
budget, along with a wealth of buttery Christmas cookies from different
lands, and once an attempt to replicate an ancient Middle-Eastern recipe,

the rich aromas of her magical kitchen having over time become interlarded in
my memory with the pungent fragrances of Pakistani cookery seeping
through the walls of a London flat,

with the smoky, fruity, rotting odors of the open-air markets of South America,
that to this day a piece of fresh papaya in my mouth will spontaneously
explode into bright colors woven into sweat-soaked garments,

mine and those of the vendors, as we encountered one another high in the Andes
Mountains or partially embraced by the luxuriant edge of a jungle that
even now stretches across the loins of a southern continent,

a jungle whose fecundity my adolescent mind could barely fathom, even as I took
pause in my youthful wonder of the natural world to read the writings of
Mahatma Gandhi and Albert Einstein, the poetry of Arthur Rimbaud,
and the novels of Fyodor Dostoyevsky and Count Leo Tolstoy,

even as I began struggling to comprehend what roles dance and music and poetry
could possibly have in a humanity so strewn with injustice and poverty,
strife and greed,

further realizing what an easy thing it would be to simply avert one's eyes, one's
hands, one's mind from the challenges facing each of us in an often
inhumane world, thereby evading the very thing which is capable of
encouraging and enthusing us,

namely the often intimidating simplicity of the compassionate heart,

yet as I traveled alone in train carriages rattling across continents, my rebellious
spirit could not envision my burgeoning life as one of such evasion, of
closing off my heart and my mind, of estranging myself from the not
undaunting world,

to then wither in false security throughout the ensuing decades of what could
then be considered a life in name only,

that I consequently found myself attempting to grapple with what it meant to
gaze across the city of Quito toward the magnificent Pichincha Volcano,
in whose shadow a metropolis was being subdued by weeks of daily
twenty-hour curfews put into effect as the government tried to regain and
maintain control of the rioting streets,

as I myself used the many hours of this enforced confinement to read books and
to listen to the Egmont Overture of Beethoven—Lamoral, Count of
Egmont, beheaded for his role in sixteenth-century Dutch attempts to
overthrow the oppressive rule of the Spanish Hapsburgs,

attempts which, years after Egmont's severed head had been shipped off to the

King of Spain, finally succeeded, opening the way for a Dutch Republic which was then and is to this day known for tolerance—

and in one of those strange coincidences in life, as I write these very words I am listening to an historical recording of Beethoven's Egmont Overture blasting forth at full volume, a performance originally broadcast on 18 November, 1939,

a mere eleven weeks after German Nazis had invaded the western border of Poland, only months before the Netherlands would itself be overrun by panzer divisions,

that we are challenged ever and again to remain joyous, to retain that sense of untarnished curiosity, of naked rapture, of humble compassion and boundless love,

in order that we might still find the courage to remove a book of poems from its shelf and upon opening it recite threads of words which form the warp of a prayer shawl which must one day inevitably lie in tatters, the weft of it fluttering in a breeze which can no longer reconstruct the many melodies lovingly woven into the fibers,

those surging melodies which were not merely the ornamentation of a life, but the very core, the truest essence of my being, those invisible and ungraspable winds which nevertheless carried aloft the wings of a paper crane whose innocent eyes watched in rapt horror as the image of a self-immolating Vietnamese monk spread throughout the media,

an image at once beautiful and tragic, that only the callous or the fearful could remain apart from the inherent human predicament it represented,

as I myself came to understand that it was not from the rhetoric of political leaders that I could seek to gain comprehension of such tragic beauty, but rather in the expressions of men and women who had gone into the great deserts of the human experience and returned bearing inconceivable and irradicable scars,

their bony hands cradling curiously charred gifts which while not explicating the journey itself nevertheless vaguely illuminated it, giving it an outline or a scent or a texture, at times with horrific honesty, at other times with voluptuous delight or intellectual exactitude, with uncompromising simplicity or overpowering grandeur,

that in the presence of such gifts we are somehow touched by an inennarable grace that knows not skin color, age, gender, class or dogma,

a spark that flickers in the queerest of places, in the most unexpected gestures of both human culture and the natural world, humbling me time and again in the face of the unembraceable universe while at the same time exhilarating my mind, my flesh and my heart to persevere, to yearn, to be enthralled by imagination, the breadth of the heart,

by the heights of the Rocky Mountains, the equatorial Andes, the Transylvanian

Carpathians and the Swiss Alps,

by the expanses of the Hortobágy and the North American prairie,

by the ever-flowing waterways of the Aar, the Charles, the Danube, the Neva, the Seine and the Thames,

by the scope of the earth's teeming oceans and the depths of the night sky as my visions carry me through and beyond the constellations of Orion and Sagittarius,

through the halls of the Musée du Louvre in Paris, where my youthfully itinerant intensity came face to face with Leonardo da Vinci's depiction of St. John the Baptist, painted on wood in 1515 C.E., four years before Leonardo's death, four hundred and sixty years before my own eyes fell upon the now unchanging brush strokes of a masterpiece beckoning me to enter into the enigma of its expression, the eloquence of the Baptist's gesture,

centuries before my young legs strode daily through the streets of London, its populace intrepidly or foolishly ignoring warnings of terrorist attacks, its eyes ever alert for bomb-filled parcels abandoned on omnibuses or in rubbish bins throughout the busy shopping districts of what was once the capital city of a vast empire,

and whether the impulse itself be intrepid or foolish, one must step into the enigma regardless, for that which is the urge to compassionate living must be fulfilled even in the midst of our perpetual mistrust of one another, in spite of our unconquerable fears of the strange and the unknown, of our incessant sundering of the very bonds which define us collectively as humanity,

such sundering shattering us daily, hourly into often irreconcilable shards of strife, that we find ourselves clutching allegiances to this's and that's though rarely clinging with any tenacity to the possibility of a synthesis of our mutual human legacy and destiny,

a synthesis hinted at in the blossom of the iris flower, its bearded petals being at once object and symbol, tangible and oneiric, its blossoming existence a lovely exemplar of the laws of nature, even as its vernal scent impels me to recall its role among the messengers of the classical gods,

its essence being then and still today the resplendently meaningful rainbow in the midst of the tempest, a potent bridge into both the heart and the mind,

the iris being also the most alluringly personal aspect of the human eye, as we turn to face one another in complex moments, in fearful moments, and in moments of quiet mansuetude, our eyes the vehicle by which we may speak without speaking, as the touch of our hands is the only way we may sing without singing,

several iris blossoms standing erect in a vase upon my desk being a fragrant reminder of how I long ago found my right hand in possession of the intellectual frameworks of our forebears, namely astronomy, mathematics, natural philosophy and physics,

while in the palm of my left hand were nestled those esoteric and even heretical
traditions recurrent within the larger bodies of Buddhism, Judaism,
Taoism, Islam, Christianity and Hinduism, traditions which were
themselves categorized onto divergent and apparently unrelated fingers,

as the accumulation of thousands of years of humankind's manifold cultural
treasures variously alit in one hand or the other, onto one finger or
another,

dependent upon the factors of its original creation or on the desires of they who
fleetingly control such treasures,

the existential universe thus being continuously and insidiously presented to me
as forever black and white, as irreconcilably broken, an antagonistic state
of affairs which from my earliest awakenings seemed absurd,

in particular the crude compartmentalizing of the known and the unknowable,
the one forever red and the other intractably white, never the two to be
brought into harmony,

or so I was told time and again by those fearful of soaring deeply into the enigma
itself, those unwilling to guide the red vessel of one's life toward the
immeasurable, unfathomable white,

and yet I sensed that were the right hand to begin working together with the left
hand, creating careful and precise folds of those seemingly estranged
sides of what is ultimately a single square of paper,

and were a person to undertake such a challenge with persistent thoughtfulness
and love,

it might actually be possible to fashion a flock of cranes from the once flat pieces
of paper,

because we shall never know the entirety of the past and the future, of the vertical
and the horizontal,

yet may we also delight and revel in the enigmatic touch of the universe upon our
flesh, in the always present possibilities of interweaving aspects of the
known and the unknowable,

of finding ourselves wholly in awe of the lovingly crafted cranes nestled in the
palms of one another's hands, cranes taking flight into the iridescent eyes
of the other within,

and upon further reflection, I suppose it ought not to surprise us that these are
the words, the life of a man who was weaned on a musical heritage
composed of men and women who, imperfect as they were, nevertheless
constructed windows through which we may envision the gestures of the
compassionate heart, gestures that cannot be fulfilled by remaining
averted, flaccid, and diffuse,

and it is this, this unmistakable truth that life be participatory, that I encounter it,
meet it, and be embraced, tattered and yes, loved by its eccentric waters,

its eloquent passions, its terrifying beauty, its unpretentious agonies,

that in the very act of opening ever wider the windows, in carefully folding the
fragile wings of a paper crane, the universe is called into existence, its
dynamic truth demanding my participation,

even as the wind buffets me, the rain drenching me,

even as I reach within and am touched by the unnameable, whether through the
contemplation of mathematics or in pondering the immensity of the
universe,

even as my body, the shuttle itself, is wasting into fragility and in so wasting is
crippling the trajectories of what I once thought was to be my life,

and even as I now find myself slowly weaving each strand of crimson silk with
stiffened, painful fingers, I feel my sanguine heart leaning serenely
forward into the pale gray future, a friend affectionately lowering the
prayer shawl onto my shoulders in the corner of a windowless locker
room,

that the touch of his hands, the song of a bird, a fragment of music, a line of
poetry, the flutter of prayer flags above the door of the Buddhist stupa
and the infinite histories of a holy fool are each capable of carrying us
into the far edges of the universe,

enlightening our journeys through all that is known into that which is yet to be
embraced,

and further into that which intimately envelops us in its knowing.

May 17, 2002

68. EYE OF THE HURRICANE

For the majority of us, what remains most revealing about ourselves—what it is still possible to interpret as our bodies deteriorate, as our abilities diminish, as our minds stumble—is that which we ourselves cannot perceive...

Namely, the eyes.

As our limbs are stilled and the mouth muted, our eyes, unbeknown to us, continue to bespeak our souls and our minds, readily conveying the constantly churning whirlpool of joy and uncertainty, determination and melancholy, delight and bitterness, angst and serenity eddying within us, ever swirling from bright to dark to sublime, from overt to subtle to essential.

It is also in the eyes of certain individuals where we may catch rare glimpses of the warrior's deep courage and gentle strength; her confident humility and supple precision; his endurance, elegance, and poise.

It was mid-morning, shortly after rush hour. The doors of a train had just closed, its disembarked passengers crisscrossing a subway station in the North End of Boston. As the noise of the train's departing, accelerating wheels was swallowed by a dark tunnel, nameless pedestrians streamed across the platform toward the city streets above, among them a meager, scraggly man in his mid-twenties, dark fedora, wrinkled trousers, worn oxfords, second-hand overcoat, a man placidly engaged in his own inner dialogue.

Thus engaged, that is, until panic-stricken shrieks reverberated throughout the subway station, a station which had in an urban moment become completely emptied, so quickly had the passengers made for the exits, dispersing onto the sidewalks above.

All of the passengers, that is, except the two elderly Italian-American women who had somehow stumbled on the escalator and were now tumbling downward...

Even as the mechanical steps carried them up,

and up,

only to let them roll down,

and down,

a mortal version of the fate of Sisyphus;

though it was not a stone but two elderly women being forever transported upward

to tumble awkwardly, continuously head over heels toward a bruised,

broken,

bloody fate,

their screams shaking the echoing concrete of the stark subway platform emptied of passengers;

emptied but for a single person—

Yes, the meager man in the fedora, now running across the station platform, leaping the moving steps two at a time to reach the women who were at this point upside-down in their bizarre journey; their frumpy, black woolen skirts flopped over their torsos, exposing undergarments of girdles, garters and hosiery, their mouths screaming in and beyond Italian.

Placing his scrawny chest against the heavy, tumbling bodies, wrapping his puny arms around the terrified, shrieking chaos, the meager man was thus able to halt the cyclic rising and falling, turning it instead into a slow, inexorable rise toward where a crowd had gathered at the top of the escalator, all the while his gently ambiguous voice trying to find its way through the swirling terror which had engulfed the two women, their distorted mouths continuing to screech, their contorted limbs entangled in widowy cloth.

Methodically,

steadily,

the mechanical steps rose higher

and higher,

bringing the odd trio toward street level,

toward where a number of hands from the growing crowd reached out to guide and bring the two women to safety, solace and medical assistance.

Having thus securely delivered the women into the competent hands of others, the darkly clothed, meager young man, being of slight build, slipped unceremoniously through the crowd and disappeared without a trace.

He simply vanished.

I know.

I was there.

The eye of a hurricane is a phenomenon of almost inaccessible stillness in the center of an immense destructive force. It comes into being, however, not separate from that force, but as an expression of that force.

Dying is also an inconceivably destructive process, exploding every psychological structure a person has necessarily and painstakingly constructed over a lifetime, drowning our presumptuous illusions in pitiless torrents of ancient, unpedigreed truth, intimidating us, that we cover our eyes, attempting to flee to higher, safer, supposedly more secure ground.

In the center of the maelstrom of dying, however, is a place of profound stillness, an event inseparable from the dying itself, which anyway continues its destruction of the physical body unabated to the very end.

High above the ocean airplanes will on occasion fly through the catastrophic torrents and winds of a hurricane to emerge alone, solitary within the stillness of the tempest's eye, a stillness that cannot be comprehended merely through intellect, doctrine or emotion, though it is readily felt in the very marrow of the bones, the flesh.

Some weeks ago, after I had electronically told one of my volunteer pool buddies what an excellent job he had done bathing and massaging me, he became silently thoughtful—a charming habit of his—as he dressed.

Several minutes later, having closed up my locker and made sure everything was in order, he wheeled me out of the locker room and backwards into the lift.

It was then, as the heavy metal doors began to close, that he chose to respond to my earlier comments, "The way I see it is this. Our job is to make sure we do a good job caring for you. Your job is to hang in there."

So you've been a truck driver your entire adult life.

Or a salesperson.

Or a diva.

Or an auto mechanic.

Or a painter.

Suddenly you are involved in a motorcar accident, or you have been diagnosed with an incurable, progressive disease—a rare type of cancer, for instance, or a form of motor neuron disease such as amyotrophic lateral sclerosis. The symptoms of the disease, whether they be weakness, pain, loss of motor control or other disabling malfunctions, make it impossible for you to continue the work you have known, and which has defined you for many years, several decades. Unexpectedly, you are now faced with a transition from doing something—doing a multitude of things, in fact—to doing...

...what?

Doing nothing.

Or so it seems by comparison.

Yet even when it seems like nothing, we are still engaged in doing so much—reading a magazine, watching television, chatting, listening, eating, shitting, worrying, pissing, sitting, sleeping, drooling, gagging, choking...

Taking things further, what would happen if a person could no longer read a book?

What would happen if she could no longer listen to music?

What would happen if he could no longer lift his arms or hold up his own head?

What would happen if she could never again write a sentence, a word?

What would happen if a person lost the ability to feed himself, if a person could not even ingest food through her mouth?

What would happen if he could not take a breath without the assistance of a machine?

And what would happen if that machine malfunctioned?

This past spring a new man joined my crew of volunteer pool buddies.

On his first day of training, after he had intently watched the needle on the sphygmomanometer descend through the systolic and diastolic measurements, after he had clearly recorded the numbers on a piece of wrinkled paper kept in my locker, I welcomed him to the Z Team.

He looked up at me with his large, thoughtful eyes and responded, "It sounds like an underground world of super heroes."

Jean-Pierre is half my age.

I sit in my wheelchair at the edge of a large room, attempting to maintain a steady rhythm of breathing in spite of the fact that the muscles in my body are uncomfortable, burning.

The room in which I am thus ensconced is filled with dancing bodies, people of varying ages, among them an octogenarian couple I have known for many years. I watch in admiration as the two of them trot, skip, stomp and turn to the varied beats of an eclectic assortment of music from around the world, hour after hour throughout the lively evening—she complete with a knee replacement. This, I learn, is the third or fourth time they have gone dancing this week.

In past years I have also encountered the husband at the state capitol. He an earnest citizen lobbying the legislature for improvements in public education; I a winged, beshawled bicyclist lobbying for human rights and health care issues.

Currently both Fred and Mary are working on a project aimed at fostering better understanding and peace between Palestinians and Israelis.

They are now almost twice my age.

One of the continuous challenges we each struggle with is how to face the unexpected—those mysterious situations when we are asked to be more than we once were.

When a gentle young man finds himself caring for the body of a stranger twice his age, his youthful arms trying valiantly not to drown the ailing man, his spirit courageously learning to bathe the unadorned flesh of another person.

Or when a spry elderly couple is confronted with strife and aggression halfway around the world, and chooses peaceful, rational action over thoughtless acquiescence to violence.

Or when a middle-aged man is handed a wheelchair for locomotion, a computer for speech, and is told, "Your job is to hang in there."

It is occasionally possible to find insects, flowers, and bits of pollen millions of years old embedded in pieces of lustrous amber.

These golden-brown gemstones, once liquid, are a window into a past we cannot directly experience, a world we can understand in no other way than to reflect upon the life held within the hardened, transfigured sap.

Similarly, it is impossible for the man cradling my body directly to experience my physical deterioration, my dying. It is only through my eyes that he can reflect upon and communicate with the life within.

To be placed aside from mere soldiery, mere admiralty, a warrior in true service to her community must possess attributes beyond obedience, brawn and sincerity. She must also embody attributes such as

> profound courage,
> gentle strength,
> confident humility,
> supple precision,
> patience and endurance,
> elegance and dignity and poise.

Each a sibling to the other, these latter three may ultimately be the qualities which enable a person to guide the airplane through the tempest in order to emerge into the placid eye, transporting a person from the unassuming acts of the ordinary into the realm of the extraordinary, which is so full of the ordinary that it ceases to be ordinary, where the ordinary has been refined so as to become unrecognizable from its humble origins, has become sublime.

As we wander through the moments and places of our lives, those markets, offices, shops, cubicles, buses, streets and odea of human culture, we encounter score upon score of soldiers, admirals and generals. There are, however, few warriors among us, and they are often so cleverly camouflaged that they are easily overlooked. Withdrawing from their touch, turning from their brilliance, we remain ignorant not only of the warrior's existence within the storm of life, but also of the latent possibility of metamorphosis within our own noisy, chaotic selves.

Are the men of the Z Team an underground world of incognito super heroes using a municipal swimming pool as headquarters?

I suppose if you were to consider Eli strolling around with a hypothetical stun gun concealed in his gym bag and a cell phone connected directly to The Boss, then perhaps there is some truth in Jean-Pierre's musing, at least as concerns one member of the team.

To be perfectly frank, however, this is a group of guys who like the rest of us are trying to understand what it means to be human, to be humane.

Perhaps in the final analysis there is no such thing as a super hero, rather each of us is capable of so-called super hero moments, that we have within us variable amounts of the fire, the blood, the strength needed to turn the ordinary into the extraordinary, metamorphosing sap into amber, carbon into diamonds, however minuscule or occasional the resultant gems may be.

And yet, as much as I can agree with this, I find it unsatisfactory. For I have found that there do exist some rare individuals who, in their acts of service, rise above the mundane, the crowd. For such men and women it is not a matter of creating an occasional minuscule gem, however worthy that gem may be. Rather, these individuals seem to speak emeralds, to breathe diamonds, often unaware, so finely have these persons, through discipline, patience and effort, sublimated the qualities of warriorhood. Yes, momentarily touched by such men and women we find ourselves in the presence of what might be described as an unexpected warmth, a simple yet piercing brilliance which exudes profound courage, gentle strength, confident humility, supple precision, patience and dignity—in other words, the breath of the warrior.

The other day as I was sitting in the passenger seat of a truck belonging to an aide from my health care agency, I was witness to a nasty altercation between him and a motorist standing beside her Cadillac, an argument resulting from a minor incident which had quickly escalated into major name-calling—dirty Mexican, white trash, bitch, black ass, whore—and spitting. More or less immobilized, I felt completely helpless to avert the needless escalation in tensions—neither could I physically intervene, nor was Max, my computer voice, of much use. Not only would Max not be heard, his pace is far too cumbersome to be of any value in such emotion-whipped wildfires.

As I listened to these two grown adults viciously attacking one another, I thought to myself, *Who among us can honestly say that under similar circumstances we would behave much differently?*

Whereto courage?
Whereto strength?
Whereto humility?
Whereto elegance and dignity?

There is mounting evidence that not only is the true warrior a rare creature in our times, as perhaps throughout history, he is dishearteningly an endangered one as well, though not yet extinct.

Jean-Pierre cradles my body in the water, trying not to drown me as Phillip
    teaches him to maneuver my limbs through the movements of my
        physical therapy routine.
During a moment of discussion between these two dissimilar men I open
    my eyes.
Almost immediately Jean-Pierre glances down at me.

Thus I find myself gazing into liquid brown eyes that are in the process of
      becoming amber gemstones,
each gesture of his arms becoming ever stronger,
each breath mining a vein of courage,
each word from Phillip a kind reminder that it will take time,
each glance of dignity within this young warrior beginning the process of
      transforming those eyes into amber diamonds,
that by the year 2063 C.E.—long after my death and the deaths of Fred and
      Mary—when Jean-Pierre will himself be more than eighty years old,
when I am nothing more than a small beetle embedded in the amber of his eyes,
hopefully he shall have become the warrior who does not turn aside, deciding yet
      again, against all odds and the apathy of those surrounding him, to create
      a humanity more humane, more peaceful, more loving.

Who among us is prepared to accept his or her final moment, to accept even the
      fleeting and final moment now flowing across our flesh?
Who among us is prepared to accept that there shall ever be a last breath, that at
      some moment, whether today or a lifetime away, there shall not be
      another inhalation, though they who bear witness to our deaths shall
      afterwards take a deep breath, rise from the bedside and step into the
      moonlight, the sunshine, the earth luxuriant with life?
And is any one of us prepared to acknowledge that we have done with our lives
      what we did—no more and no less?
Are we prepared to acknowledge that with more profound courage and strength,
      with more patience and dignity we might have come closer to calming our
      strife and our greed?
Are we prepared to embrace the unavoidable fact that we did, once upon a time,
      save a life, or two, or perhaps twenty?

Am I then willing to accept that my dreams were only that, dreams? That my
      goals were only that, goals?
Am I willing to accept that my hopes were nothing more than that, hopes? That
      my thoughts were just that, thoughts?
Am I willing to accept that my opinions, my perceptions, my habits were only
      that, opinions, perceptions and habits?
Am I willing to curtail my greed for even a moment, long enough to be grateful
      for the gentle sunrise, the brilliant sunset, for the dying which gives our
      living potency?
Am I willing to relinquish my fierce attachments to objects, ideas, memories,
      abilities, dreams, bodily functions...?
Attachment to my beloved clouds, for instance, with their majesty, their ferocity,
      their nurturing,

to a past so very replete with music and poetry and love;
or to a future once envisioned as noteworthy, luxurious and comfortable.

Can I surrender my vanity, lowering the self-knotted veil of the ego enough to
        peer upon a landscape of unanticipated marvels,
to perceive even faintly the suffering of the person beside me, across from me;
to notice the famished young rabbit incessantly searching for a blade of
        nourishing grass in the midst of a severe drought?
Am I willing to relinquish my imagined autonomy and simply be a body within a
        body, floating upon the arms of the warm water?
Can I be content to be a small, nameless sapphire held in the hands of a man who
        has understood that there is little more to be said, that he and I are in a
        realm beyond words, that no verb or noun can speak of what we are to
        one another?
Can I remain supple beneath the crushing weight of destiny, the heat of death, to
        become in these days, weeks and months a shimmering diamond in the
        care of this man or that, or yet another
not one of whom is aware that there are silent jewels murmuring in his eyes, eyes
        which eloquently express the growing strength, courage, and dignity
        behind the unassuming façade?

Can I, as I stumble in the very midst of my journey, stop grasping long enough
        to realize that my illusions about the future, about non-being, are being
        destroyed by the arms, the chest of a young man,
the water challenging me to relinquish my fear of dying long enough to open my
        eyes to this moment,
to see, in the warm, dark amber or the glittering sapphire of another's eyes,
that I am safe, that I need have little fear of this journey toward a final breath,
the rhythmic pulsing of the heart of one man or another carrying me through the
        diamond clear water,
here where words and names cease to have power,
where my entire body has become merely another eye within the ancient, jewelled
        eyes of the Beloved,
where the only voice remaining is that of the water, the blood, the sap?

No longer are we two individuals peering at one another,
rather we have become the Eye that perceives Itself.

July 10, 2002

69. I TURN TO YOU

After a decade of living in this quiet, high desert landscape, I will soon be relocating to what was once the edge of a nearby city but is now its approximate though not historic center, to a neighborhood bustling with traffic, schools and shops, a move prompted by the fact that my deteriorating body can no longer endure these bucolically dusty, bumpy, and occasionally muddy roads, plus the additional thirty-five kilometers of asphalt whose traversal is required simply to get me to the swimming pool. While there are certainly many timely advantages to be gained from such a relocation—else I wouldn't bother—it is undeniable that there are also pangs of loss and moments of lamentation.

There is, for instance, the imminent adieu to the ever taller oak tree, planted ten years ago by my own hands expressly for ME, ME, ME, that I might enjoy the deep red of its regal autumn leaves in MY fiftieth, sixtieth, seventieth and so on, years; this now four-meter-high tree so like a lithesome adolescent, a tree which, in one of those pranks which the frolicky universe is daily playing upon my rickety life, I discover to my humbling surprise was in fact planted for someone else's gratification, for another's seventieth year. Of course I philosophically understood this when I put the little bastard twig in the ground, and yet isn't it true that most of us have scant physiological comprehension of our philosophical fancies, that when they up and slap us full in the face we run about in circles, whimpering and whining, entirely affronted by such pugnacious attitude and wanting nothing less than to plot utter revenge upon what amounts to little more than our own thoughts, our own beliefs?

Oh lamentations, I tell you, lamentations!

To think of my furry, feathery beasty friends, and how they will miss my scintillating monologues, the innocent little creatures ever ruing the day of my departure, for who other than ME, MYSELF and I will take the time to listen to their Arcadian woes and their adorably humble dreams of a better life? That this relationship is a complete falsehood nurtured in the human imagination does not keep me from pining for these anthropomorphized creatures before I've even packed my pearls—the gliding hawks and hooting owls, the glee clubs of impudently bawdy coyotes, the blue-tailed lizards and the non-blue-tailed lizards, the fuzzy bunnies and the lanky jackrabbits, the family of quails all in a strutting line, the industrious beetles, the migratory flocks of birds. . .even the black widow spiders in the decrepit outhouse, the raucously omnipresent indigo crows and the occasional tarantula or rattlesnake. Truly, as I write these prophetic words those creatures are keening their lamentations over my departure—or are they merely expressing a cackling of immense relief, a cacophony of victorious delight at the removal of at least one of the destructive, polluting, imperialistically domineering hominids in their midst?

As you may well imagine, I will certainly miss the vistas and the solitude, the former for their grandeur—five seemingly eternal mountain ranges plus an entire opera of majestic clouds performed daily—the latter for its sustenance of that queerly human creative urge which so often needs to sit and suck its thumb, or to meander off on aimless strolls, pondering the formal structure of the universe, the rhythm of life, and the cadence of death. Additionally, the nocturnal vistas here can be nearly as stunning as those of the daytime, for without the intrusion of urban lights, nor a veil of low altitude humidity, the edge of the universe feels startlingly near as one peers into a starscape abundantly ornamented with comets, constellations, and galaxies, with meteors, moons, and nebulae, with wandering planets and human-made satellites, as well as the ever familiar merry-go-round of a Milky Way, that great swath of stellar gauze populated by an immense family of solar sisters and brothers, planetary comrades and neighbors, the lot of them held together from a central throne by a domineering, secretive old aunt of a black hole.

There is also for me the necessary abandonment of any former illusions of vigorous autonomy, those meager and disastrous efforts to grow one's own food in the middle of a drought-riddled desert, of building one's own house, of maintaining one's own motorbike, and of one day dying self-sufficiently and in a timely manner, without niggling bureaucratic interference, undue fuss or prolonged agony, certainly without an entourage of volunteers, aides and nurses. Truly, the number of our illusions is superceded only by the near infinite noise of our unruly thoughts, these latter so apt to scamper about without supervision, throwing tantrums whenever we tell them to behave, insidiously sneaking up on us from behind and scaring the shit out of us just when we had an inkling of devekut, of satori, of bliss and the me-less nature of four-dimensional space-time, of an eleven-dimensional universe burbling among an incalculable roster of multiple universes.

Certainly living in the middle of the city not far from where I do my water therapy will make the logistics of transportation much easier, a definite boon. Presumably guys will more willingly take ten minutes out of their schedules to tote the gimp homeward than eighty minutes with no assurance of ever getting disentangled from the maze of dirt roads cunningly rearranged each night by coyotes howling with ululating laughter at the looks of desperation on the faces of confused motorists. Though for Lou, since he currently lives somewhat near me out in the middle of nowhere, it has been merely a matter of a few additional kilometers beyond his own destination, thus making it relatively easy for him to fetch me home from the pool in recent months.

In my worthy opinion, I think you would like Lou.

Yes, if you had to choose a guy to be in a car accident with, I would without hesitation recommend Lou.

Or Phillip.

Which is precisely how Phillip and I met Lou—a car accident.

It occurred the very first time Phillip gave me a lift, kindly offering to drive me from the pool to the cathedral where I was to meet up with Pete, and in one of those ironies of life, as Phillip was stowing me away in the passenger seat he jokingly warned me about the risk of getting into a vehicle with a New York driver.

Then wouldn't you know. . .

A woman ran a stop sign at full speed and broadsided us.

I hasten to assure you that the accident was NOT the fault of my New York driver; nor did the now flustered, distraught woman appear to be pursuing a vendetta against New York drivers. It was just one of those moments in life, complete with wheelchair stowed in the back, a rather dramatic smash-up which we each survived without major injury, except for the vehicles, one of which required a mortician, the other a cosmetic surgeon. Much to my great misfortune, however, neither Phillip nor I had the presence of mind to inform the attending police officer that my face had been wrinkle free and my tummy as smooth as sculpted marble BEFORE the accident and consequently I myself would be needing the services of a cosmetic surgeon every bit as much as the damaged vehicle. In spite of this lapse, and with the magic of cell phone technology, calls were placed to such and whom, including one to Pete's office whence a short time later Lou arrived, a knight in shining armor camouflaged for the sartorially casual early twenty-first century as an unassuming engineer, a complete stranger gallantly prepared to finish toting me and my wheelchair the short distance to the cathedral.

If transporting a gimp within the city limits is this complicated and requires that many people, imagine how much more complex it becomes when adding thirty-five kilometers of motorway and a labyrinth of gnarly dirt roads. Oh that Zsolt were merely content to sit at home and watch endless, nauseating hours of television. But no, the bloke's got it in his droll head to go splashing about in the municipal swimming pool, and to attend performances of theater and music, thus wheeling along public thoroughfares in his powerchair, inadvertently upsetting unsuspecting motorists who had been led to believe that the last of his kind had been locked away following the HOMELAND CIVIL DECENCY AND SECURITY ACT OF 1849.

Yet, in spite of such attempts at a normally functioning life, and even with my routine trips to the pool and an occasional excursion hither and yon, the tangible world is for me ever decreasing, becoming ever more restricted as my body deteriorates. And perhaps it is this particular aspect of illness or decrepitude which so confounds each of us as we in turn journey toward death, the nine-year-old boy with leukemia alongside the ninety-nine-year-old woman whose body has simply worn out. It is also this which is perhaps the most dominant characteristic of the culture of dying, for each and every person in the process of dying, regardless of age, locality and personality, will experience and can speak of loss in ways that the more-or-less healthy simply cannot grasp, vivaciously as they may try.

Imagine for yourself that you have just awoken from a pleasant sleep, discovering to your immense consternation—for it would be that—that you cannot speak, for example, or you cannot walk, and you can no longer drive yourself in your beloved car or truck; you cannot cook your favorite meals, you cannot hope to go to Africa as you had planned, and after paying off the medical bills there is now no longer enough money for you to go shopping for new clothes, even though the ones you have are stained because food keeps falling out of your mouth, and even when it does go in it tends to go into your lungs as often as your stomach and in the process of choking you lose control of your bladder, pissing in your pants, a mess you haven't the strength to clean up because in addition to everything else you are in constant pain and discomfort. . .

Without a doubt you have made valiant attempts to imagine yourself in such a position. Yet I would wager that you failed utterly—unless, of course, you are already for whatever reason living in such or a similar state. There is no need to feel embarrassed at being incapable of imagining such an existence of extreme loss. After all, many of you, if you are not killed suddenly in an accident or do not happen to die swiftly of a heart attack at the healthy-ish age of, say, fifty or sixty, will eventually find yourself in a position in which you need not imagine such loss, as it will be by then the dominant dynamic of your life, monthly, daily, hourly.

Certainly you cannot imagine *how* ruthlessly lonely it is, even when among a lively crowd or in the midst of loved ones.

You cannot imagine how you could ever feel so useless and burdensome, let alone superfluous, needful and unappealing. . .

How the truth of your life is now this pang of physical agony, this ever-present lassitude and weakness, and perhaps waves of recurrent nausea; is this leg that won't walk, this arm that won't lift, and perhaps a bladder or sphincter you cannot control; is a mind that forgets what it forgot and a breath that refuses to breathe. . .

How most people around you have little to no experience of the dying processes of the terminally ill, offhandedly negating the depth of your needs and denying the intensity of your feelings; inadvertently clothing you in their anxiety your eyes and nostrils and ears. . .

How out of a worldwide population of over six billion people and from among the thousands who have crossed paths with you, a small cadre of individuals will become immensely, intensely important to you, the contours of their hands carved upon your faltering heart. . .

How your true comrade will show himself by the quality of the stillness he engenders as he holds you during your moments of deepest anguish, by the touch of his wordless hand upon your flesh, unhurried, without judgment, and neutral with love; a comrade in whose presence you feel neither lonely nor superfluous, neither needful nor burdensome. . .

And with each enlightening loss, with each pang of remorse allowed to float away, each twinge of frustration permitted to blossom and then wither, the realization gradually unfolds within you that these days, these hours are blessed with a richness of being, of existence quite unlike those of any other time in your life, though the details of these hours are so terribly banal, my friends—truly, an exciting travel brochure they would not make.

On this point you can ask Lou.

Because once again we are sitting in his truck, riding over the arching back of the earth, a mostly nonverbal journey occasionally shaped by Lou's humorous comments on life, a brief anecdote from his day at work or a story about how his almost-three-year-old son refers to his mother's yoga classes as her "yogurt classes;" Lou's few sentences accompanied on my part by squeaky attempts to chortle, attempts which due to my weakened chest muscles erupt more as falsetto belches than any laughter known to humankind, more coyotic than anthropic;

> the constant purr of the truck's motor interwoven with the flight paths of crows and finches,
> Lou's occasional words followed by long, comforting silences,
> and asphalt;
> our journey hallowed by azure blue skies,
> and more asphalt;
> then dust,
> dust,
> and more dust;
> the atmosphere textured by dramatic clouds one day, eternal blue another;
> a hawk above us, layers of receding mountains on the horizon.

One month we were accompanied by blossoming clover along the roadside, while in another sunflowers struggled to bloom in the serest of reincarnations.

And soon enough, in the weeks ahead, these kilometers of asphalt and dirt will be replaced by the shorter increments of city blocks; the mountains by layers of juxtaposed houses, humble in their huddled demeanor, inhabited by a variety of people young and old.

Pigeons will take the place of the hawk and the vulture; domestic dogs and cats standing in for antelope, coyotes and rabbits.

While the choruses of crickets, easily and happily placed in fictitious bamboo cages for the transition, will come along; for to be sure, it appears crickets are as happy there as here.

And it is this, this evening chirping of the crickets' legs, ever a delight to my ears, which reminds me once again of a fundamental choice in the human predicament, namely that while this imminent and necessary relocation does indeed provoke moments of poignancy, in the end I can and do opt not to be sorrowful, for the light in my heart goes with me wherever, if I so choose, and needs neither stunning landscape nor pristine solitude in order to fulfill its destiny, this light that need not be darkened merely because of a change of abode, or because of the deterioration of my body. Nor need I let it be extinguished by the anxiety, the discomfiture, and the shame felt by some when in the presence of what for a few of us is an unexpectedly long, autumnal Dance of Death, an elongated cadence of an ever slowing, ever quieter pavane.

As I gaze transfixed into the swath of a carousel which has been quaintly dubbed the Milky Way, its starry milk pouring out of a celestial teapot, I turn to you, confirming with unabashed joy that the journey, in spite of the physical anguish, the daunting changes and the ineffable loneliness, is totally awesome, my friends, totally awesome.

September 2, 2002

72. HANUMAN'S GIFT

Thousands of years ago, long before this you and this I were born, a most unprecedented event came to pass on the Indian subcontinent...

In order to show the depths of his devotion to Sri Rama, Hanuman the Monkey ripped open his own rib cage to reveal his pulsing heart, a heart upon which were emblazoned the letters of his beloved friend's name, not once but a multitude of times...

Rama Rama Rama Rama Rama...

Rama...

Rama...

Rama...

Rama...

Times being what they were, the faithful Hanuman did not perish from this selfless display of his devotion; instead he insouciantly closed up his rib cage, blithely ignoring the wet blood tangled in the hairs of his chest, before giving Sri Rama a friendly thwack on the head for being such an insecure little twit of a deity, then scampered off into the forest from whence he would continue his amity with Rama throughout the latter's ensuing lives.

Yes, eons ago one of the world's great religions taught humanity the foundations of caring. Had there been no intervening technological advances, no new religious developments, no additional cultural or political innovations, we would yet know how to care for one another. As it is, in spite of the births of new religions, in spite of humanity's astonishing trajectories, one might say fireworks of technological innovation and cultural efflorescence, we are today little nearer to comprehending the ancient gesture of Hanuman and consequently making it our own, than were the men and women who first heard this tale of the abiding friendship between Hanuman the Monkey, Son of the Wind, and Sri Rama of Ayodhya.

With this in mind, one wonders what words we would discover today were we to metaphorically open the rib cages of any number of caregivers among us, be they family, friends or professionals, thereby exposing those hearts to scrutiny? To be perfectly frank, it is doubtful we should find an abundance of golden glyphs scattered in among the viscera, let alone entire words of a devotional, compassionate nature. We would rather be more likely to find an unsettled, indistinct mass composed of varying syllables expressing impatience, weariness, inattention, peevishness and ennui, possibly even selfishness, resentment, repugnance and malice. After all, these are individuals who, though generally of good intentions, often find themselves at the bedside of the invalid solely because of professional duty or familial obligation, rather than from any selfless devotion to the person in their care.

Well do I know, having been a caregiver myself, both by profession and as a volunteer; hours, days and years caring for strangers as well as friends. And while I was considered a dedicated, sensitive caregiver, I can nevertheless state unconditionally that there were moments when my own heart bore few words remotely resembling compassion, to say nothing of devotion, as I trudged sleepily from bedside to bedside at three o'clock in the morning, pushing before me my designated cart loaded with adult-proportioned disposable diapers, with a paltry assortment of medical supplies and the ubiquitous plastic waste bag for soiled diapers, my heart certainly not in any mood to hear the seventy-eight-year-old Lloyd screaming, "GET AWAY FROM ME, YOU SON OF A BITCH! YOU'RE A FUCKING BASTARD, YOU SON OF A BITCH!!!"

I cannot deny that there were times when I barely had it in me to brush the few rotting teeth hidden inside the clenched mouth of a recalcitrant patient or to clean the feces and urine off the withered body of yet another lonely, bewildered elder, my mind fixated only on being somewhere else, walking in the resplendent mountains, for instance, or being pleasantly ensconced at home playing the piano or writing poetry, drinking cup after cup of stout tea, a sip of sherry—bon vivant and so forth and so on—anything but being burdened with the never-ending needs and gluttonous desires of the Lord of Death, feelings which to varying degrees were unmistakably evident in the eyes of the rest of the nursing staff as we wearily reconvened after our rounds, even the eyes of those I considered most compassionate, most devoted. Yet there was also, particularly in the faces of these latter individuals, an unmistakable sense of contentment from having at least attempted to make the lives of these elderly and disabled citizens more comfortable; of having worked together as a team; of having brought succor, possibly even joy into the solemn hours of the darkest mornings of the year; of being the randomly chosen guides who unwittingly and unpretentiously accompanied many souls toward the *bardo* and into a world beyond our ken.

To be sure, many were the times when my heart simply overflowed with devotion for the patient in my care, from the almost adolescent, severely disabled Jeremiah to the elderly, white-haired Bess. It would be a meager heart indeed that did not find itself sincerely devoted to gentle Bess, she who was eternally grateful for anything and everything we did for her, whether bathing and massaging her wrinkled skin, or putting a clean diaper on her plump, naked body, or brushing her long snowy hair; her round face ever content as I kissed her good night, no matter that it was already the third time in eight hours and very nearly daybreak, Bess's mind easily drifting back into the enchanted arms of sleep.

On the other hand, undoubtedly many of the elderly people I cared for found me to be little more than an energetic nip of a nelly, rather like an exuberant dog they once owned, a puppy they thought would never learn to sit still, those many years ago. After all, my institutionalized patients were, with the exception of a few severely disabled children and young adults, much older than myself—one of the women in my care celebrated her eighty-second birthday while I myself was gaily prancing about in my mother's womb inventing words to rhyme with orange. In order to keep you from the psychological angst of a mathematical story problem, I will tell you without delay that Isabella was indeed 106 years old, her tiny, tiny body often curled up in a fetal position, her mind still lucid enough to express her annoyance whenever the aides and nurses moved too quickly or too abruptly in the never-ending cycle of trying to care for a full roster of patients with an understaffed crew.

I suppose it could be said that for the most part I was very patient, even indulgent with those in my care. One particular resident, who lost her sight and had a leg amputated as a result of her advanced diabetes, referred to me as *mi conejito* (my little bunny). A rather cantankerous, strong-willed woman, Flora was quite capable of easily and flawlessly recognizing my footsteps in the corridor—a little too much prancing, perhaps, or an irrepressible pirouette erupting among my steps?—and woe to me if I passed by her room without an encouraging word, or more precisely, an accommodating ear for her unceasing miseries, unburdened to me during the darkest hours of insomnia.

Yet in spite of my own self-motivated dedication to quality care, I nevertheless erred now and then, at times rather indecorously. For example, I will never forget the day I yelled at a patient, a man who grabbed my beard, essentially pinning me into a kneeling position, and yanked and yanked until there were tears of pain in my eyes. I suppose one could call my explosion of annoyance self-defense. Even so, it isn't something to be proud of, is it?

What can I say? I was young; I was barely experienced; I did the best I could in the midst of these decades, these centuries of ours in which citizens are shown how to read a few words, how to sum a few figures, how to consume products rapaciously, how to fulfill their desires and cater to their private needs, but in which few are taught anything remotely resembling compassion, leaving most of us to flail about in the very situations in which no other action will suffice except that of the compassionate heart, this arcane gesture which in the end eludes many if not the vast majority of us simply because it is so utterly nonsensical, so mythically simple.

Certainly the concept of devotion as the foundation of a caring ethos has been mostly nonexistent across the world I have encountered, regardless of the rhetoric flouted by adherents of various religious, ethical and medical systems.

Yes, a person is expected, sort of, maybe, to be devoted to one's family or clan, possibly a religious figure, a reigning monarch, a dictator or, very often, a current popular entertainer. But to one another? You have *got* to be joking! Only a fool would propose such silliness. And do tell, where would such a preposterous notion lead us? Devotion to the homeless chap on the street corner? Or the felon locked behind bars? Or the suicide terrorist strapping herself into carefully-assembled bomb-laden clothing?

Ah, but such is compassion—which is not to be confused with approbation or condonation—and believe me, it ain't easy.

And it ain't easy because most of us cannot grasp the paradigm of an infinite love dwelling in a finite heart, opting instead to insist that there simply isn't enough room on our hearts to engrave the names of over six billion human beings—a disproportionate number of them rather distasteful to us—let alone extending such graciousness to the often violent and always unpredictable processes of the natural world. Therefore we begin early on to make categories—one person fits into our hearts because she is beautiful or successful or has a respectable religious or reputable professional affiliation that neatly aligns with our sensibilities, while another person is excluded because, well, you know, her body has an unusual odor in addition to the obvious fact that she wears the most outlandish hats and espouses the weirdest ideas. Of course the most ludicrous aspect of this categorical game is that each of us to some extent firmly believe ourselves to be in the former category, when in fact we are quite as likely to fall into the latter. I myself have often been placed in the latter—the rejects, as it were—by upstanding, civic-minded citizens. For instance, some years ago I stopped by the office building of one of my adult students in order to discuss a scheduling problem. Panting slightly as I removed my bicycle helmet, I politely asked the receptionist at the front desk to point me in the direction of my student's office. Without bothering to take my name, the receptionist quickly disappeared behind a door and did not return for nearly a quarter of an hour, at which point my student herself appeared and said with an unusual inflection, "Oh! It's only you, Zsolt."

I later found out that the receptionist was convinced I was dangerous, carrying a bomb or something, and that they had spent the quarter of an hour trying to decide whether to call in the police.

To detain *me*?

Me?

El conejito? The little bunny?

How, I ask you, how could there not be room in her heart for a little bunny!

But to proceed with the tale, my friends, by returning to ancient India…

Here, or rather then and there, we have Hanuman the Monkey with his chest flagrantly open for any and all to witness this extraordinary display of devotion to his friend.

What then is Sri Rama's response?

What is the only dignified response available to him?

Gratitude, of course.

Yes, gratitude, my friends.

And now you are laughing!

You chortle and snortle, snickering and sniggering.

Somehow you find the answer even more silly than the question.

So perhaps you think it is easy to be grateful.

Well then, just you go ahead and try it.

Come back in a week and tell me how well you managed.

Then, you tell me, were you grateful?

Were you grateful when some chap cleaned your butt for you? If you were lucky, he was gentle.

Were you grateful when your legal guardian made arrangements to place you in a dismal, foul-smelling institution? It really is for the best, you know.

And how grateful were you when the aide assigned to your bed decided she couldn't be bothered to change your diaper because you're too tall or too fat...

Too black or too white...

Too crazy or cranky or smelly and anyway nearly dead.

Think how many lives it took Rama to learn gratitude, and you sit there sniggering as though it were the silliest notion in the world.

No, no, no, being grateful is no such easy task.

Believe me, yes, I should know about these things.

You see, several years ago when a couple of guys first started helping me at the pool, I would naturally tell them, "Thank you." But these two little words, they seemed so insignificant compared with what these chaps, blessed be their names, were doing for me.

So I decided after a while that three words were better than two, that I would no more say, "Thank you." Instead I would say, "I love you," and say it with sincerity!

Well, ladies and gentlemen, you can just imagine, two guys there at the edge of the municipal swimming pool, and one guy turns to the other and he says...he says, "I love you."

You still think it's easy, eh?

Then you try it this week.

You take your mechanic or else some chap you've met in passing, and you take this fellow down to the swimming pool locker room and you say to him in front of a bunch of naked guys, "I love you."

Then you come to me and you tell me whether it was easy or not.

Because this is one of the core gestures of caring, and these gestures, they
    are all related, you see, like links in a chain...
    ...devotion-love-gratitude-love-devotion...

Truly, it takes a surprising amount of grace and acceptance to learn how to be
        fully grateful, and to express it with one's entire being—
not a sniveling, obsequious gratitude, not a haughty, moral gratitude, nor a
        superficial, obligatory gratitude,
but a warmth of deep thankfulness, a sturdy bridge built one stone at a time, year
        upon year...
realizing that as I have been painstakingly building the pier of such a bridge in
        the watery shallows on my side of the river,
there on the distant shore an odd, anachronistic chap with several heads
        and many arms has been building a similar pier upon which to secure the
        stones and beams of what would become a bridge constructed between
        two distinct embankments,
each of the stones, each of the steel girders being set into place through careful
        observation and diligent practice.
On his part, his several heads and many arms are dedicated to making sure my
        needs are faithfully met,
on mine, a surrendering to the truth of this eternal moment.
Through such diligence on both our parts it was perhaps inevitable that there
        would come a moment of synchronicity,
in which the final stone was duly set into place, its perfect fit creating a solid,
        beautifully arcing structure,
the two of us wordlessly facing one another high above the ever-flowing river, my
        blue eyes peering into his many, our glistening rib cages torn asunder
        by life.
And as with any structure seen by those who had no role in erecting it, no one
        will ever truly know the amount of effort, of attention, of devotion and
        gratitude needed to keep the whole thing from collapsing in midair, or
        from ultimately not meeting in the middle,
that as the shadow of Hanuman himself scampers off into the twilit forest,
we are in this hallowed moment, as the wintry night long ago wreathed the snowy
        head of gentle Bess, blessed by Hanuman's selfless gift.

September 26, 2002

73. IN THE FINAL SURRENDERING

In the final surrendering tides of our mortal lives,
we will be astonished at how intransigently wrong,
how preciously smug we were about a surprising number of things;
and though such a tolling of tides be far distant from the worldly fury
        of everyday activities,
the subtle waves themselves rise to the fore within the demanding stillnesses
        of silent meditation,
these quiet valleys of gentle contemplation,
of routinely dying to the grand old bustle
and facing an uncompromising, unornamented truth.

Stripped naked in the presence of an unbounded nothingness
and relentlessly shown one's prodigious opinions,
one's sanctimonious, stone-throwing judgments,
one's ceremonious schemata of self,
a person is humbled almost beyond endurance,
certainly beyond structure,
beyond yesterday and tomorrow;
until the nearly insufferable stillness expands into an unmitigated depth within,
into this garden of simple delight
and cosmic jest,
suffused in first light,
made lustrous by the pure, opalescent spectrum of being;
one's very blood radiating an insouciant respect for the kaleidoscopic progeny
        of nothingness.

Ever after is the parody of parodies revealed,
that to hear again the earnest soliloquies of one's former days played out
        in the theaters of memory,
or propounded anew in the splendid mouths of others,
is agonizingly comic in the extreme;
and perhaps this then is wisdom—

this realization,
at some subtle point within,
that like the universe itself,
one ought simply have said nothing at all—

that it is enough to be
intrinsically,
graciously
radiant.

October 2, 2002

75. SLAUGHTER

Undoubtedly the common housefly is a domestic annoyance
of a truly unrepentant sort,
utilizing the most sophisticated of guerrilla tactics,
ranging from expert dive-bombing to psychological intimidation.

And what pesky rogues we are in return,
monstrously rampaging through cozy kitchens,
our frenzied, impatient arms slicing the air;
our reputedly intelligent faces peevishly bloated, offensively distorted;
our miraculous hands brandishing plastic fly-swatters ingeniously manufactured
        for the sole purpose of killing;
our cute and morally superior mouths unhinged with ungodly expletives
as we gleefully encourage the cat to paw and devour a devious fly;
while above our coiffured heads innocent creatures torturously perish,
their wings, feet and proboscides mortally glued to fatally sticky fly strips
        hung enticingly from innocent ceilings—

such imaginatively gruesome slaughter,
it may be noted,
as has traditionally
and historically
been perpetrated
upon a colorful panoply of undesirable creatures,
among them the unrepentant martyrs of many faiths.

October 10, 2002

80. CLOSER AND CLOSER

While there are no clear and easy solutions to humanity's dilemmas...

All across Hungary, as I had trekked hundreds of kilometers on foot toward this border, passing numerous military installations vacated in recent months by the once occupying forces of the Soviet Union, I had been told countless times not to enter Romania; that with political upheaval and civil strife quickly escalating into what could become civil war, it was sheer madness to even consider crossing the border. Additionally, were I foolish enough to insist on going, then I would be even more of a fool to utter a word of Hungarian, its use severely restricted by the Romanian government in an attempt to suppress and assimilate the large Hungarian minority bequeathed to it upon the dissolution of the Austro-Hungarian empire at the conclusion of what was called the "War to End All Wars."

Thus, irrepressibly daft as ever, I found myself walking along a lonely road in Transylvania, in the western region of Romania, toward what my map indicated was an Orthodox monastery. To the east, the capital city of Bucharest was awash in riots, the government was being more ruthless than ever in its suppression of a burgeoning democratic movement, many of its roots here in the western regions. The political tension was extraordinary, yet the mulberry tree I had just walked by was in full fruit, my youthful limbs warmed by the sun's sumptuous summer rays.

Late in the afternoon a car stopped alongside the road. After pointing to my destination on the map, I was offered a lift the last few kilometers to the isolated monastery, which turned out in fact to be a convent occupied by three very elderly nuns who accepted my unannounced arrival with aplomb and accommodatingly welcomed me into their simple world, our entire dialogue consisting of pantomime, laughter and the few words of Hungarian which one of the sisters had learned growing up among Hungarian neighbors, years and years ago, before the governmental proscription of these nouns and verbs.

The following day, after a good night's rest, I asked the sisters what I could do to be of help, an offer which, once understood, was immediately and unanimously rejected. Even though I was a complete stranger who had appeared out of nowhere, I was their guest. In spite of this generous policy, I persisted in my offer. There had to be something that needed doing, something that only a fuzzy-chested young fairy of an antelope could accomplish.

"Cherries," the one sister replied obligingly after some persuasion on my part.

So cherries it was, and throughout that warm, soft day and into the next, I climbed the massive old cherry trees on the quiet convent grounds, picking basket after basket of succulently ripe sweet cherries, to the utter pleasure of the three elderly nuns.

On the Saturday evening a priest arrived and invited me to join him in the common room, where he was watching televised news stories about the tension spreading throughout the country. Not understanding much Romanian—in fact, I could only count to twelve—I thanked him for his invitation and instead returned to the kitchen to assist the nuns, who had more pressing things to deal with than watching people get coshed on national television, namely mounds of freshly picked cherries which, when preserved, would last them throughout the coming winter, were they to survive that long.

> *While there are no clear and easy solutions to humanity's dilemmas,*
> *I shall nevertheless continue to believe...*

The kid was twelve years old.

I will always think of him as a kid, though by now he would be approximately thirty-five, if he remains alive. And I thought of him then as a kid because I was so much older. On that evening of our encounter, as a graceful autumn bowed to an insistent winter, I myself was a wise old man of nineteen, my vigorous, lithe body, so recently that of a child's, protected from the wintry elements by an enormous hand-woven alpaca poncho purchased some months earlier on the far side of the globe.

It was a cold, wet December night when I alit from a train in northern Germany only to discover that the British friend who was supposed to greet me was nowhere to be found, nor was I able to reach her by telephone. For an hour I waited and called, walked about and called again, but to no effect. It was at some point during this vain searching and unanswered telephoning that the solitary Turkish boy joined me in my dilemma, and however it happened that our lives converged, it seemed the most natural turn of events. When it became apparent that my friend had been seriously waylaid and detained, the kid suggested we set off on foot in search of her flat, which he felt fairly certain was not too far from the train station. Dividing my worldly possessions betwixt us, we jauntily set off through the cold wintry streets, he chattering to me delightedly about his favorite pop music stars and asking me about mine, causing me to ponder whether Beethoven would be a proper answer to his dark, alert eyes, the kid obviously enjoying this badinage, this unexpected camaraderie blossoming in the midst of coldest December.

After a short time and a bit of travail we found my friend's flat and the note on the door telling me she had been called away at the last minute for an unscheduled rehearsal and would be back at such and such a time; that if I had made my way this far, I was to wait for her here. I translated the note for the sake of the kid, whose command of English consisted mostly of names of pop stars, along with some parroted lyrics from their songs, which was anyway more than I knew of Turkish. Having reached this denouement in our story and not knowing what else to do, I reached beneath my voluminous poncho and into my pocket for a few Deutsch marks to proffer him as recompense for assisting me. Perhaps I assumed this was the only reason he had offered to help me, to get some money; or perhaps I simply wanted to be courteously reciprocal. Whatever the impetus for my action, his response was a dramatic gesture of refusal.

"Remember," he said, "we're friends."

There we stood, two kids in the dim light of a chilly, nondescript postwar corridor, his lustrous dark eyes, my shining blue.

For the first time since our lives had coincided at the train station we both became quiet, as often happens on such occasions when the rallying assignment is over, the search complete.

After a few silent moments, he said he ought best be getting home, as it was already quite late.

Emulating the world's leading statesmen, we shook hands, the only acceptable international adieu for emergent manly men.

There we were, two kids, emissaries on the verge of forever, whose spontaneous coming together and subsequent engagement in human dialogue across chasms of culture and language would in the ensuing decades rarely be emulated by purportedly mature world leaders who would instead claim specious moral superiorities as their basis for shunning one another.

Then it was just me, sitting on my baggage in a lonely corridor in the industrial north of Germany, waiting for my friend to come home, thankful for the intervening companionship of a Turkish boy guiding me perceptively through the city's streets, all the while entertaining me with soprano renditions of the latest popular songs.

> *While there are no clear and easy solutions to humanity's dilemmas,*
> *I shall nevertheless continue to believe*
> *that vibrant, flexible minds...*

Many years ago, on a nearly blossoming spring day during the labyrinthine darkness of the cold war, I was among a troupe of young dancers touring the Soviet Union. Though our schedules were generally tightly controlled, we were nonetheless given one or two free mornings to roam about and do as we pleased. On one of these occasions two British friends and I decided to search for a museum of musical instruments which we had read about in a guidebook. Finding the building with relative ease, we entered its massive doors and were politely told, using pantomime along with a strange mélange of German and French verbs, since the three of us were not even vaguely conversant in Russian, that the museum was closed for renovation—indeed, one could see corners of display cases covered in cloths.

After being unexpectedly turned out of the museum, we found a nearby bench to sit on in order to discuss the altered situation. And there we remained a few minutes later, three ballerinas in their mid-teens with nothing better to do than gossip and dream, when the door of the museum opened and we were beckoned back inside. True, the museum was closed to the public due to the renovations, but the director, for some reason, had decided to show us through the museum in spite of its official closure. Thereupon and during the ensuing hours he proceeded to peel cloths off of displays in order to show us the treasury of musical instruments under his care—Chinese pipas and Indian tablas, peasant dudelsacks and mediaeval sackbuts, baroque clavichords and Japanese kotos, Russian balalaïkas and Hungarian cimbaloms, ancient lyres and plaintively silent hurdy-gurdies—other members of the museum staff joining us at intervals.

Why this courtesy to three unknown, unimportant kids remains a mystery to me to this day. The leaders of our respective countries were sworn enemies barely capable of sitting in the same room, though certainly capable of obliterating most of life on the planet with the weapons of mass destruction they had amassed in only a few insecure, nervous decades. Yet, without even a basic knowledge of one another's languages, and certainly without official sanction, a small group of citizens from these ideologically warring empires had spontaneously joined together to marvel at the tools, the instruments of humanity's music, of that which is capable of bringing joy to our hearts, of expressing our inconsolable sorrows, of elevating us to dignity, and of also serving as a rowdy outlet for our innate bawdiness.

Following this unexpected and thoughtful display of entente, the three of us courteously bid the Russian adults farewell and stepped into a future that might, just might be created through joyfully constructive, mutually beneficent sharing rather than undignified warmongering, imperiously pompous threats and puerile name calling.

> *While there are no clear and easy solutions to humanity's dilemmas,*
> *I shall nevertheless continue to believe*
> *that vibrant, flexible minds*
>   *and fearlessly loving hearts...*

It was a habit of mine during my magically ambidextrous days in the theater, that after smoothly applying the foundational makeup to my face and neck, I would then use my left hand to apply assorted greasepaints, rouge and mascara onto the left side of my face, before proceeding to the other half and using my right hand to do the same for the right half—truly insufferable idiosyncrasy, to be sure, but there you have it, ladies and gentlemen.

One fine summer's day while on tour in provincial Ecuador, as I gazed through the window of the dance troupe's official bus, I noticed a fascinating old building standing unaccompanied alongside the thoroughfare. Later, as I sat alone applying my makeup for the comic role of an old man, I overheard the company director saying that our performance would be delayed an hour or two—I had already arrived at the theater much earlier than the others, who were undoubtedly still shopping for souvenirs or enjoying one last *cerveza*—and that he needed to run an emergency errand, a task which would take him past that same intriguing building. Interrupting his conversation, I precipitously asked him if he remembered the lonely building we had passed earlier in the afternoon, and could he please drop me there on his way, to fetch me on his return, a request to which he readily consented, whereupon he, the chauffeur and I hurriedly climbed into the big, empty bus to retrace the last leg of our journey.

Shortly thereafter, as I strolled around the grounds of the decrepit building looking for an unlocked entrance, I encountered a young lad about ten years old. After explaining my curiosity about the building, I was led to his mother, who happened to be the impoverished caretaker of what turned out to be a vacant schoolhouse. Though I don't suppose it is quite right to say the building was empty, for it was obviously the repository of a great number of untold stories floating about and embedded in its three-storied structure. Forthwith the woman and her son politely escorted me through the rooms of the desiccated building, quietly explaining bits and pieces of its history, before I bid them a courteous adieu, not wanting to spend too much time inside lest I delay the bus's return to the theater where, after all, we were still scheduled to perform.

Strolling out through the massive wrought iron gates that were the entrance to the school grounds, I took up my expectant position by the side of the road, peering contentedly along a bucolic ribbon of asphalt. It was as I stood there waiting that I suddenly realized to my chagrin that not only was my eighteen-year-old face wearing the heavy stage makeup of an old man, but only the left half of my face was finished. From the moment I had leapt up from the dressing room table and jumped eagerly onto the bus, I had completely forgotten I was wearing greasepaint of any kind, let alone only half a face full of cosmetic details such as wrinkles, hollows and a carefully limned bag under my left eye.

Several minutes later, the company bus pulled to the side of the thoroughfare and opened its doors, not even coming to a full stop as it swallowed me up to deliver me for what would turn out to be a most impressive performance complete with finished makeup and appropriate costuming.

Truly, I will never forget how utterly gracious the caretaker and her son were to what must have been the oddest of apparitions appearing at the end of an ordinary day in the life of an abandoned schoolhouse.

While there are no clear and easy solutions to humanity's dilemmas,
I shall nevertheless continue to believe
that vibrant, flexible minds
and fearlessly loving hearts,
will get us closer to sustainable, enduring answers
than will estranged hearts and intolerant minds.

November 7, 2002

81. MONDAY MORNINGS

—For Ramón Lucero

Here upon the rising shoulders of the distant sun,
in the early hours of this humble morning,
there is not a trace of colored glass to be seen,
nor the sculpted folds of an ancient cloak.
There is instead a mattress upon which you sit,
an edge of existence to which few are called,
an edge which few can inhabit with any nobility,
and fewer still will ever hallow by their mere presence.

Prior to this white-walled winter morning,
we had met only once, you and I,
in the early springtime of a shimmering window of stained glass;
you, unbeknownst to yourself, a saint
wrapped in a vitreous carmine cloak;
me, the arabesque of a leaf
ornamenting the edge of light.

Now in December,
as I awaken from a difficult sleep on an uncompromising morning,
my face partially covered and sealed with a mask
            connected by a tube
            to a whirring machine
            gently forcing air into my sluggish lungs,
you
are here
beside me, only the two of us;
and even after you have removed your black leather jacket,
I hardly recognize you
            without your paned cloak of saintly carmine.

No longer a vibrant window of leaded glass,
we are now a quiet painting painted centuries ago,
during a decade when we knew one another well;
a painting in which you, robed in iridescently sacred silks,
        were an angel;
me, a falcon perched on the gnarled branch of an oak tree,
        a falcon which,
when the painter turned briefly away,
glided down onto your shimmering sleeves,
resting on the bones and muscles of your arm;
this you who has come to rouse me from a stiffly curled sleep,
to care for me on this wintry morning.

And whoever you are, you are not the stranger you appear to be,
this much I know,
even as I motion you to accept the most honored seat in the house,
that of the caring comrade,
in this, our second meeting.

Nor do I know why you have volunteered to assist me,
what it is that prompted you to extend a warm, generous hand
        on a frigid day
        in the midst of a world
        rife with unrelenting need.
Yet regardless of your motives, be they simple or complex,
you have arrived on the flaming tongues of the rising sun,
entering the clear light of a nameless, numberless morning
to sit beside my silent body,
here upon the blanketed edge of a quiet bed.

You have come that the pain in my muscles might be dispersed
        through the warm, powerful touch of your hands;
that the once tepid urine in the now cold bottle might be emptied
and flushed into the bowels of the city;
that I might hear your resonant voice recite words
written by poets of justice,
        poets of ecstasy,
                poets facing the unutterable, the cruel, the sumptuous.
You have entered this plain room,
a pentagonal space smaller than any cathedral, mosque or synagogue,
that I might better understand how the wastelands of my existence,
this sweating skin,

these phlegmatic lungs,
        and the pungent excrement,
are to be redefined as symbols and maps
      guiding us toward kindness;
that I need not fear the shadow which falls upon us both,
a shadow not of darkness, nor of dread,
but of an ancient, fearless fraternity;
a shadow, a veil which envelops us, stirs us,
its rare filaments set aflutter by the movements of your hands
as you unlock the night's final door,
as you step through a strange, unfamiliar house in search of my bed,
as you take your place in an old painting which many have admired,
but few have ever touched,
and fewer still have explored, this landscape of fierce tenderness,
of one man tending to the needs of another
simply because it is the right thing to do,
his actions speaking as much of justice as of mercy.

And in this, though the path you tread be sparsely traveled,
you are not wholly alone,
for on another morning
      and another
          and another
in the cyclical unfolding of the recurrent weeks,
men whom you know and men you've never met
shall arrive to sit beside me,
      rousing me from sleep,
          to begin again this ritual of nursing.

A man's words come and they go,
the facts of his life are ever suspect;
but the simple truth of his hands remains unchanged,
pulling aside the warm blankets of these cold December mornings,
then the cotton linens,
      the gray clouds,
         the azure skies,
            the shadow itself,
to uncover these naked limbs
touched by the noble hands

of a tender soul
fierce enough
to face
the unknown
and not
flinch.

December 19, 2002

82. THAT WHICH WAS REVEALED

Now that I am living in a situation more conducive to visiting, several people have inquired about visitation protocol. Second only to bureaucratic paperwork, this is conceivably one of the most complicated aspects of living with an illness or disability. Unlike the drudgery of paperwork, however, the complications are not merely logistical but also emotionally and psychologically entwined.

In the past I would listen patiently as terminally ill people, or those who had become disabled through serious accidents, would lament the fact that many former co-workers, social cohorts and even some of their own children had incomprehensibly ceased to visit them. While nodding sympathetically, I smugly reassured myself that this would never happen to me. MY friends were much too devoted, you see; and had I had children, they would never do anything so pugnaciously unfilial. Alas, it is the things we are most smug about that turn around and slap us hardest in the face when push comes to shove.

A friend of mine who is dying was recently in the hospital undergoing major, though not life threatening surgery. By no means antisocial, she nevertheless requested no visitors, with the exception of a couple of friends who served as couriers. In the past, when imagining myself in such a situation, I would never have considered this option, and innocently assumed I would want to see everyone I knew, had known, and would ever come to know. At this time in my life, however, I fully understand her decision.

Truly, the rules are different now; indeed the whole game has been subverted, converted and thoroughly redecorated in a mishmash of seemingly confusing hues. What worked before no longer holds sway. In the lives of the ill and the disabled, all manner of subtleties arise to alter the physical and spiritual landscape, including the home environment along with one's relationships to those who cross its threshold.

Just today a woman and her daughter came for a planned visit. They were both in different stages of a vile stomach flu and had come simply to cancel the visit. As the daughter stepped to the edge of my bed to embrace me, the mother blurted out, "Don't get near him!" Since her work is in the medical field she was well of aware the havoc that stomach flu would wreak upon me. And while I was disappointed to miss the rare opportunity to catch up on the news of their lives, I was at the same time relieved to see them depart, because I really don't want to catch the stomach flu, nor the elbow flu, nor any flu, for that matter. Admittedly, I am not nearly so cavalier about pathogens as I once was in those halcyon days when I would recklessly taunt germs, because we'd all live forever anyway, thanks to youth and modern medicine, and anyway why let the specter of a little discomfort rule one's life?

Yes, in terms of visiting protocol, I find myself in an odd position, since this is not a hospital, in which visitors come and go as they may during specified visiting hours. Nor is it an able-bodied home, where the resident can readily scurry to the door and take care of a guest's every question, every need, in a traditionally hostess-like fashion. Nevertheless, though it may not be the latter, this is still a person's home, literally and figuratively, and some amount of respect is in order. For instance, how would you feel if someone walked in on you in your bedroom or bathroom without permission, without asking? I should imagine you'd be rather unpleasantly surprised, perhaps even mortified. Yet, this has happened to me more than I would have thought possible, making for some needlessly embarrassing moments for all involved. And how would you feel were a visitor to boss your pets around without permission, move your wheelchair or turn off your music without asking? These things have also occurred more often than I could have imagined. And perhaps most galling, I have even had guests tell me that if I don't like their behavior, tough luck for me.

Perhaps you have seen Bette Davis and Joan Crawford in *Whatever Happened to Baby Jane?* They didn't make that up, you know. It isn't science fiction. They took the everyday lives of the disabled and the invalid, exaggerating the experience for horror, but not so much that it became farcical. In some sense, that film is potentially the life of every invalid, though usually—I say usually—without the sinister intentions. For instance, the other day someone used my computer, then left the house without putting back the chair he'd needed, therefore I was unable to get to the computer until someone else came along to move the chair. And it is surprisingly not uncommon for visitors to forget to put things back where they found them, often frustratingly out of my reach—an unobservant habit that would be truly cruel in the house of a blind person. This may seem insignificant to you, but it points out how different the rules are, because our every minor action as guests, those habits that in the able-bodied world would be nearly insignificant, now take on magnified proportions and possibly disastrous physical or psychological consequences.

What to do? In terms of guests bursting in at inopportune times, my aides know to tell visitors to wait until my personal needs are taken care of before the visitor is asked into my room. In spite of this, people often follow my aide right into the bedroom without waiting for him to prepare me for their visit. On one occasion when my guests did just this, they walked in while I was using my urinal in order that I wouldn't have to worry about a full bladder during the ensuing visit. I realize that these mishaps shouldn't matter in the greater scheme of things—it's just a piece of meat, as they say—and while you may consider this a great personal flaw, I am not terribly thrilled about having any old Tom, Pat and Mary wander in to watch me piss and shit. Meanwhile the solution is so simple— listen to my caregiver, respect his position in my life and wait until he gives the go-ahead.

Matters are different when I am alone, though the premise of respect remains much the same. This is a very small house, so it is quite easy for a guest to announce him- or herself, then sit and wait. If I am in the middle of meditating or writing, it may take me a few minutes to transition and get myself into a different mental framework before wheeling out to see someone. Or I may be in the midst of a few minutes of personal care and really don't want guests involved. If a person is in such a hurry that he or she cannot sit for a few minutes reading one of the many books from the bookshelves, then I am not convinced that his or her visit would have been of much value to either party.

If I am in bed, and therefore unable to wheel out to see a guest, I can ring my bell to let him or her know that the coast is clear—or I can not ring it if it is an inappropriate time for a visit. A couple of times people have arrived just when I am dozing off or waking up, times when I am not in a condition to see anyone other than a caregiver. In these instances I simply chose not to ring my bell and after patiently waiting a few minutes the visitors departed, hopefully without taking offence. It is worth remembering that there is no reason for us to be offended by the simple fact that a friend or relative does not feel well and has no wish to see us—or to see anyone, for that matter.

You see, in spite of the pain killers I take I am often in a lot of discomfort and having to be a politely social host and a good listener is simply too exhausting. And here we find ourselves once again in a paradox. I may sit here all alone thinking how nice it would be for someone to drop by, and at the same time hoping that nobody does because I simply haven't the energy to deal with a guest. What to do, what to do? It is my opinion that in these situations much thought and reorientation is required from us as visitors. Whereas in other relationships an equal give and take is expected between parties, in our relationships with the ill or disabled we must accept that they simply haven't the wherewithal to meet us on the same footing that we might expect from others. Therefore it becomes our responsibility to stop and think, to reorient our habitual patterns in order that our visit be appropriate. This may require introspective preparations on our part. It may require interacting with caregivers in order to discover new ways to associate with our loved one. It will definitely require some sacrifices on our part. Regardless, it isn't as easy as popping through the door. And perhaps it is for this reason, namely the amount of effort involved, that we shy away from visiting the elderly, the disabled, the infirm, or we do so only under compulsion—i.e. guilt, remorse, duty, duress—which makes for a most bizarre and dare I say unhealthy dynamic.

Another complicating issue for visitors is that none of this etiquette is applicable to caregivers, who must come and go as necessary. The caregiver, whether professional or volunteer, whether spouse, friend or nurse, has a unique relationship with his or her "patient"—a relationship which brings with it special privileges as well as great responsibilities. Regardless of what our prior relationship was with the patient, it must now necessarily take second or third place to that of the long-term caregivers involved in our loved one's life. This can cause quite a lot of tension, especially when the caregiver is a newcomer. But this is just another example of how things have become topsy-turvy, unexpected.

On a regular basis, I have wonderful professional home health aides who are with me for forty-four hours a week, and I have a volunteer team of about fourteen remarkable men who assist me in various ways with my personal care needs. In the best-case scenario, the roles of such individuals in the life of a disabled or ill person are necessarily ones of deep intimacy and trust, of searing truth and loving tenderness. Their presence in the home, their skills, their relationship to the patient, are to be much respected. When we ignore or demean these quality caregivers, or attempt to wriggle our way into these relationships, we are only creating needless strife.

So why, you may ask, go to the bother of visiting the disabled, the infirm, the homebound, especially when it requires such demanding personal exploration on our part in order for it to be worthwhile for our loved one, or when, like my dying friend, our loved one is in the process of detaching from personal relationships preparatory to dying? There is, alas, no simple answer to this question. It is a conundrum we each have to answer for ourselves, and answer anew for each person in our lives who becomes disabled or who steps on the path toward death.

And here I must confess that I myself was generally speaking a better caregiver than visitor. Nursing the disabled and the dying came somewhat naturally to me, bringing me great joy, while just visiting them was more of a challenge for me. Interestingly enough, a couple of my finest volunteer caregivers fall into this same category—completely open and unflappably fearless in caring for me, while self-consciously awkward when merely visiting. It may be that a person cannot be good at both. If so, then perhaps we can come to recognize our natural talents and thereupon find for ourselves those situations which will best nourish our innate skills.

If we do choose to visit our loved one, it is tempting to follow the advice simply to act normal, rather as though nothing were amiss, which is I suppose what we most want to do because it does not require confronting the challenging inner issues that can lead us toward a deeper awareness of life. For truth be told, our visit can be an excellent opportunity to leave our little selves at the door and enter into the greater Self, for want of a better term. In those years during which

I spent time visiting and being with the disabled and the dying, the most beautiful and stressless visits were precisely those in which I'd left behind at the threshold my self-will, my stubborn prejudices and pompous self-determination, all my dreams and hopes for my ailing friends, my pretenses of knowing what is best or worst for them, and even my basic desire to love them. In a sense, I was then figuratively approaching them completely shorn, naked. You see, so much has been stripped from them physically, emotionally, environmentally, that if we are willing to surrender some of our overladen emotional, psychological and spiritual baggage at the door we will be going a long way toward creating a clearer, more compassionate meeting.

Once we cross the threshold of the infirm, whether it be the door of a house or that of a room in a nursing home, we must recognize that we are no longer in our accustomed and artificially supported worlds. Habits that served us well enough in those realms are suddenly useless, gauche, or even cruel in the context of this strange land. It is not that this new land is special, as some might erroneously maintain, merely that it is different, alien to most. And the worldly tourist who has a propensity for complaining about the coffee in foreign restaurants, for making snide comments about unfamiliar religious customs, or mocking the dialects of others is not likely to be a good guest in this strange landscape. A friend once asked my advice about travelling. My response, eerily applicable as we enter the rooms of the disabled and ill, was, "Expect nothing, accept everything."

Earlier I mentioned the lamentations of those whose formerly chummy friends and family had gradually ceased to visit them, rather a pathetic image as I left it. If, however, one waits around long enough, he will discover that the lamentational narrative gradually shifts and the person begins to speak warmly of new faces, new names, and even the occasional re-emergence of an almost forgotten face, individuals who are unafraid to step into this strange landscape that requires so much surrender. And quite honestly, we cannot seriously expect old comrades to stick around in a world they never wanted to be in and haven't the skills to inhabit, but we can readily accept those who now step across the threshold and are earnestly, thoughtfully willing to learn the distinctive vocabulary, to discover a different way of drinking coffee, to be shorn within the wordless dialect of the greater Self.

Returning to the question of why bother to visit, the truth is that there is no reason at all to visit the elderly, the disabled, the infirm. As far as I know, failure to visit such people is not anywhere listed as a sin or a crime. Indeed, in some cultures such individuals are not visited at all; rather they are simply left behind to die in peace, alone with the universe. Furthermore, the invalid in question is likely to be dead in one, ten or twenty years, and every last one of us, even the babies among us, will be long gone in two hundred years, so one stupid little visit ain't gonna alter world poverty, religious strife and ecological sustainability—indeed, reducing global warming. . .

If it is ultimately so unimportant, why did I myself make at least feeble attempts to visit my disabled and dying friends? I suppose it was precisely because it was an unknown, challenging landscape, an opportunity to spend an hour or two learning about life in an environment where the breathing, the light and time itself were slower, quieter, and ultimately forever inexplicable, an environment in which harmony presented itself only when I was willing to surrender my preconceptions, my cherished ego, and the security of my self-made matrices, an environment which, when I was able to step outside of the past and the future, to strip away the encrusted layers of my self and enter nakedly the compassionate Self, revealed to me. . .

And here my narrative must end, for it is well nigh impossible to communicate in words that which was revealed.

This, if you so choose, my friend, you must discover on your own.

December 29, 2002

83. A Delicious Poem

—For Courtenay Mathey

Laboriously shifting my body minute by minute,
arc by arc through a vast semicircle of waking,
I come at last face to face with Borges,
this handsome, full-lipped young man,
his photograph printed on the spine of the dust jacket protecting a volume of
        verse collected from the *oeuvre* of this twentieth-century Argentinean, a
        librarian, a poet, and ultimately a man of sightless visions.

The poems themselves—
many composed by a middle-aged or elderly Borges
gone blind too early in life to become a painter in his dotage,
though arguably not too early to nourish the visions of a poet—
are hidden, tucked away inside this large, bedside tome;
yet, in the blossoming morning of this placid moment,
the complex fragrances potent in those mute poems
are wordlessly spilling
from the photographed eyes,
the succulent lips,
of this intense young poet,
a man who breathed time into cadence
and cadence into histories.

As I open my eyes within the yawning mouth of this early morning,
there is no need to lift the thick, heavy book from the small, whispering table;
another hand is gathering it up, caressing its lovely design,
his slender, winter-chilled fingers opening the cherished volume, his smooth lips
        and articulate tongue randomly revealing dreams and oblivion; Oedipus
        and the Sphinx; Archetypes and Splendors;
and, turning the page,
Spinoza the Jew, centuries after his death,
once again polishing the stubborn lens.

Reverently replacing the well-read Borges on the table,
my tall friend leans across the blankets covering my body,
reaching toward the small library of books
which carelessly nestle among the pillows and bedding,
their thicknesses and thinnesses sleeping nights with me, resting days with me,
        his warming hand alighting on the ecstatic Hafiz,
        a poetry of divine laughter,
and love;
of rapturous dancing, exultant song,
and love;
of camelshit, flatulence,
and divine love;
Hafiz's vividly flaming words now escaping through the mouth of a friend,
reminding us what we have lost in the intervening centuries, that godliness has
        become merely politics and prudity divorced from truth, while holy love
        has been disembowelled of its universal laughter,
its intimate spontaneity, its embodied everness.

Thus from the printed word, through the spoken oracle,
utterly within the fragrances, the laughter of an absurdly honest love which
        succinctly destroys the imprisoning monuments of hesitation, along with
        the trepid pretenses of naming and separating,
this day has dawned upon the tongue, the lips of a slender man holding in his
        hands a voluptuous photograph, a delicious poem, the unhesitant sunlight
        caressing the morning contours of nothingness.

January 2, 2003

84. LONG-TERM CARE

The previous eighty-three instalments of this Zsoltgossip chronicle have served many purposes, from the lofty to the profane, the complex to the simple. Each instalment has been inspired by diverse and even divergent factors—the flight of a bird, for example, or an everyday observation, a memory, a sensuous melody, a strident fragrance, the touch of a hand, the words of a poet, a moment of indignity. Additionally, this chronicle has been, among many other things, a vehicle by which to pay tribute to the remarkable people in my life who assist me in various ways. Therefore, in the spirit of past tributes, though perhaps without much in the way of poetic nuance, I bring you household management.

Household management is part and parcel of life on earth, regardless of one's religion, culture, education, class, gender or species. In your home it is likely taken care of by you and your household members—a litter of children, perhaps, or a gaggle of roommates, a robot or two—with possibly some additional help from outside, a missile, for example, aimed to perfection. In an institutional setting such as a nursing home, the responsibility for orderliness, cleanliness and overall maintenance of the facility falls to the general management, the janitorial staff, and to some degree the nursing staff. In my neither black nor white situation, the household management requires an odd assortment of people, each providing bits and pieces of the puzzle, including for instance many generous folk from around the world who recently sent donations to one of my home health aides to ensure that the brakes on his vehicle could be fixed in order that he may safely transport me to physical therapy.

Beyond such sporadic, occasional assistance provided by a diverse range of people, both professional and volunteer, I am fortunate to have a small clutch of individuals, plus one remarkable agency, who have in the past couple of months become responsible for making sure the house is run with efficiency, cleanliness and safety. Without them things would be a real mess, figuratively and literally.

My aides come to me through an agency which receives federal and state funds from a government social program—God bless those tax-and-spend liberals—that seeks to provide a range of at-home services to indigent disabled or elderly people in the hope of delaying institutionalization, potentially and preferably until near death, when hospice programs can intervene to allow the individual to die at home, presumably with more comfort and dignity than in an institution.

Emmy and Randi are two long-time friends who recently resurfaced in my life, initially volunteering to assist me with deliveries of food, to augment what I receive from a local nonprofit agency. Within a few days of my move into this residence, I had scribbled down a list of household necessities that needed to be purchased, from cat paraphernalia to cleaning supplies, not having a clue how these sundries were going to be obtained. At that point Randi came by with some food, noticed the list on the refrigerator—a list which had not the least thing to do with food—and whisked it away only to return later bearing gifts of the entire list. Toward the end of the week, Emmy did the same thing with a newly scribbled list.

At the time I assumed these were merely thoughtful gestures meant to welcome me into my new residence and to help set it up. These were not isolated incidents, however, but the beginning of an informal routine wherein one or the other woman comes by every few days to take the list from the refrigerator in order to keep the household supplied with cat litter, cat food, cleaning supplies, toilet paper. . . Additionally, they have generously continued with their original mission, that of providing food, some of it deliciously cooked by Randi's spouse, Shelly.

It is also worth mentioning that Randi has become a paragon of interfacing with my aides to ensure a well-run house. From the first she has been willing to communicate with them and to respect their position in my life. For instance, she'll stop by on her lunch break, pick up the list, discuss household needs with the aide on duty, then quietly depart without disturbing my physical therapy or napping.

Emmy's work schedule is precisely that of my aides and therefore she has had less opportunity to interact with them, though this will likely change as my aides' hours increase in the coming weeks, and I have no doubt that she will get along with them as well as Randi has. It was Emmy, however, who within days—or was it hours, minutes—of my arrival heartily lugged one of her spare televisions and a VCR into my new bedroom, precipitating my decline into hedonistic debauchery. It is only a matter of weeks before she will have me puffing away at cigars, drinking gouty supplies of port, abusing my meds and renting pornographic videos.

On those days when I am away at the therapy pool, Emmy and Randi will each let themselves in as needed, put away the supplies they've brought, and if necessary leave messages concerning those supplies. Indeed, I rarely see either of these women, but their tactful, supportive presence in my life is palpable and integral. Believe me, without their consistent generosity, things around here would quickly go downhill.

Gregory is the Van Man. While a wheelchair van is not strictly speaking part of a house, it is part of the needs of some people in wheelchairs. This easygoing, unassuming, kindhearted man has been an invaluable help to me in many ways over the past several years. Only recently has he taken on the role of Van Man, which entails taking care of the vehicle's paperwork and minor maintenance—all of which he does with consummate ability.

Though they do not live nearby, my dedicated parents have been and continue to be an important part of the household management, consistently shipping supplies of clothing, lotions, and various odds and ends to assist my aides in their work.

A local beneficent organization supplies me with a daily meal large enough to serve me as two meals, five days per week. Staffed by one hundred fifty volunteers, this organization ensures that savory nutrition is cooked and delivered to indigent, homebound individuals.

Other than my aides, none of the above people are paid for the services they render to provide for a well-run household—and the homecare agency pays the aides such a pittance that they might as well be considered volunteers.

Long-term care—it used to be the province of the family or neighborhood.

Long-term care—some feel it should be tucked away in institutions where only a few citizens are required to take responsibility for the direct, hands-on care of these admittedly cumbersome lives.

Long-term care—the truth is that it requires the participation of all sectors of society, including government social service programs, private nonprofit agencies, family members, the business community, the religious community, the neighborhood, and most important of all, individuals, whether friends or strangers, who are willing to lend a helping hand in order that those in need of long-term care can live out their lives in a humane fashion.

If you yourself know someone who is responsible in small or large ways for the personal care or the household management of an individual needing long-term care, do me a favor—take him out for lunch now and then.

Buy her a spectacular bouquet of flowers, some gouty port, or a fat cigar.

Give him or her a kiss, nay, a dozen kisses, for no other reason than that these people are willing to do what others, for whatever reason, cannot—or simply will not.

January 5, 2003

85. THE HOUR OF THE WOLF

The legendary hour of the wolf has already passed.
It is now seven o'clock in the morning.
> Listen to the sound of the rising sun.
> Cars driving by in the busying street.
> The constant whirr of a breathing machine.
> Two cats stretching, leaping onto the tiled floor.

Here a man of varying heights unlocks the front door.
He comes quietly to sit beside my waking limbs.
He removes the plastic breathing mask from my face.
Then he reads a poem or two or three.
The cats gather round, listening intently, seeking warmth.
Now the man beats the hell out of my lungs.
First the chest, then the back, to loosen the phlegm.
He massages my cramped, burning muscles.
The hips, the sacrum, the butt and the back.
The feet, the belly, the hands and the neck.
Fully pummeled and kneaded, it is now time for dressing.
Then the toilet, along with some tidying up.
Before leaving he brews half a pot of stout tea.
> The sound of the water coming to a boil.
> The clink of spout against cup.
> A buddy's spontaneous laughter.
> The quiet motor of my shiny black powerchair.
> Sometimes the characteristic tone of a wolf's low voice.

And already it is between eight and nine o'clock.
The hour when this dedicated buddy, or another, must depart.

(It is true he has a name same as any other guy I know though I will not refer to
it here in order to somehow somewhat protect his roguish soul from undue public
harassment because it goes without saying and by the monstrous proof of his
actions that he is utterly guilty beyond doubt and yet in order to proceed with the
narrative I must use some referent for him and will therefore refer to him

forthwith as The Rogue this man of many coats for whom being a good boy is not nearly as tempting as being humane and compassionate.)

Alone, after drinking the milky tea, I try to write.
>	*The hum of the fan inside the computer.*
>	*The constant swell of traffic.*
>	*Perhaps some music.*
>	*The slow click-clack of the computer keyboard.*
>	*The heater turning itself on and off.*
I also meditate each and every morning.
I take my vitamins and minerals, my synthetic opiates.
I piss the morning's tea into a plastic urinal.
I empty the pale-ale-colored urine into the toilet.
Then I try again to write, typing with one finger.
On certain days I await the arrival of my aide.
By midmorning I usually feel lousy.
Some days I feel even lousier.
So I tumble from my wheelchair forward onto the bed.
>	*A fleeting memory of the wolf's voice.*
>	*The sound of my labored breathing.*
>	*The rustle of the blankets.*
>	*A dog barking outside.*
>	*Radio opera on Saturdays.*
Here I take a deep breath, staring at the ceiling.

(Were you to meet The Rogue you probably would not think of him as a rogue in any traditional use of the word and this is because he is in some sense the proverbial wolf in sheep's clothing and therefore you are likely to presume he is a respectably commonplace citizen perhaps not unlike yourself who would never in a million lifetimes rebel against the dominant social fabric and here I must regretfully inform you that in your espousal of such an opinion you will have fallen prey to The Rogue's masterful though not intentionally deceitful subterfuge because there is one thing you gotta realize about The Rogue which is that when you are absolutely certain he is thinking or acting like any other brainwashed citizen he BAM WHAM does something so lovingly original and compassionately out of the ordinary that it shreds your convictions of a common sense norm and causes bystanders to stare dumbfoundedly as the confident Rogue lopes across the tundra leaving timid folk behind.)

As my aide cooks and cleans, I do physical therapy.
Then I eat lunch.
I nap with the breathing mask secured over my face.

Some days my aide takes me to the doctor.
Four afternoons a week I go to the therapy pool.
There, one friend or another assists with my water therapy.

> *The primordial rhythm of lapping water.*
> *The sound of air being forced through massive industrial vents.*
> *Swimmers conversing in scattered words of liquid confetti.*
> *The inhaling and exhaling of my buddy's lungs.*
> *Water dripping from a wolf's sodden pelt.*

By the edge of the pool he offers me water.
Then my buddy bathes my chlorine-saturated skin.
He massages my muscles, applies deodorant, and again offers water.

> *Boys squealing in the locker room.*
> *Toilets loudly flushing.*
> *Lockers being slammed shut.*
> *Water splashing from showers or faucets.*

Finally my buddy dresses me before driving me home.

(As his lanky limbs trot in and out of my days with an athletic precision and a
natural intensity the cunning Rogue of many coats is by turns my advocate and
my barber and my bather and my butt wiper and my chauffeur and my comrade
and my confidant and my janitor and my masseur and my nurse and my physical
therapist and my pummeller and my sleuth and my tea-brewer and on occasion he
also recruits and trains latent Rogues-of-Compassion hidden in among a generally
unremarkable humanity and ever the while in everything he does for me he is a
selfless volunteer this regal wolf this man of unpretentious love who invariably
arrives and departs the flow of my weeks with a look of joy that is more than
happiness and more than pleasure and more than self-satisfaction this joy which
springs from his sinews and muscles this burning joy that radiates from the wolf's
blue eyes as he turns again to lope unhesitantly across the tundra of a daunting
human landscape forever inaccessible to the faint-of-heart and lethal for any soul
not in possession of The Rogue's impudent mastery of the nearly forgotten skills
of the Knights Hospitalers this man whose humble gestures are unbeknown to
himself graced by the light of a ruthless compassion nourished for countless eons
by motley crews of crazy-wise Bodhisattvas.)

During the afternoon a dedicated friend may deliver some food.
He or she may run an errand or two.
A hot evening meal is delivered by a local agency.

> *Hear the sound of the humming microwave.*
> *Possibly words or music from the radio.*
> *Or the screenplay, the soundtrack of a video.*

After eating, it is time to retire.

Occasionally someone is here to help me safely to bed.
If not, I once again tumble forward onto the mattress.
Here gravity is as much my helpmate as my nemesis.
Huffing and puffing, I work my way beneath the bedclothes.
I attempt to hold a book, to read a poem.
I listen to the muffled traffic, an ocean of humanity.
The two cats settle themselves atop or beneath the blankets.
I carefully adjust the face mask of my breathing apparatus.
I turn off the soft light.
Again in the velvet lap of darkness I can hear. . .

> *The purring of this breathing machine.*
> *The now faint echoes of the once setting sun.*
> *Distant murmurings of enigmatic quasars and bellicose supernovae.*
> *The pattering of the wolf's paws on the nocturnal streets.*

Then sleep.
Blessed sleep.

January 12, 2003

87. SMALL BOY

Once upon an inexplicable afternoon,
in the hither-thither history of a summer-moored locker room,
as I were being scrubbed by a sailoring chap, swabbed
upon the saltedly naked deck of a wave-tossed wheelchair,
there beside the mirrored portals of a blimey row of sinks,
a small seven-year-old matey swaggered his sea-sung self
all the way up and to my anchored ship.

And though my water-weary eyes were shuttered
to the heave-hoing bustle around me,
I could easily discern this shanty-squeaking boy
asking my buddy what-ho! had happened to me,
and why was it I was beach-scuttled in an oarless wheelchair,
and why did I not hue and cry the waves of time.

After listening to the sailor-spelled answers
spoken across the monster-infested sea of a locker room sink,
the new little lad fell silent.

Then,
unexpectedly,
I felt his small fingers touching my ruddy face,
not invasively,
nor with any disrespect,
gentle even;
a small boy quietly searching for ways
to read this unmapped world he had found himself in,
to navigate the perilous latitudes and mutinous longitudes,
to understand horizons which haven't any verbal language,
his fingers wandering without timidity over my features—
the short, bristly hair;
a Neptunian goatee;

the full and silent lips;
a pirate-boned jaw;
the robust, sea-sprung moustaches;
a long neck easily severed by the Corsair's bloody blade;
these contours and textures once read and studied
by a seal pup of a small boy I've never seen since,
a boy with the rare gift for sounding the sea with his hands,
for reading the epic stillnesses
of a string of unspokenly becalmed moments.

February 4, 2003

89. PEACE AND WAR

It seems almost silly to continue sending out these Zsoltgossips in the midst of war, but one of the greatest tragedies of war, and one of the ways in which governments utilize war to their advantage, is the fact that it causes us to forget that there is so much more happening in our lives than war. While world leaders of all persuasions strut about in peevish hubris, this is no time to forget that in our own communities there is still racism, misogyny, poverty and anger that each and every one of us must face, even the self-proclaimed saintly among us.

In these tense days I hear citizens, regardless of their point of view, speak of their anger about this current war—anger toward Saddam Hussein, toward Bush, toward Blair, toward the Americans, the French, the Germans, the Chinese; toward one another. But in many ways this anger is precisely what our leaders want us to feel, because it helps to perpetrate their wars, their dogmas and ideologies, and provides them the mechanism by which they may hope to stand in glory upon the confused minds of citizens and the dead and maimed bodies of soldiers.

It is better, I feel, to transform that corrosive anger into powerfully thoughtful indignation, and then to funnel that potent and legitimate energy proactively into our own struggling communities and neighborhoods.

Somewhere in your community during this hour a woman will be battered by a tyrannous husband, father, boyfriend, girlfriend, or even son or daughter. In her realm she is consumed by war, a refugee from her own home, completely ignored by world leaders who see no glory in coming to her rescue. You, however, can go to your local shelter for battered women and offer your love, your compassion, your resources. For these women, who are as bruised, bloodied and demoralized as any exotic refugee, there will be no American relief aid packages miraculously falling from the sky, parcels filled with candy bars and pamphlets urging her to overthrow her government, to choose freedom over oppression.

All around you, in your own neighborhood are people who need your energy, your time, your love—an elderly invalid, a young boy who is struggling to learn his multiplication tables, workers who have lost their jobs, families living in poverty. (If you happen to be a committed misanthrope, there are libraries, animal shelters and city parks that also need attention.) The war will go how the war will go, and certainly we must be mindful of our leaders' assumptions that we are stupid enough to forego our deepest beliefs in freedom in order for them to climb to ever higher power and glory. Yet we are no better than they if we remain unwilling to reach out to those in our midst, both neighbors and strangers, in order to make our communities—especially those that have been abandoned by the same government intent on saving communities elsewhere around the world—better places to live, so that when the war does end, in a week or a decade, our own neighborhoods will be safer, cleaner, and friendlier, less burdened by oppression.

I understand that this current war, from the perspective of the Americans, is called "Iraqi Freedom." Where, I wonder, is the offensive called "American Freedom?" If it exists at all, it resides, my friends, in our hands, yours and mine. As you are well aware, the weapons of such an offensive are love and compassion, but also the courage to reach out to the oppressed, the persecuted in our own neighborhood, that we might create civilized, tolerant communities in which we may together celebrate the joyous births of healthy babies, the creation of paintings, music and poetry; to contemplate humankind's exciting journeys ever deeper into space, time and molecules, along with the apricot blossoms mingling with the falling snowflakes, the arrival of the spring migration here in the Northern Hemisphere.

Personally I am not very good at theories, schemata and systems, and thus am a dubious and insubstantial commentator on current events. But I do know that putting your arms around someone in need and holding them close against your own beating, uncertain heart, does make the world a safer, calmer place for all of us, does create peace in our souls. I urge you, for every angry, snide, confused or prejudiced comment you spout, please turn to someone you despise and put your arms around him, hold him close, to feel his beating, uncertain heart next to yours. This, my friend, will do more to bring peace than all the demonstrating, the placards, the rhetorical propaganda, the bombs and policy making you could ever imagine.

If you and I are incapable of embracing those whom we loathe or with whom we disagree, how can we seriously expect our political and religious leaders to do so, and in doing so take the necessary steps toward civility and tolerance, toward peace?

March 21, 2003

90.   THE TIMELESS HOUR

One Tuesday afternoon, I was floating as usual in the warm water of the therapy pool, held afloat upon the arms of a buddy. As he proceeded with my physical therapy, gently pulling my body this way and that through the clear water, the ebb and flow of my breathing became ever shallower and more dispersed, not at all an unexpected result of being in the relaxing water. On this particular afternoon, however, and unbeknownst to either of us the shallowness of my breathing crossed onto a new threshold as my body gradually began the process of shutting down, so gradually in fact that it appeared from the outside to be a kind of sleep or torpor, but was instead a state of suspended threshold, bathed in unearthly light, resplendent with scenes of my life played out in striking clarity and nearness, peopled with fellow adventurers whom I hadn't seen in years. Only the vibrations of my buddy's own breathing, now faint and far off in the distance, remained to strangely, vaguely define the earthly dimensions of this unfamiliar, otherwordly threshold. And for another hour or so, as I wandered back and forth through those dimensions, I am not sure my buddy, nor I, nor the lifeguard were at all certain the direction my life was going.

How quickly things shift, how in a blink we move from peace to war and back again. And how, with no presentiment, no forewarning, I might have slipped across a painless threshold into nonexistence on a specific Tuesday evening in March, having said goodbye to no one except the man who was holding me in his arms—not a farewell of any conscious act or turn of phrase, but an adieu expressed only by the presence of a slackening body becoming lifeless against his body in the quiet turn of an hour in which no one expected me to die, and neither did anyone expect you or the strapping young soldier on the battlefield to perish, and yet one of us, somewhere on the planet, did die.

For an indeterminate time after being lifted from the water, I floated in and out of awareness, even as my physical body contracted with waves of heaving and convulsing, horrifying efforts to get air into my lungs, oxygen to my brain, the exertion leaving my mouth dry, my muscles sore. On a deeper level, however, I felt strangely unattached and serene, both in the beguiling calm of the water and in the convulsions of land, accompanied throughout by those same clear, almost tangible presences of old buddies rising from the pages of a life lived across three continents, guys I hadn't seen in years comforting me by their attendance, showing me again the rich tapestry of my decades, confirming the remarkable twists and turns that were a life hewn not so much from bizarre events but from an unabashed nearness to living, a *joie de vivre*; a life forged and constructed from an irrepressible delight in the sensuous fragrance of a budding hyacinth, in the enigmas of the structure of universal matter, of Beethoven's late piano sonatas, in the unique shape of a man's jaw, or the texture of his hair, as well as the almost overpowering grandeur of the changing clouds in an undying sky, the deep time embedded in a simple piece of stone, a fossil, a garnet.

How in these past days I have tried to write something pithy, something poetical or philosophical about the shift that occurred on that Tuesday evening, that timeless hour during which I was suspended in an unspeakably fluid light; this I who had become no me of any substance, straddling the edge between life and death, a boundary which in truth was no edge, but a peaceful, brilliant expanse, so clear, so warmly illuminated, and not in the least fearsome. Yet each strand of poetry seems to fall flat, each philosophical phrase pales, and ultimately, as in so much that I have been through in these past months, such an experience remains nearly incomprehensible to anyone not present in the eloquent moment, because the eloquence of such an intimate moment withers in the harsh simplifications of public light.

There is, however, one last image I would like to share with you from that intense, surreal evening, and this is the image of a lifeguard standing beside my wheelchair in the corner of a locker room, resting my head against his torso as my buddy puts on my socks and laces my shoes, a lifeguard reciting the only poem he can remember from his school days, his articulate recitation of Robert Frost's words calling me firmly and fully back from the threshold of light into the realm of life.

March 29, 2003

91. Chains of Events

The *Story of the Three Bears* did not begin, as you might have supposed, on the feast day of Saint Valentine. Rather it began a week earlier, on 7 February, the selfsame day a neighbor kid knocked on my door for no other reason than to introduce himself, and no doubt to satisfy his curiosity about this new neighbor whom the boy had occasionally seen through the wintered windows as he'd walked home from school.

In the first four or five sentences of our initial exchange—me writing, him talking—I was able to ascertain the kid's name, where he attends school, and that he was fourteen years old, turning fifteen in five days—all the trappings of small talk, you know. It was in his fifth or six sentence, in answer to a blandly routine question about school, that he incongruously, though not inappropriately confided, "I'm gay." I say not inappropriately since the simple fact of being an openly gay fourteen-year-old can completely alter the safe trajectory of one's school experiences. Generally not for the better, I might add.

BEAR #1—Five days later, on the kid's *quinceañero*, his fifteenth birthday, I wheeled myself over to his house to give him a celebratory pink boa, which, it must be admitted, looked especially striking against his all-black ensemble and dark, dark hair. I do not mean to imply by my choice of gift that every gay teenager would want a pink boa for his or her fifteenth birthday—some might prefer red, you see, or black, while others would be most happy with battle fatigues and an unfettered opportunity to enlist in the army. Yet I sensed correctly that for this kid a pink boa was indeed a most appropriate gift, delight spreading across his face as he tossed the end of the boa dramatically over his shoulder. His mother then said to him, "Go get the Valentine present you bought for your new friend." At her instigation the kid disappeared back into the house, its humble doorway inaccessible to my electric wheelchair, returning a moment later with a medium-sized red and white teddy bear hugging a packet of candy.

BEAR #2—The following day, 13 February, I returned from physical therapy to find a not unexpected stack of video cassettes sitting innocently and quietly on the kitchen counter, part of a rotating loan system instituted and maintained by my friend Emmy. Atop the stack of videos was a lovely heart-shaped box which, when I lifted it felt empty, but which, when opened revealed a tiny ecru teddy bear in such proportion that it nestled perfectly in the lap of the red and white bear given me the previous evening by the neighbor kid.

BEAR #3—A day later, now the official feast day of Saint Valentine, aka Our Laddie of Lovers, I once again returned home from physical therapy, this time welcomed by a large brown teddy bear sporting a polo shirt and sitting comfortably in the huge armchair in the front room, its poised paws holding a box of assorted chocolates. Mute like me, he has consistently and insistently refused to tell me who brought him here, and to this day I have no idea which thoughtful friend delivered him. The search was easily enough narrowed to the two dozen people who have access to my home, but no farther. I cannot even dismiss Emmy from the suspects, her mug shot lined up with all the others, for it would not be unlike her to bring me two teddy bears. Furthermore, and not implausibly, this last bear could quite conceivably have come from the warden himself.

Thus, in a rather oversized nutshell, you have the story of the three bears—medium, little and big. Whereas these individual and vaguely related stories of the teddy bears culminated on or before the feast day of Our Laddie of Lovers, *The Saga of the Sour Candy Boy* began most explicitly on that day, almost simultaneously with the unobserved and mysterious arrival of the last and largest teddy bear. Therefore I now bring you *The Saga of the Sour Candy Boy*...

14 FEBRUARY, 2003 C.E. Tucked inside the paper bag which contained an evening meal delivered to me by a beneficent organization, there was a Valentine's Day card made by a local school child. Obviously someone in the community had gone to a lot of effort to coordinate this craft project, because it wasn't just an anonymous valentine, but was actually addressed to me and signed by the child, a boy who had put much effort into making the card. While the design included the ubiquitous heart-themed artwork, this card was unusual in that the boy—and presumably all the children involved in this project—had written sentences and paragraphs about himself, cut them out with scalloped edges, and glued them onto the card. Thus interspersed among the paper cutouts of hearts and stars, many of his words expressed his enjoyment of the sounds and scents of rivers, and in one of the paragraphs he also told me about various flavors and foods that he enjoys, including among others, shrimp and sour candy—though not necessarily in the same recipe! Not that the idea of someone eating a *pot-au-feu* concocted of shrimp and sour candies would upset me much, since I don't really give a damn what people put in their mouths, so long as they don't vomit in the streets and scare the horses. Nevertheless, I do not want to be giving an incorrect and possibly pernicious impression of a little chap I've never even met.

Several weeks later, as I was lying exhausted in bed, a plainly-wrapped package sat plump and patient on the kitchen counter, a modest package addressed to the young lad. It was, quite naturally, a collection of sour candies swathed in a page torn from a magazine. That particular day a buddy of mine was planning to arrive shortly after four o'clock in order to assist me with bathing, and would therefore be able to hand over the package to the volunteer who would be delivering my meal. She could then take it back to the agency's offices and with any luck make arrangements to have it delivered safely to the lad's school teacher. As things sometimes go in life, my buddy was delayed in his arrival and the efficient volunteer brought my food early, which meant that they missed one another by a minute at most, during which I lay mutely incapacitated in my bed. Undeterred, I asked my buddy if on the following day he could please drop off the package at the agency's offices, which happen to be located quite near his own office.

To make a long story short, and since I cannot possibly convey the subtle twists and surprises that filled the next ten minutes, it turns out that my buddy actually knows this lad. He even knows where the kid lives and how to contact the family via telephone. Because of this remarkable coincidence, the package was duly and easily delivered within a few days' time—end of story.

In the very first paragraph above I spoke of things beginning, which of course they always do from a certain perspective. Yet on other and diverse levels one can always find a gesture, a word that was a precursor, all the way back to the singularity that was the Big Bang, and theoretically beyond, dipping tantalizingly over the edge of that astonishing event's horizon. Similarly with endings—they never really do end. The memory of a parcel of sour sweets delivered to an unsuspecting boy will be with him the remainder of his life, even if only in his subconscious, altering the cycles of that life in subtle, unimaginable ways.

Thus to conclude, if I may be permitted to call it a conclusion...

There was once a certain day, perhaps a year-and-a-half ago, maybe two, when I happened to be in a book shop, my body innocuously ensconced in my manual wheelchair and being aimlessly wheeled around by a friend. I wasn't sure I wanted to go in the direction he was going, but neither was I convinced I wanted to go anywhere else. Suddenly from around a display of books a strikingly handsome man appeared, almost tripping over me. As usually happens in such cases, we were both rather stunned at the suddenness of the encounter. There was also, gazing unequivocally into one another's eyes, a sense of recognition, of familiarity. In truth, however, we did not know one another, and had never met before. In spite of this, we spoke congenially for a few moments—at that time my voice, though hoarse and quiet, was still what most people consider a voice to be—then he offered me his e-mail address. I duly put his name on the receiving list of these essays and heard nevermore from him. Indeed I was not absolutely sure I was using the correct e-mail address, nor whether he was receiving my missives, nor whether he even wanted to receive them. His name lost in the depths of my cyber address book, I mostly forgot about him within the sublunary day-to-day concerns of life.

A couple of months ago, out of the blue, as they are apt to say on the planet Venus and elsewhere, I received an e-mail from this same man, a collection of delightful photographs culled from a body painting contest in which the bodies of

203

men and women had been painted with images such as tigers, alligators and landscapes, the artists using the natural curves and protuberances of the bodies as blank canvases. I duly wrote back, thanking him for the fantastical, inventive images, and since then we have maintained a relatively consistent cyber dialogue, our musings ranging from nursing—he is training to be a nurse—to poetry, to whether or not he should enlist in the Air Force. Additionally, he has continued to send me odds and ends of photos, images of popular culture sent speedily to all stretches of the globe via the internet, ending up most incongruously in this quiet room of a corner of the universe.

As quickly and as inexplicably as this striking man arose in my life, not once but twice, he may one day vanish unexpectedly into the thrilling river of greater Life, caught up in a demanding career, or consumed by the joys of raising a family, or downed in a burning airplane in some future skirmish bitterly fought among the world's self-aggrandizing, proselytizing plagues of nations and religions, his charred face only ashes of its former beauty.

Furthermore and inevitably, one fine day in the onrush of the future the middle-aged characters in the above stories will all be dead. The young adults will be old and the children will be middle-aged, their lives and deaths unfolding from unforeseeable instances of serendipity and labor, violence and love—small ripples flowing exponentially into complex biographies. Truly one cannot foresee the great chains of events, whether tender, absurd or tragic, that will arise from a simple conversation, the gift of a teddy bear, a few kind words, a parcel of candy. Yet, in spite of this uncertainty and perhaps because of it, to gaze lovingly, openly into the eyes, the life of another being, especially a stranger or an outcast, remains to this day an act of profound merit, of potent consequence for the entire world.

Therefore, gaze deeply, my friend, fearlessly, and be not afraid to be gazed upon.

July 15, 2003

92. LOSS AND SOLACE

—*For Mike Baca*

1. ONE AFTERNOON

The late winter walls are unadorned;
baseboards torn away, layers of old paint revealed.
The unremarkable ceramic bathtub is stained with age;
towels are frayed; the sink small, plainly utilitarian.
And I am sitting on this nondescript toilet—
mute, utterly naked, clothed only in coarse body hair.

Standing beside me in this cramped space dominated
by the commanding presence of my electric wheelchair,
is one of my buddies, his able stance
supporting my exhausted torso, the cotton cloth of his shirt
pressing softly against my stubbled jaw,
my severe temple, my carved collarbone.

Another day of disease has left me weak and weary,
depleted and vulnerable,
the mighty universe reduced to this meter of space,
this clockless time marked by the steady rising, falling,
rising, falling of my buddy's diaphragm.

Amid this unpretentious calm, without warning,
without precedent, his hand begins to stroke
the coarsely haired pelt of my back and shoulders,
his touch thoughtful, tender.

Neither a patronizing pat-pat,
nor a hurried, timid brushing of the hand,
his is instead a gesture of dialogue predating language,
therefore no word, nor even syllable, exists for it.

2. THE SECOND WEEK

Imagine a person's home, her belongings
and the richly varied nuances of her lifestyle,
being plucked from her grasp one by one—
even those dearest objects and daily customs
she'd carefully packed in a valise placed
near the door in case the uninvited
Angel of Death arrived sooner than later.
Imagine a person being ineluctably stripped
of his distinctively accumulated wardrobe;
his favorite shoes and eyeglasses;
his prayer wheel, yarmulke, or crucifix;
along with the means to shave himself or clip his nails.
Imagine a person being inexorably divested
of most everything that expresses her sense of self;
including her intangible name, her discursive gestures;
her cosmetics, her idiomatic language;
her honorific and social titles;
her hairstyle, whether flamboyant or demure;
the successful fruition of her generous desires
and ardent hopes,
the subtle articulations of her innermost feelings
or her wit and wisdom...

Now,
my friend,
attempt a human definition of this person's nameless,
irreducibly naked existence.

3. THE THIRD YEAR

Loss of mobility, of independence, of habitat,
not exempting removal to a situation far
from cherished domesticities
and lifelong habits...

Neglect
by spouses,
children,
friends,
comrades...

Loss of identifyingly personal sacred objects—
furniture, vehicles, clothing, jewelry, tools,
even one's toothbrush—
to be replaced by the haphazard dross of a system,
any system,
trickled down,
carelessly scattered among the weeds,
as readily revoked today as proffered yesterday...

Deprivation of livelihood, status, power,
and each of one's names—
whether given, marital or honorific—
names originally concocted
from letters of the world's alphabets,
becoming gradually numerical,
translated to room #212,
client #522 944 09 558,
case #9478531...

Loss of bladder and sphincter control,
loss of vision and/or hearing,
of speech and/or appetite...

4.   A MOMENT TO CONTEMPLATE

Throughout an arduously debilitating,
often humiliating disease,
what becomes of a person's long-held,
hard-won material and psychological vanities?

What now of one's lifelong fear of walking naked,
utterly, irreducibly naked?

What now of a person's terror at being flayed alive,
stripped of one's identity,
layer by layer;
each cultural affectation, from rituals and friendship
to language and marriage;
from art, blasphemy and cigars
to whiskey, storytelling and underwear,
sinews-of-self excruciatingly peeled
from the bones of persona,

to become against one's will a mythic creature
incapable of survival in the wild,
yet generally unwanted in the culture of humanity,
narrowly surviving in a far corner of an ersatz zoo
that exists on no known map of society;
a creature mutely awaiting extradition to the local butcher,
its tidily packed valise long since looted?

5. SEVERAL MONTHS LATER

Having assisted me with bathing, physical therapy
and dinner, my buddy is now sitting comfortably
on the edge of my midsummer bed,
here in this simple, book-cluttered room.

As often happens after eating, I am not feeling well.
Today, however, the resultant discomfort and dyspnea
are especially acute,
causing my body to curl fetally, instinctually.
After watching in silence for several minutes,
my buddy once again does something wholly novel,
wholly unexpected,
yet fiercely compassionate…

…he deftly removes his shoes
then crawls onto the bed with me,
curving his lithe body to shape my anguished form,
wrapping his clothed arms around my bare torso,
his gracious action executed without words,
without ceremony;
an incisive act of compassion piercing layer
upon layer of vanities, mores and shames—
the sublime beast
crawling into an unfamiliar, unmapped corner
to succor
the sublime beast.

6. THIS EVENING

When stripped by the whimsical blade of life
to these stark moments embedded
in mornings and evenings barely ornamented

with the veils and artifices of identity;
when lying nakedly vulnerable in a landscape
beyond the edge of linguistics,
swirling in an uncharted legendary river
known to history as the Narrows of Anguish,
it may happen that the injured beast, alone in his agony,
comes face to face, eye to eye, hand to hand
with a creature whose unerring response to feral suffering
is the simple gift of bodily warmth,
the intimate breath of succor.

Within this twilit fold of time and space,
here beyond the vanities, beyond the shames,
here at the far edges of definition,
nearest the obscure boundaries of self,
exists a man's compassionate embrace;
a tender raft, a silent solace
of inexpressibly primal warmth.

July 30, 2003

94. THE UNFOLDING JOURNEY

Tomorrow
I'll be gone.
—Thich Nhat Hanh

1.

My bags are nearly packed,
tomorrow I'll be gone; I'll be journeying
into the eastern whisper, the western echo.

2.

This day of now unfurls from its ancient genesis—
its morning light, its afternoon thunder blossoming
into the eastern whisper—

       the western echo
slipping toward tomorrow.

      I'll be gone by then—
silken nights of further centuries shall not know me,
this insolently enraptured I-of-Time having vanished.

3.

Accept my humblest apologies—I will not be witness
to the distant opening of the butterfly's elegant chrysalis,
this insolently enraptured I-of-Time having vanished.

For now, however, the slight yet refreshing rain falls
onto the gray asphalt, dampening our umbrella, here
on this today in the past when tomorrow I'll be gone;
I'll be boarding a nameless yesterday train
whose accelerating wheels shall carry no knowledge of
your dying, your own inimitable death.

4.

Standing in the delicate rain, one wonders, my friend,
who will ever comprehend, let alone contemplate,
your dying, your own inimitable death—
and will the memory of the butterfly's fleeting life
be thrust aside during your lonely last breaths?

What then of the hauntingly slow Bulgarian dance
whose living fate I'll never know? What then?
Because tomorrow I'll be gone—
I'll be dancing a day in a somewhere of a when,
in a why of a where I've never been,
my bags fully packed,
utterly empty.

5.

In a subtle yet breathtaking moment, the world shifts—
all that one is and was and might have been, is stilled.

Utterly empty,
the sky of thought opens toward the vastness—
the abyss gathers in the blood.
Carrying my bags neatly packed with nothing—
I loiter in the middle of the street, the melody of life.

Once upon a time I would have begged you,
>   *Remember me, remember me because*
>   *tomorrow I'll be gone.*
But that vain future of eternal eulogy
is no longer of any consequence to me. Rather,
I want only this tender moment alone with you,
to ponder the arrival of a certain man,
the touch of his hand, the lilt of his smile.

6.

In these days the shadowy yet uncompromising
Angel of Death is no longer a stranger to me.
The touch of his hand, the lilt of his smile
arrive with random ease to taunt, tease or intimidate;
startling me with terrifyingly beautiful visions—
that to say I do not know the sensation of his zephyr,
the uncompromising touch, the crushing weight
of his intense whisper,
would be a monumental lie.

My experience, however, is not unique,
for although it is true that in an unpredictable sometime
of a tomorrow I'll be gone, having journeyed
from yesterday's unfurled today,
the same can be told of you and the yellow butterfly;
life finding itself circumscribed, shaped, created
by the transfiguring Dance of Death,
by the austere boundary of not being, by the curve of
oblivion's generously awesome emptiness.

7.

This fragrance of warm summer air captivates me,
enthralls the torrid afternoon with nuances of
oblivion's generously awesome emptiness—
its ever transfigured survival
felt in the final whisper of the butterfly's wings;
in the wafting pungencies of a meal being prepared, cooked;
the calm odor of a musty book opened in the dying twilight;
the stilled photograph of a girl gazing across the ocean;
the cadence of a musical phrase dissolving into faint echoes
of a dance more subtle than anyone could ever dream.

In the midst of the keening, a waterfall plummets
into the heart's depth. At the base of the falling water
is a resonant pool, ever deeper, ever stiller, into which
tomorrow I'll be gone forever from this here
and that there, the empty chair, the unslept bed.

This ambiguous poem of life,
now nattily accoutered for the journey,
shall then blossom into your ears, you who hear these lines;
perhaps the same you who once stood in the street with me,
damp with life and love; the both of us laughing and leaning
into the eastern whisper, the western echo.

mouthing
the ocean names of night.
—Audre Lorde

1.

Surely the humanly cultivated culture of the normal
is no safe haven for the mad poet;
                              the ecstatic gazelle;
this wanton dove of myself mouthing the ocean names
of night;
            I who am of no proper utility, no production;
my wheelchair-bound, bed-floating body slowly
degenerating beyond usefulness into neediness.

Truth be told, there is, in this society, no acceptable place
for dead poets still panting, still keenly listening
to the echoes of the universe's initial thunder;
                                          no place
for this me-of-now in an economic production force
based primarily on profit and consumption;
                                          nor is there
likely to be any role for me in the reproductive success
of our species, my living merely
an iridescent dead-end in the genetic maze of hominids.

As it is, these fervent days of my vulnerable, uncharted
journey are precariously balanced on the fingertips
of a few individuals who rally to
keep alive an increasingly lame body, its limbs capable
of little more than hovering, its resplendently pulsing heart
dumbly mouthing the ocean names of night.

2.

For those disabled or elderly citizens who proudly hail
from the ranks of common normalcy—and each
succeeding generation engenders its own defining norm—
life in a nursing home can have positive medical
as well as social benefits—

MEDICAL: proper dosages of medication;
constant monitoring of symptoms or decline;
timely use of appropriate assistive technologies;
regular attention from qualified nurses.

SOCIAL: residents watching their telly sports and sitcoms together,
reminiscing about childhood and favorite pop stars, discussing
how prices have changed through the decades;
                                                   the food, the décor
the atmosphere, everything comfortably inoffensive for the
majority of the population, who while they may not prefer this
institutional setting to their former homes, can at least rest
assured they'll not be brazenly terrorized or sinisterly ambushed
by sinuously woven poetry, exotic spices,
          and probable discourse on quantum mechanics;
by strident aesthetics and ecstatic grandeur;
          by dissonance and dissidents;
by sensuality of flesh, explosion of mind,
          and the arduous study of Urdu.

3.

As things stand, can you imagine any nursing home
staffed and qualified to nurse the mad Poets;
the irrepressibly Curious;
the wanton Geniuses;
the Divas of Love;
                    those who Unrepentantly,
                    Masterfully,
                    Ferociously
transform the catholic tedium of humankind
into gem-filled kaleidoscopes pointed toward the
burning rays of the sun;
                         or the others, the tender
souls mouthing the ocean names of night.

What then are we to do with these embarrassing
oddments, these silken rags of humanity?
                                          Where
are they to go when the body is decaying but the mind
glitters with the sudden shapes of exhilarating
supernovae;

when the crippled flesh continues to house
a soul aglow with soaring calligraphies;
                              when it isn't
a done thing that tomorrow I'll be gone.

Some such individuals have, of course, solved
the dilemma for themselves, using various methods
of guns, bridges, or rivers;
                        also automobile exhaust,
oven gas, or natty neckties of jute;
                              alternatively,
plenty handfuls of pretty pills—
                            such solutions
often premature, though admittedly effective.

Others, forced by circumstances to conform to an ersatz
social norm founded on entrenched superficiality, ubiquitous
TV, and blindly shared assumptions of a common cultural
destiny grounded in so-called common sense and common
morality, simply retreat into substance abuse, or go clinically,
—as opposed to aesthetically—
                            insane,
the once scintillating luminescence of their gifts sullied
to less than a spark of a spark of a sputtering quark.

4.

For the time being—and considering the sorry fates
of other subversively mottled elements, past and present—
I myself remain blessedly if tenuously fortunate,
in that some few valiant seraphim camouflaged as citizens
have reached the ever unpopular
and highly seditious conclusion that the alien,
the eccentric,
the luscious,
the enigmatic are worth caring about and caring for;
that my living hour,
may continue to course through these blood-sculpted veins;
that the small but broad library of books—
                              so at home
        in my heart,
        my hands—

                    might remain alive and literate
for some few more months, perhaps years;
                                    my buddies
trekking valiantly through volumes of poetry, reciting ideas
and cadences that ever challenge us
to encounter the unknown
that dwells just the other side;
                              to touch it,
                        know it,
and be unexpectedly destroyed, astonishingly transfigured
by its unveiling.

Thus for the foreseeable future I remain neatly huddled,
cuddled, and clandestinely smuggled from uncertainty
to uncertainty in an obtusely angled corner
of this roundly unbounded planet,
here where I may pant and breathe the thunderously Sublime,
the obstinately Kind,
the uncommonly Tender;
                        mouthing
                              the ocean names
                              of night.

II—THURSDAY

> *come with a burst of song.*
> —Rabindranath Tagore

Come join me on my park bench;
come share this irrepressible absurdity of a picnic.
You need not feel embarrassed—
I am well aware that it resembles less a park bench
than a floating bed cradling a scrawny, muted invalid;
I realize the magnificent beech and oak trees
look suspiciously like straight white walls,
and the elegant Parisian avenue at the end of the pathway
is in truth the unpredictable, grueling road of compassion,
which you travel faithfully, gallantly
in order to be at my side.
Nonetheless, and regardless this simple setting,
your presence—
          your strong limbs and soft mouth,
          that warmth which has often brought me succor—
is requested.

Come with your picnic hamper filled with delicacies...
those pungent cheeses, succulent strawberries;
volumes of delightful elegies from miscreant poets,
these sweet almond pastries, a slab of grilled salmon;
the residual fume of burnt tobacco on your fingers,
the scent of your sweated shirt, your laundered trousers;
this musky cup of tea, that bowl of aromatic *sag paneer*—
a blanket, too, to spread across the mown grass mattress.

Come with a bottle of wine,
Bull's Blood with which to toast
this odd confluence of rivers on the central plateau;
to celebrate the eerie survival of the once gamboling gazelle;
to sit among proud skeletons bound for Calais, Callisto,
and kaleidoscopic ports beyond.

Come with a bursting light to hew the shapes
of my park bench as you open the curtained window,
your simple gesture flooding the fleeing night
       with liquid day.

Sit beside me as you always do, so unlike most;
your actions, your voice,
the warmth of your torso seldom in a hurry;
your demeanor uncommonly serene,
as though you alone have fully understood
and embraced
the possibility that tomorrow
I'll be gone from these labyrinthine alleyways of melody.

Come with a burst of quiet ripples across my chest,
my legs, my arms and face,
soothing the day's agonies, the night's deep labors.

Come, my friend, with a burst of song unlike any other,
to enrapture my encompassed life,
to push away the white walls,
to anoint the parklands of my bed, my body, with music
echoing from the ceiling of boundless inner sky—

>Come exhaust the blood of imagination
>before interring it forever in tombs of books
>and sepulchers of documentary films—

>>Come, my friend—
>>sup with me,
>>here on this park bench,
>>the two of us nestled
>>in the shimmering valley
>>of the shadow
>>of death.

III—FRIDAY

drinking nectar with Allah.
—Nikki Giovanni

Not today, I say,
but tomorrow,
I'll be gone.

Because today, you see, I have this fervent desire
to listen to velocities of dissonantly ravishing music,
to sail the unbounded edges of the universe,
to dance the loving curve of your neck,
drinking nectar with Allah.

Yes, today I am hell-bent on enjoying
the green leaves quaking in the breeze,
if only during that short time
when despite the pain pinned and sewn into my body
I wheel myself outside to meet Elijah
in the vast
blue
ceiling
of summer, drinking nectar with Allah.

Today I yearn to write a few new words, a poem,
for no other reason than to bring the unconquerable abyss
nearer my flesh; to open the gates of my heart,
letting the lovely doving blood
flutter onto your shaping shoulder;
to weep with joy,
with sorrow,
with unabashed tears,
drinking nectar with Allah.

Today—and I shall not deny it—
I want more than anything
to hold you near, my friend;
to curl in one of the bountiful laps of the Buddha,
to feel again your pulsing heart of life,
because tomorrow I'll be gone, you see,
I'll be in the next street but one,
drinking nectar with Allah.

IV—SATURDAY

the weight of sweetness.
—Li-Young Lee

I certainly can't speak for you,
but personally I have a difficult time
grasping
this concept of oblivion—
to not feel the weight of sweetness.

No matter my earnest endeavors,
I simply cannot envision *Not-me,*
or *Supra-me,*
or *Me-without-the-me-part*—
whatever the abyss calls itself
when I'm not laughing at its merry pranks,
or caressing its dark, full-lipped mouth.

Sometimes, it is true,
the powerful Angel of Death comes dancing for me
in the inner reaches of night,
occasionally the bright of day—
and I can tell you,
wrestling disembodied oblivion is too surreal for words.

The travail leaves me exhausted
yet desirous,
            finely desirous for the weight
            of sweetness,
for the touch of your earthly, living hand.

Despite such ephemeral reprieve, however,
the consoling weight of that sweetness
must eventually diminish and disperse into the thinnest
of echoes,
until the rare story, the one that tells
of your gentle hand comforting my face,
is one day known only to you,
the sun's virile rays piercing the canopy
of the great tree,
the solar light dappling
my cold,
sky-blue body.

V—SUNDAY

Dressed in its own naked enigma
—Octavio Paz

I am lying in this rumpled bed of torrid July,
my life dressed in its own naked enigma.

Golden urine has leaked
from a small puncture in the plastic urinal.
Now more piss is dribbling from my penis as I look
to see how much has already soaked
into the bedding beneath my crotch.

Curious,
how quickly warm liquids seep and disperse,
turning the mauve cloth a damp shade of royal purple.

I glance at the clock—it is 1:00 in the morning,
the drunken, ravishing hour of the poet—
and me,
I'm waiting for the moon to dry the piss on my bed.
It won't take long in this arid climate,
only a few minutes,
the wet patch draped in dark stars.

No matter,
tomorrow I'll be gone for the day,
maybe a lovely lifetime or two,
elegantly dressed in enigmatic indigo;
my echoing caress lovingly haunting each generation
to the seventh, then no more.

VI—MONDAY

The privilege to die—
—Emily Dickinson

Now grant me the privilege to die—
not only the privilege to die,
but to die fully alive to the wondrously dancing universe,
even the thrilling possibility of a vast bubbling multiverse;
 to die ridiculous in my infatuations,
  my mind supple and clear,
  my chest resplendent in pearls,
  my life draped in its ubiquitous prayer shawls.

Grant me the privilege of grimacing without shame
when the pain shoots through my flesh, my limbs;
or when the dull, constant discomfort
becomes grave and irreducible;
 at the same time, grant me the privilege,
  in my bizarre circumstances,
 to brazenly touch your life,
  transforming this now holy moment of your living;
allow me to ruthlessly shatter untenable stereotypes
of nursing and caring,
stereotypes of compassion and brotherhood.

Grant me the privilege of not having to laugh
at peoples' sincerely hearty attempts to cheer me,
and yet to gleefully chortle at inappropriate times
simply because life is defiantly absurd;
 the privilege to rudely ignore
 the incessant drivel of fools
 in order that I might quietly contemplate
 with inner delight the sensuous unfolding
 of the splendid clouds—a mundane sight
 for the majority of motorists and pedestrians,
 yet potently miraculous for prisoners,
 visionaries,
 and invalids;
 for the little girl whose sight
 was blindingly destroyed by a mortar attack.

Grant me the privilege to not always make sense,
to be frustrated,
fickle,
withdrawn
or disoriented
in this disabled body;
>grant me also the privilege to love
>fiercely,
>haphazardly,
>chivalrously,
>with a selective suddenness inexpressible
>in the propriety of words;
yes, grant me this, for tomorrow I'll be gone;
a tomorrow when all my pain and my joy,
my life and my death,
shall be beyond the reach of your living—
when they'll be dumb and icy cold to the touch
of your trembling, feverishly alive fingers.

Grant me the rare privilege of being tenderly alone
with my fondest friends,
while feeling devastatingly isolated
upon their inevitable departures;
furthermore, grant me the privilege
of loving you, my friend,
in irrefutable ways nobody else ever has or ever will;
ways hauntingly ornamented
by the hallowed presence of disease
>and the long, patient shadow of death.

Grant me the privilege
of clasping your hand against my weary chest,
of touching your face with this mute truth that is my lot—
>of leaning my head against your warm torso,
>of curling my body beside yours,
>of one fine day dying small and frail, yet blissful
>in the comfortable shape
>of your strong, devoted arms,
>a shape I've come to know and trust.

Grant me just this, my friend,
then bury my ashes
in the sky's delightfully
laughing
belly.

VII—TUESDAY

the ones who name each piece of stained glass
—Dionisio Martínez

The ones who name each piece of stained glass
haven't forgotten you.

As patterns of colored light fall across your life,
unnoticed persons are witness to each dissolving event.

Yet, when in a given moment
you turn to acknowledge that person,
he or she seems to have vanished.

In spite of this, the letterless names of each fragment
of stained glass remain subtly lit by the universe,
whispering you a portion of the mysteries,
whispering you news that tomorrow I'll be gone—
　　　　followed by your departure in the evening.
We'll be nestled among the ones who
since sand first melted into glass
have insistently, fearlessly mouthed the emergent stars.

Stained, ravaged and mottled by living,
I remove windowpanes of colored glass
from the morning, evening and night.
With each tender caress of your neck,
each wordless kiss of your cheek,
I am proffering you a vision of azure light;
a ruby one to you,
and an emerald one to you—
metallic dreams,
bejeweled fevers,
opalescent waterways carrying each of you
toward your own pavilions of kind oblivion.

Now I am weary.
Please be good enough to close
      the amethyst door when you depart.
Tell the malachite god among you to return alone,
for he shall understand best
how to kiss these spectral tears of starlight
scattered across my bony cheek;
how to peer through the eyeless, sun-bleached skull
toward the enduring depths of the universe,
there where my body gradually curls
into dimensions of existence
that dwell beneath
and beyond.

Epilogue

Your tea is cold now.
—Edna St. Vincent Millay

You've been waiting for hours, possibly days or years.
Your tea is cold now.

True, I once assured you my departure
would not be for another day yet;
saying it'll be tomorrow I'll be gone.
I know I told you that today I would
under no circumstances be late or absent;
yet tomorrow has come sooner than expected.

Your tea is now cold—
there's little use waiting longer.
It's time to pay the waiter and be on your way.
For my sake, tip him well,
tell him he's charming,
kiss his bony, unsuspecting hand.

If on a coming September, January or May afternoon
you chance upon one of my buddies,
tell him he's a good man;
tell him I couldn't have done it without him;
tell him the replenishing rains have come,
but the laughing tea has gone cold, icy cold.

When instead of reply he gazes thoughtfully
toward the horizon, his eyes reflecting the blood
of the setting sun and the silver of the emerging stars
        of autumn, winter or spring,
rest your face against his shoulder, his chest—
listen to his beating heart,
feel the warmth of his body,
gather strength for your own inimitable journey.

For after all is said and done,
your bags are nearly packed.
Tomorrow you yourself shall be gone—
journeying into the eastern whisper;
the western echo hovering amidst the falling rain,
its evanescent song descending
toward the distant seventh generation,
then no more.

August 18, 2003

95. Moonlight to Flood the Soul

—*For Tyson Reed*

*I should like
to put aside
everything
that is merely
envelope, an
appearance, a
surface, in
order to go
directly to the
heart of the
rose, to the
bottom of this
sweet chalice.*

—Marguerite
Yourcenar

Years ago, in those blithely innocent times of forever, I would gather with friends several evenings each week to learn and dance a variety of dances collected from diverse regions of the globe, including Africa, Argentina, Armenia, the Balkans, Britain, Cuba, Hungary, India, Israel, Mexico, Poland, Russia, Scandinavia, Transylvania, Turkey and the U.S.—line and circle dances, couple dances—tango, kolo, salsa, kujawiak, pols, contra-dance, swing, dzanguritsa, waltz, hora.

During the winter months we danced in various venues—social halls, sports gymnasiums, dance halls. But in the summertime a group of us would congregate weekly to dance outside on a public plaza at the university. It was a large bricked area surreally lit with outdoor lighting intermittently veiled by tree limbs fluttering with leaves, creating phantasmagoric shadows, breezy undulations of dappled light. Along one edge of the space was a retaining wall upon which people would sit to watch; those who were waiting out a dance, or passers-by enthralled by the richly folkloric dancing, by the exotically eclectic music—sounds of balalaïka,

It is in these and other similar gestures, as we briefly dissolve the edged barriers of ignorance, arrogance and fear, that we may at last submerse ourselves in exquisitely topsy-turvy carnival realms in which each is teacher *and* disciple, each is lover *and* beloved, each is named *and* unnamed, mortal *and* immortal.

*Putting down
all barriers,
let your mind
be full of love.
Let it pervade
all the
quarters of the
world so that
the whole
wide world,
above, below,
and around,
is pervaded
with love. Let
it be sublime
and beyond
measure so
that it
abounds
everywhere.*

—Digha
Nikaya

bandoneon, cimbalom, clarinet,
dudelsack, dumbek, fiddle, hurdy-gurdy,
nickelharp, oud, panpipe.

One evening, as the music was starting
for an especially lively couple dance, an
unfamiliar young man—I too was a
young man at the time!—appeared from
the depths of night, unexpectedly leaping
from the crowded wall to land at my feet.
Was this a bizarre attack from a madman?
Or the asinine antics of an inebriated
graduate student?

Hardly anything so violent or
undignified: Straightening himself up,
the scruffy-faced, floppy-clothed man
asked enthusiastically, "Would you dance
with me?"

The music was fast, athletic. The guy,
though nimble, had no idea what was
going on, yet was electric enough in his
limbs to equal my own passionate
enthusiasm for dancing. Consequently the
two of us spun, stumbled and galloped
through that queerly illuminated outdoor
air; a couple of blissfully crazed,
centrifugally embraced gazelles. Did it
matter to him that he had no idea what
to do; that our dancing was less than
graceful; that this awkward yet exuberant
escapade was unfolding in public view?
Apparently not. In recalling my years of
social dancing, he is one of the few
partners I danced with—and I have
danced with a wide range of men and
women—whose eager countenance was
unabashedly radiant from the moment I
agreed to his request until the final note
of music brought our dancing to an end,
his exultant face flashing me a smile of

Thus,
inexplicably
and on
luminous
waves of
existence,
does paradox
disappear;
one is
immersed in
experiences
of
unbounded
scope.

It is also in
such
strangely
beautiful
encounters
that we can
finally
comprehend
the often
obscure or
didactic
words of the
sages
concerning
love or
compassion;
ever flowing,
ever
changing
rivers in
which *Love
thy neighbor*
is no longer
a mere

231

rapturous gratitude before trotting off into the teeming night of the city, never to be seen again. A mere two, possibly three dozen words had been exchanged—indeed I never even learned his name—yet in those few minutes he and I galloped and swirled a galaxy of delight.

Why he leapt from the night sky to dance with me, I'll never know. And I need not know. The ecstasy of dance, like love and compassion, has its own laws, not beholden to the written or spoken word—this account of mine is therefore and necessarily a crude interpretation from that nonverbal language.

Long ago, in those distant days of our forefathers; Rabban Gamaliel, blessed be his name, rose in greeting and kissed Rabbi Yehoshuah, may his name also be blessed, saying to him: *Come in peace my teacher and my disciple.*

Shoulders beshawled and collarbones bepearled, I am sitting in my wheelchair at the entrance of a small, popularly hectic bakery. Slightly overwhelmed by the noise, unable to enter any farther than the wide entrance, I readily relinquish the logistics of the situation to

concept, law or creed, but a vibrant act filled with warmth of breath, breadth of mind, and the unsettling touch of lunacy.

Furthermore, by weaving together such actions hour upon hour, day upon day, we engender a living tradition—a tradition that belongs to any individual of courage, commitment and frank daring; a vital tradition that does not require

From all the
offspring
of the earth
and heaven
love is the most
precious.

—Sappho

my buddy Pete. Even so, though my attention is primarily focused on a few nearby baskets filled with bagels, baguettes and other breads, I look up momentarily to discern a face behind the counter, there amidst the bustling clutter of the shop—I look up to see two eyes turn from serving tall Pete in order to peer with curiosity at me in my wheelchair, a glance, nothing more. Yes, only a glance, yet it is enough to set in motion a most marvelously unrehearsed scene.

What now occurs seems quite natural to me, but likely surprises onlookers; namely, the young man races to the end of the counter and lithely clambers over a low section of the display case in order to wrap me lovingly in his arms, kissing my delighted face, jubilant in his words, his beaming smile.

For much of Grady's childhood and adolescence I was his piano teacher—who else would have taught him to eschew all propriety and clamber over a counter for no other reason than to kiss a diseased, middle-aged man he's not seen in several years? Who else would have given him the tools, the chutzpah to become in his turn a momentary master of zany delight? Though only recently grown out of adolescence, he is obviously capable

specialized knowledge or secret laws; nor is it limited to close kin, trusted friends or like-minded believers.

Rather a living tradition that in its fearless and hourly enactment embraces the *known* and the *unknown*, the *dark* and the *light*, the bosom *buddy* and the new *neighbor*, the *master* and the *disciple*, the aromatic nocturnal *flower* and its pale breath of *moonlight*— transforming

My heart has become capable of every form: it is a pasture for gazelles and a monastery for Christian monks, and a temple for idols, and the pilgrim's Ka'ba, and the tablets of the Torah, and the book of the Qur'an. I follow the religion of love: Whatever way love's camel takes, that is my religion, my faith.

—Ibn Arabi

of fearlessly perpetrating this gallant act of love amid a bustlingly, even antagonistically unaffectionate clutter of humanity.

And me, though once teacher, master, professor, I am become student, disciple; humbly yearning to touch the universe, learning anew its shapes, its sounds, its aromas; my soul, my life enlightened in this fine moment by the unexpected kiss of another.

Born in present day Afghanistan during the thirteenth century of the common era, living much of his life in Turkey, the Sufi poet Jelaluddin Rumi wrote the following quatrain,

> *I asked for one kiss. You gave me six.*
> *Who was teacher is now student.*
> *Things good and generous take form*
> *in me, and the air is clear.*

Recently, in the midst of summer's unforgiving heat, a neighbor began assisting me with my personal care. For several months we had been waving to one another on the street, but little more. Each of us taciturn in his turn, I knew little of the texture of this man's voice, not to mention any of the sordid details from his FBI dossier. Despite this utter paucity of data, it was decided that during our customary stroll Pete would ask him whether he'd be willing to help me on Thursday mornings, a request

isolated points, confrontational lines and unyielding polygons into curves of circles in which the *you* and the *I*, the beginning and the end, intermingle then dissolve; circles in which a person may scruffily, brilliantly leap from concrete walls into the vibrant arms of the spinning dance...

which was initially and succinctly declined. A quarter of an hour later, however, as Pete and I ambled past on our return journey, the guy approached us, offering to try.

Therefore and two days later, early on a summer's morn, this same stranger was sitting on the intimate sanctuary of my bed, adeptly learning the care routine from my friend Ramón. Hardly had this first morning passed; hardly had I begun to discern let alone trust the voice of this man's hands, his body, when he was called upon to accompany me to a concert. Thus it was that I found myself traveling alone with him in the middle of a clear night, the two of us laconically traversing the city streets after enjoying a succulent, sensuous evening of Portuguese folk music.

Suddenly, without warning, he veered onto a lonely side street, precipitously abandoning the van with nary a comment. Weary and slightly disoriented from the day's events, I found myself stranded alone in the palm of the night's hand, partially trying to make sense of this odd turn of events, partially beyond caring whether this was some bizarre murder sequence from a film I never auditioned for. Was this guy, for example, involved in a clandestine drug ring? Was he mentally unstable in some manner such that I'd now be stranded here until the baker and the candlestick

and clamber over bakery counters of propriety to become master of a moment of love, bestower of blessed kisses...

I chose a wild willow branch and plucked it to send it to you. I want you to plant it by the window where you sleep. When new leaves open in the night rains, think it is I that have come to you.

—Hongnang

maker came across me in the dawn light of the twenty-third century? After all, it isn't a "normal" person who swerves onto side streets and abandons vehicles, consequently stranding mute gimps in the dark.

Within a few minutes, at a nebulous point between thought and dream, he returned, the reason for his oddly abrupt behavior now cradled in his hand. Not riddled with gang-flung bullets, nor bearing a week's supply of narcotics, nor foaming at the mouth, he quietly reached across urban constellations of concrete, metal and humanity to offer me a heavenly blossom of night-blooming datura, its richly scented, voluptuously shaped bloom plucked from an incongruous plant we'd passed on the main thoroughfare, a blossom that would not last the hour, let alone the night, hence the necessity of sniffing it, kissing it, enjoying it now, in this darkly abundant moment of learning.

Living in the late seventeenth and early eighteenth centuries, the Japanese haiku master Kikaku wrote,

> *May he who brings*
> *flowers tonight,*
> *have moonlight.*

Might I add, *moonlight to flood the soul, the body with love and delight.*

and pluck the blossoming, heaven-scented night, proffering it to the stranger who may or may not be the Prophet Elijah, but who is without question a human being, same as you and me.

August 29, 2003

236

97. WISP OF GREED

There's no denying
I were a right greedy rogue I were,
then in my yorish days gone by,
wanting fervently to inhabit and absorb each
      and every continent,
         even the stunning ice castles of Antarctica;
wanting to speak 927 languages,
        not to mention chanted mantras,
        unspoken mudras;
wanting to hone my body into a virtuosic machine,
         my mind into a symphony of knowing,
         my ethos into acts of grace and nobility.

Yes, it was me who wanted all the visions of the universe
and both sides of the coin at once;
'twas I who salivated to hear every note of celestial music,
as well as that what they call voices of poets.

And more and more and embarrassingly more.

Now, however, as I dilly-dally along the autumn streets,
my stiff neck narrowing the panorama though not the vision,
I'm wont less to grasp and cuckold the riches of the world
than to rest in this delicate moment,
my body a frumpy canvas upon which time and space play
with sensuous abandon. . .
        a caress of warm sunlight on my thigh,
        the cacophonic songs of migrating birds,
        trees shedding their leaves,
            each uncataloged but beloved—
                at least by me, a fellow leaf.

Nonetheless, my innate greed remains embellied in me,
though now my clutching, my wanting is simpler:

    A cup of tea.
    A whisper of fresh air.
    The softness of your mouth.

A gracious wisp of greed is after all a touch of curiosity,
and a touch of curiosity might conceivably
enrich and strengthen one's life
toward even the bitterest of deaths.

September 15, 2003

98. WORDLESS POETRY

The flutter of my winged hands across your skin; the gentleness of your lips against my face; the whisper of your breath upon my neck, are moments of expression, of language; are symbolic not of grammar but of narrative, this wordless recitation of thoughts and feelings, this poetry that can no longer be expressed through the spoken eloquence of the word, the melodic phrasing of syllables; nor in the cold remove of the printed text.

Simple caresses of quiet fingers and utterless lips, these living symbols have become for me language of a profoundly personal nature, a private language evolving within this intimate landscape I inhabit, a landscape not of space, nor of time, rather of tenderness.

Like most forms of communication, it is a language of dialogue, yet one which no matter how public, how peopled the venue, must always remain a language of *two*-ness, of *us*-ness, our silent conversation inevitably an enigma to others, this uniquely intimate dialogue that is nevertheless capable of expressing the marvelous, the subtle, the caring, the here and now, as my fingers follow and decipher the story of your jaw; the texture of your coarse hair, your fine hair, your coifed hair; the stubble of your whiskers, the scent of your cosmetics; the woven threads of your cotton shirt, your denim jeans; the smooth skin of your young face, the epic wrinkles of your ageing flesh; your eyebrows, lips, shoulders; your bony hand; the contours of your belly, your hip against my tilted brow.

In these muted days of my still vibrant life it is this rare language of tender nearness which is most comforting for me, most communicative; the now effortful use of scribbled or typed words ever more wearisome, ever more elusive; words which while they may be superior in explicating details of a person's complicated life, seldom illuminate the finer hues of living, those vital colors and textures which for me are graciously, exquisitely expressed through and within the nearness of our moments together, this silent language in which few are fluent.

Therefore, as happens to visitors in a foreign land, the spoken language of the majority swirls and burbles around me, while my idiom, which knows no national borders, no religious barriers, is used by only a handful of scattered individuals who in cyclical waves of meeting ever and again engage me in unspoken embraces of the unscribable mysteries of life and death.

Here at last, with my head nestled against your neck, my fingers shaping the contours of your face, I may express not the grammar but the rich subtleties of life, nuances of gratitude and sorrow, kindness and serenity.

In the close comfort of this slow and tender language, I may at last lower the mask of the stoic fighter, of enduring strength, that studied mask of civility one dons in order not to burden others with the tedium of illness.

And whereas words time after time fail to convince me fully of the sincerity of anything, the nearness of your hand, your body creates an ambience of comfort, an unspoken gentleness within which the private truth of my life may be expressed openly, unashamedly, utterly.

Finally, in the timeless encounters of this elegantly intimate language, the rigors, anguishes, and camaraderie of long-term illness may be nakedly, fully expressed; a wordless poetry punctuated occasionally with tears, often with laughter, shaped always with the hallowed touch of love.

September 21, 2003